Praise for
MESSI VS. RONALDO

"Deep and intelligent . . . a portrait of football greatness."

—Arsène Wenger

"Excellent . . . a brilliant follow-up to *The Club*."

—Independent (UK)

"Impressive."

—*Boston Globe*

"A comprehensive primer into the entwined histories of the two titans and the commercial forces that have molded their careers and, by extension, the sport."

—*New York Times*

"An absorbing cautionary tale for soccer fans and students of sports finance alike."

—*Kirkus Reviews*

"While these two soaring greats are known for their transcendent wonder on the field, this rollicking narrative plunges into the complex backstories and entire ecosystems that propelled their colliding trajectories. With a pair of epic hero stories like *The Last Dance* or Homer's *Odyssey* in cleats, this book traces the journey from aspirational prodigies to global commercial billboards, explaining how these two juggernauts and their rivalry shaped the most popular, and lucrative, era of the world's most beloved sport."

—Roger Bennett, founder, Men in Blazers Media Network

T0286443

"This rigorously researched book avoids becoming hagiography. The result is an ambitious and valuable study for all those who want to understand the modern world of football that Mr. Messi and Mr. Ronaldo have helped forge."

—*The Economist*

"A thoroughly enjoyable and interesting read . . . packed with insight. . . . Highly recommended."

—All Sports Books

"This book explains the brilliant backstory behind how each player became a star and how that stardom changed the footballing landscape not just in Spain but in the wider world as well. . . . I read it in a day."

—Rebecca Lowe, NBC Sports

MESSI

v s.

RONALDO

ONE RIVALRY, TWO GOATs,
and the Era That Remade the World's Game

Joshua Robinson and Jonathan Clegg

MARINER BOOKS
New York   Boston

HarperCollins books may be purchased for educational, business, or sales promotional use. For information, please email the Special Markets Department at SPsales@harper collins.com.

A hardcover edition of this book was published in 2022 by Mariner Books.

FIRST MARINER PAPERBACK EDITION PUBLISHED 2023.

Designed by Emily Snyder

Library of Congress Cataloging-in-Publication Data has been applied for.

ISBN 978-0-063-15718-7

23 24 25 26 27 LBC 6 5 4 3 2

To our parents, with love:
Aline & Jeffrey, Lizzie & Ant

And to Evie and Cooper, almost certainly future Ballon d'Or winners

CONTENTS

AUTHORS' NOTE

There are countless ways to tell the stories of Lionel Messi, Cristiano Ronaldo, and the era of soccer that bound them together. On the pitch, every weekend they spent in the Spanish league was its own miniature soap opera. Every major-tournament summer became a magnificent psychodrama. And away from the field, Messi and Ronaldo built global empires that put them on a level of fame normally reserved for US presidents and popes.

Taken individually, each one offers his own portrait of all-time sporting greatness—and plenty has been written about both. But any story focusing on just one of them necessarily comes with a gaping hole shaped like the other. Whether they like it or not, Messi and Ronaldo are inextricable from each other's narratives. In the twilight of their careers, they're now secure enough to admit this. For nearly two decades, they drove each other on. Being the GOAT meant first being better than the other guy.

As it turned out, this wasn't an isolated battle. In their intertwined quests to make history, Ronaldo and Messi also turned into the twin centers of gravity in the world's most popular sport, exerting their pull on everything and everyone that came within their orbits. Even at a time when the sports world was changing more dramatically than in any 20-year period since the invention of the TV set, the most remarkable thing about this one was that the players at the very top stayed the same.

This is the era that we grew up in as reporters for the *Wall Street Journal*. We came of age when Messi and Ronaldo did, and we have chronicled their careers—and their ripple effects—ever since. For nearly 15 years, we've chased their exploits on four continents. We were there for Champions League finals, World Cups, and European Championships. We saw them raise and re-raise each other with moments of supreme glory, from Messi's fourth Champions League title in Berlin to Ronaldo's exorcism with Portugal at Euro 2016. We also witnessed them confront crushing disappointment. None was more dramatic than the evening in Rio de Janeiro when we trudged to the Maracana Stadium, sunburnt and sleep-deprived, fully expecting to see Lionel Messi win his World Cup on South American soil.

That was the day Messi had a chance to become a world champion and gain a decisive edge in soccer's all-consuming debate, "Messi or Ronaldo?" When he didn't, as Argentina lost to Germany, we came away with a realization: the Debate is never really over. More than that, the Debate is beside the point.

That's why this is not merely a dual-biography of two brilliant players. The whole point of this book is that it isn't just about them. It could never be just about them.

Messi vs. Ronaldo is an exploration of how two footballing geniuses emerged at the same time to alter the sports world and accelerate the changes within it. In this account, they are not only a prism through which to understand modern soccer, but also a study in power, reach, and influence. The rivalry went so far beyond the field—where they have met only around three dozen times—that it disrupted entire business and cultural ecosystems, even though the individuals themselves had little awareness, or control, of the consequences.

There have been biographies of these guys, but there has been no serious journalistic treatment of their global effect on the game, the business of sports, and the nature of global celebrity.

Implicit in all of it is the mutual understanding from Messi and Ronaldo that their most important business partner is the other one. The rivalry generates so much energy and zeal in otherwise rational people that their currency is no longer sports. Instead, as their soccer careers wind down, their stock in trade is whether you love them or hate them, a conversation that Messi and Ronaldo have long stopped trying to manage. And in many ways, they made it easy for fans to pick sides, because these two extraordinary players are so extraordinarily different. They are opposites in every meaningful way: One is big, one is small. One likes to burst past defenders, the other likes to weave through them. One is a finisher, one is a playmaker. One is shy and humble, the other a strutting peacock. You already know which is which.

For years, Messi made it look simple, scoring effortless, dazzling goals. Ronaldo made it look impossible—you could see every carefully honed muscle and sinew stretching as he smashed the ball in.

Neither's art required translation. Kids from Beijing to Brooklyn instinctively understood that the global order was these two and then everyone else. They scored in practically every game they played, and they played every three days all year-round. Yet the deeper we got into the story, and the longer their careers went on, the more similar they started to seem.

Based on deep dives through confidential documents and years of original interviews from around the soccer and sports business world, with executives, teammates, and coaches, this book is a snapshot of the galaxy they created, with the two massive stars in the center. In many cases, those close to Messi and Ronaldo only agreed to speak to us anonymously, since their relationships (and occasionally their livelihoods) hinged on discretion. Where we have recounted whole conversations, they are reconstructed from the firsthand accounts of the people in the room or those briefed on them immediately afterward. And through it all, over and over, we did the most important thing anyone in soccer could do in the Messi vs. Ronaldo era: we watched them play.

—JOSHUA ROBINSON AND JONATHAN CLEGG, APRIL 2022

PROLOGUE

Zurich, December 2007

Two of the greatest soccer players who ever lived sat awkwardly in a Swiss opera house wondering why they'd bothered to show up. There was the floppy-haired Lionel Messi in a dark suit that draped over his narrow shoulders. And there was Cristiano Ronaldo with diamond studs in his ears and wearing a tuxedo, even though the event was expressly not black tie. Neither of them wanted to be there. Neither of them was allowed to leave.

The reason they slouched like punished schoolboys was the empty seat between them.

At their first ever FIFA World Player Gala—an annual celebration of dazzling skill, relentless drive, and uncomfortable banter—Messi and Ronaldo had both been voted *not quite* the best men's player of 2007. Instead, that honor had gone to a Brazilian playmaker named Ricardo Izecson dos Santos Leite, or Kaká for short, who was now up onstage collecting his trophy. He was older than Messi and Ronaldo, and as far as they were concerned, he was also worse at soccer.

At least two other people in the velvet opera house seats that night agreed.

One was a Portuguese former nightclub promoter named Jorge Mendes, who was remaking himself as a slick-haired soccer agent by moving Iberian and South American players around Europe as casually as he juggled his many cell phones. Putting Ronaldo on that stage was a key piece in his master plan to make his client the richest athlete on the planet.

The other Jorge in the room was even more outraged. That would be Jorge Messi, father of Lionel, who still spent much of his time in their hometown of Rosario, Argentina. It had been barely seven years since he bundled his sobbing son onto a flight to Spain in the hopes of impressing some coaches at FC Barcelona. Now the former supervisor at a metal factory was an agent too—with one client who happened to share his last name—fumbling his way through the most cut-throat business in sports.

That night, they all learned a vital lesson. Award shows like this one had never counted for much in soccer before. The trophies that mattered were the ones handed out on the field, at the end of a struggle, with everyone wearing shorts, not designer suits. But that was about to change. The game they grew up with had never known an era-defining rivalry between two soloists. What no one could predict in Zurich that night was that the guys who finished second and third were about to transform soccer into an individual sport. Award shows would become their unlikely battlefield—just as soon as Messi and Ronaldo could start winning them.

Still, Messi, Ronaldo, and the Jorges couldn't get over the fact that this event, with potential long-term effects on transfer fees and sponsorship deals, was run like Sepp Blatter's personal cocktail party. Long before he was found to be paying himself tens of millions of dollars in illicit bonuses—which is to say, while he was still enjoying those bonuses—the longtime FIFA president concocted the awards ceremony as yet another way to surround himself with soccer legends and supermodels. And this year, for the first time, the gala was being broadcast live, in its entirety, with Blatter playing his favorite soccer role that wasn't center forward: center-stage emcee. Next to him was a pair of Swiss TV personalities whose job it was to keep the proceedings moving and repeat Blatter in French, English, and German. But to present the marquee award of the night, the FIFA president needed more heft. He called on none other than the most prolific goalscorer and soccer pitchman of all time, the three-time World Cup winner Pelé. It was the FIFA equivalent of the Grammys trotting out Paul McCartney.

The organization that Blatter had built up from a small promoter of soccer tournaments into a global monster of marketing and television rights was sitting on roughly half a billion dollars in cash at the time. In its day-to-day operations, FIFA was more like a record label or a medium-sized insurance firm than a sports body. And just like any self-respecting record label, it held a vital stake in manufacturing its own stars.

The problem was that in the mid-2000s the soccer skies were a little dimmer than usual. The four men who had shared every award from 1996 to 2005 were now in their twilight years. Age and weight had caught up to the Real Madrid *Galácticos*—Zinedine Zidane, Luís Figo, and the Brazilian Ronaldo. The two-time winner Ronaldinho, meanwhile, was barely finding time to play matches for Barcelona between all-night beach parties. Things were so thin at the top of the soccer food chain that in 2006 the distinction for the world's best, most exciting talent went to Fabio Cannavaro. He was a defender.

Now, it was Kaká's turn. The clean-cut, middle-class kid from Sao Paulo ran AC Milan's midfield with an easy grace that belied what a nightmare he was to face. Kaká, a freshly minted European champion, had been the golden boy before Cristiano was the golden boy and long before Leo had finished growing to five-foot-seven.

"Ladies and gentlemen, the crucial moment. I have some practice to open envelopes," Blatter said, without a hint of irony. "Ladies and gentlemen, the winner of the FIFA World Player 2007, of this gala here in Zurich, is Kakaaaa."

Kaká got up. Pelé, a man who had shilled for everyone from American Express to Viagra, proudly endorsed his countryman. Messi and Ronaldo stayed benched.

Making matters worse for the sulking pair, they'd been through the same drill two weeks earlier in Paris at the Ballon d'Or, a separate player of the year award that would later be unified with the FIFA prize. So the element of surprise was somewhat dampened. "To be honest, I was expecting it a little bit," Kaká said. "I won the Champions League and was the competition's top scorer. . . . That is the key. You have to play in a winning team."

Not that Messi and Ronaldo were playing for pub sides. Messi, 20, had broken into the starting lineup at Barcelona under the former Dutch great Frank Rijkaard, who was doing his level best to figure out what position this dribbling Argentine actually belonged in. And Ronaldo, 22, was a bona fide star at Manchester United, where his manager, Alex Ferguson, had spent four years toughening him up to become the most complete attacker in the game. Messi and Ronaldo were already world-class, with Champions League and Premier League winners' medals at home. Yet Kaká had captured more votes than both of them combined. As a final indignity to the losers, Blatter invited them up onstage to pose for photographs. Pelé handed each of them a little trophy, smaller than Kaká's, only to realize that he'd mixed them up.

Somehow he'd handed the second-place prize to Ronaldo and the third-place trophy to Messi. Blatter had to intercede, shuffling between the soccer geniuses to make sure everyone was holding the right hardware. "Second, second for Lionel," said one of the two other hosts onstage, in the kind of generic European accent that populates world soccer. "Could you change it please?"

For a moment, Ronaldo came as close as possible, for him, to feeling embarrassed. He had discovered something even more awkward than showing up to this event and losing: showing up to this event and being made to turn his trophy over to Messi. They traded second and third places while Ronaldo hoped for the opera house to open up and swallow him whole. When that didn't happen, he endured one last shot. "You tried, you tried," one of the hosts said as the crowd giggled. "But you didn't manage."

He didn't manage a smile either. Ronaldo and Messi were forced to stand onstage through the end of the show until an orchestra played them off with "The Impossible Dream" from the musical *Man of La Mancha*. They hadn't come to the opera for Broadway numbers. And they certainly hadn't come to not win.

As it turns out, that wasn't a problem for long. By the time someone not named Ronaldo or Messi won the award next, it would be 2018, 11 years later. No matter what Kaká said about winning teams, this prize was the ultimate yardstick for individual achievement in the world's favorite team sport—and the award Messi and Ronaldo cared about most.

This was also the rare arena where they could be compared independently of their teammates or circumstances. Here was a live measure of all-time greatness, Messi or Ronaldo, Ronaldo or Messi. For an entire era of the game's history, one man or the other would claim soccer's top individual award every single year—a decade defined by their personal duels, their staggering numbers, and the wreckage they left behind.

PART 1

Two Geniuses

ONE

Across the Sea

I T WAS NEARLY 1:00 a.m., and Cristiano Ronaldo was winding down in the cool of the Sporting Lisbon locker room as if nothing had happened. Out there, in the summer heat of 2003, fans were still giddy about what they'd just seen: a ceremony to christen the club's new stadium, a 3–1 victory over Manchester United, and mostly, the performance of the youngest guy on the team.

Even Ronaldo's teammates were beside themselves as they ripped the tape off their ankles and tried to make sense of the past two hours. *Can you believe Cristiano?*

The 17-year-old with blond highlights in his hair and pimples on his face had been sending signals for days that something big was on the way—his teammates could see it at practice. Ronaldo oozed hair gel and intensity. Sporting manager Fernando Santos had told him he'd be in the lineup for the big exhibition against Man United, and he'd been locked in ever since. "Cristiano didn't have to say what he wanted or what he had in mind," says João Pinto, who scored two of Sporting's three goals that night. "It was clear in his face how he felt and what he wanted."

What he wanted was for Manchester United to take notice.

Down the hall the cramped visitors' locker room was in chaos. The United players were sunburnt, jet-lagged, and also trying to make sense of the past two hours. They could barely tell what time it was or where they were, having landed in Portugal from their US preseason tour at 4:00 a.m. the previous day. All they were certain of was that they'd been taken to the cleaners by someone who looked like he owed a teacher some homework in the morning.

Every time the ball came to Ronaldo, electricity ran through his feet. He tore up and down the wing, beating defenders with so much speed and skill that, as United manager Alex Ferguson said, fullback John O'Shea came in at halftime with a migraine. Roy Keane, a combative midfielder, was less charitable. O'Shea, he felt, had played like a "fucking clown."

"It was not just the fact he was going past him," says defender Phil Neville. "It was the stepovers, the tricks, the flicks, and the confidence of this guy that struck me more than anything. . . . It was chest out, 'This is my arena.'"

The United players didn't want to be there before they'd been embarrassed by some kid in a friendly, and they definitely didn't want to be there now. They were only in Portugal as a favor. United and Sporting had signed a memorandum of understanding years before to increase cooperation between the clubs, though really it was to allow the English powerhouse to keep tabs on any players coming through the Portuguese youth system. So when Sporting asked if United might grace the new Estádio José Alvalade with its presence on opening night, it made sense to oblige. The whole affair was very much a Sporting showcase—the team even switched out its kit at halftime from the traditional green-and-white home jersey to its gold away shirt. The United players hardly registered the wardrobe change since they had no idea who the guys across from them were anyway.

Forty-five minutes later, they'd noticed at least one of them. Senior players hounded Ferguson at full-time to hand a contract to this kid, the one who'd made their night so miserable. "We need to sign him, boss." What they didn't realize was that the plan was already in the works. Everyone down the hall was in the loop on Ronaldo's immediate future. "By the end of the match," Pinto says, "we already knew it was very likely he would go to Manchester. It was all we talked about."

Beyond the Sporting dressing room, three other men in the stadium knew exactly what was going to happen that night: Alex Ferguson, an agent named Jorge Mendes, and Cristiano. All over Europe, anyone in the business of paying attention to these things also had an inkling. United's gobsmacked players may have been the first outside Portugal to feel what he was capable of, but they might have been the last to learn his name.

By the summer of 2003, Cristiano Ronaldo was a secret to no one.

THE CRISTIANO RONALDO origin story is soccer's equivalent of Peter Parker getting bitten by a radioactive spider. Years later, everyone has heard the tale of the unknown kid who took down Manchester United and earned a move to the most famous club in the world.

The truth is far different. Ronaldo's superpowers had been incubating for years. Inside Portuguese football, they were already comparing him with some of the game's greatest players. The academy kids at Sporting had nicknamed him "Kluivert," because his rangy frame and technical gifts resembled those of the famed Netherlands striker. The manager of FC Porto would name-check a different Dutch goalscorer. "The first time I saw him play, I told my assistant, 'There goes van Basten's son,'" says José Mourinho. "I didn't even know his real name."

Ronaldo's reputation grew so fast that it reached a former video-store clerk who was busy trying to carve out his own future in the game. Jorge Mendes was starting out as a soccer agent. Not long after, Cristiano Ronaldo would become his most important client.

Mendes was still relatively new to the profession in the early 2000s, but he'd already grasped the secret to the whole game. Instead of waiting for buying clubs to approach him with an offer, he would work in cahoots with the sellers and create the markets himself. In late 2002, he informed Sporting Lisbon's general manager, Carlos Freitas, that Cristiano would not be renewing his contract, which had 18 months left to run. It was time to put clubs on alert that he was available.

Mendes had nailed the timing. He knew that most of Europe's top clubs were tracking Ronaldo, including much of the cash-rich Premier League. Led by Man United and riding a new wave of television and commercial income, English teams were on their way to becoming the

most powerful in Europe, ending more than a decade of Italian su-
premacy. Arsenal had brought Ronaldo out to train in North London,
and the club's vice chairman, David Dein, flew to Portugal to make an
offer. Newcastle United was sniffing around him too, having shopped
successfully at Sporting for a player named Hugo Viana the year before.
Liverpool was watching Ronaldo closely and actually made a move,
though it worried privately that fans might take it badly if the club signed
another young prospect when it was supposed to be chasing silverware. Even Everton, the second most famous team in Liverpool, knew
about Ronaldo. The club had the chance to buy him for £2 million in
2002 before deciding that it was happy sticking with the awkward teen
it already had on the books, a boy named Wayne Rooney.

At one point, Mendes and Sporting ginned up a deal to take Ronaldo
to Juventus in Italy in a cash-plus-player arrangement, only for the transfer to collapse because Chilean striker Marcelo Salas refused to move
in the opposite direction, Freitas says. The same problem occurred
when Sporting offered Ronaldo to Olympique Lyonnais in France: the
mullet-haired French striker Tony Vairelles wouldn't make the jump to
Portugal. Mendes also held talks in Lisbon with Real Madrid director
Ramon Martinez, though they went nowhere.

The most lucrative proposal came from the Italian club Parma, which
offered single-digit millions to Sporting and sweetened the pot with an
extra €4 million to Mendes personally and another €4 million to Cristiano.

Except it wasn't about the money. Not yet. There would be plenty
of time for all that, for the big house, the 400-diamond watch from Ja-
cob & Co., the Bugatti, the other Bugatti, and the custom cryotherapy
ice chamber.

Mendes knew that what Ronaldo needed then was something much
harder to acquire than cash. He needed minutes.

SPENDING EVERY POSSIBLE minute playing soccer was pretty much all
Cristiano Ronaldo dos Santos Aveiro had wanted to do since learning
to walk.

As a kid growing up on Madeira, a craggy lump of volcanic rock in the middle of the Atlantic Ocean, Ronaldo was just three years old when he was given a soccer ball as a Christmas gift. For the remaining nine years he lived on the island, he was almost never seen without it. The ball went everywhere with him. It followed him on the way to school most days, and it followed him on the way definitely not to school on other days, when he skipped class to play with the older kids in the narrow street behind his family's home. He took it with him to church, to meals, and even to bed, in the tiny room he shared with his older brother and two sisters.

All of which is perfectly standard behavior for soccer-obsessed kids across the globe—and perfectly standard origin-story stuff in the retelling of any footballer who makes it—except for the part about a lump of volcanic rock in the middle of the Atlantic Ocean. Situated 650 miles off the Portuguese mainland, closer to Africa than Europe, Madeira is an island with many qualities, including its temperate climate, exotic flora, and charming harbor, where Margaret Thatcher stayed on her honeymoon. But its roads are completely bananas—steep, crooked, uneven, and often perched on the edge of a cliff. It was on those twisting, treacherous streets that Cristiano Ronaldo learned to dribble a soccer ball, and if his childhood precocity teaches us anything, it's that nothing forces you to master the fundamentals of close control like knowing a heavy touch could send your ball careening two miles down a hill. At six, Ronaldo was able to maneuver so expertly that adults would come to watch him perform tricks behind his house in the evening. "The ball never touched the ground," says a neighbor who lived across the street. "It was as if the ball was attached to his foot."

When he joined the local soccer club at age seven, the other kids quickly came to the same conclusion. Not that it would have taken much to cause a stir at the club he joined, a tiny semipro outfit named Andorinha. Nestled high in the Madeiran hills and deep in the fifth tier of Portuguese football, Andorinha CF amounted to little more than a ramshackle clubhouse, a couple of small dirt fields covered in potholes, and a coffee stand. But Ronaldo's father, Dinis Aveiro, was the equipment manager there, which explains how the most famous soccer player in Portuguese history began his career at a club so obscure that even most people on Madeira had never heard of it.

With Cristiano Ronaldo on board, Andorinha didn't stay obscure for long. Word of his talent made its way to the other clubs around the island. In 1993, CS Marítimo made the first formal approach, submitting an offer of 50,000 escudos, roughly $300, to sign Ronaldo to its youth team. It was a preposterous sum for an eight-year-old, more than most people on Madeira earned in a month. It was also rejected immediately. Andorinha executives knew they had a rare talent on their hands. They weren't going to let Ronaldo go until they received a truly blockbuster offer, one that better reflected his immense potential. That offer duly arrived the following year from Marítimo's main rival. This one was much more valuable to a club like Andorinha—its beleaguered equipment manager, in particular. In the summer of 1994, Ronaldo joined Nacional in exchange for two seasons' worth of fresh kit and training equipment.

The move to Nacional represented a major step up. The facilities were better, the coaches were better, the other players were better. But the results were just the same. Matches and training sessions consisted mostly of Ronaldo running around with the ball and everyone else failing to take it off him. That was partly down to his superior skill, and it was partly down to his new habit of dropping deep into his own half, picking up the ball, and attempting to dribble past every opposing player before launching a shot on goal. It was an exhilarating sight, one that drove Ronaldo's opponents crazy, and Ronaldo's teammates only marginally less crazy. No matter how many opposing players encircled him, he never passed them the ball. "They asked me to pass, but I could never see anyone to pass to," Ronaldo says. "I'd only see the ball."

Not only was it practically impossible to get the ball off Ronaldo, it was also highly inadvisable. On the rare occasions he lost it, or on the even rarer occasions he lost a match, he would invariably burst into tears and could be found sobbing inconsolably even hours after the game was done. "Even if the team won a game, if he thought he hadn't played well, he would cry," says Pedro Talhinas, the Nacional youth coach. "He couldn't deal with any failure."

Fortunately, failure didn't happen very often to Cristiano Ronaldo. Within a year of his arrival, he had led Nacional to the regional championship, which was a cause for great celebration for everyone except the Nacional coaches. They were already resigned to the fact that Ronaldo would soon be moving on. The boy who had gotten his first soccer ball for Christmas clearly had a gift.

"We knew he could not stay," Talhinas says. "A player like this does not stay for long in Madeira."

EVERY PORTUGUESE KID who ever dreamed of making it as a pro soccer player invariably winds up at one of the country's three big clubs: Benfica, Porto, or Sporting. Known as Os Três Grandes, the Big Three have won all but two of the championships in the 88-year history of professional soccer in Portugal.

Yet all those titles tell only part of the story. As much as the Big Three have had the Portuguese title on lockdown, their grip on the country's top young talent has been even stronger. Almost every Portuguese player of note in the past 40 years has come up through one of their youth academies, and the competition to recruit the best young prospects is as fierce as anywhere on Earth. That's because the quest for talent is as much an economic priority as a sporting one. In Portugal, where TV and sponsorship money is substantially lower than in the other top European leagues, even the likes of Porto and Benfica can't afford the astronomical transfer fees and salaries needed to lure the best players from overseas. Rosters are mostly composed of homegrown players, who are recruited as young as nine, housed in dorm rooms, and carefully molded into professional soccer players. By the age of 17, those who are good enough are fast-tracked into the first team, while those who fail to make the grade are encouraged to sign with one of the other 15 clubs in the Primeira Liga. Which helps to explain why Os Três Grandes end up taking home the championship every year.

This intense focus on youth development has made footballers Portugal's most popular export this side of sardines. When Europe's richest clubs go in search of the next big thing, they invariably start by looking in Portugal and at the rosters of its Big Three clubs. For young Portuguese players, the Big Three aren't just the best chance of glory in the Primeira Liga. They're also the gateway to Europe's top leagues and all the riches and fame on offer there.

So there was no doubt that Cristiano Ronaldo would eventually find his way to one of the country's Big Three clubs. The only question was which of them would find him first.

A road-worn veteran scout named Aurélio Pereira was already on the case. For almost his entire adult life, it had been his mission to traipse around Portugal and sign the country's most promising kids for Sporting. By the spring of 1997, that mission had progressed with remarkable success. While Sporting had fallen behind the other members of the Big Three on the pitch, with no league title in 15 years, the club was in the midst of a golden age of youth development.

That was almost entirely down to Pereira, a quiet, watchful man with thick eyebrows, a thick mustache, and a rapidly thinning hairline. As a coach at Sporting's academy, Pereira had personally recruited some of the most talented youngsters that Portugal had ever produced. Paulo Futre and Luís Figo both joined the club under his watch and developed into world-class players. Jorge Cadete, Luís Boa Morte, and Simão Sabrosa were among more than a dozen other kids brought to the club by Pereira who would become mainstays of the Portuguese national team. In 1991, when Portugal won its second consecutive World Youth Championship, its squad was composed largely of Sporting players, including Emílio Peixe, who was named the tournament's best player. Pereira had first spotted him when he was nine.

It was a gift Pereira had always possessed, going right back to his own days as a 14-year-old hopeful in the Sporting youth team. The first person to realize that Aurélio Pereira wouldn't make it as a top-flight player was Aurélio Pereira. Yet all those years later, he still struggled to explain how exactly he could watch a bunch of scrawny adolescents chase a ball up and down a field and instantly pick out the one diamond from the rest. Often it was some minuscule detail other scouts didn't notice, like the way a kid shaped his body to receive a pass, or how he carried himself on the field. Pereira says he knew that a 12-year-old Figo was destined for stardom from the way he tied his shoelaces.

Even in a country with more than 100,000 registered youth players, Pereira was certain he could identify the best of them. His only challenge was covering enough ground to lay eyes on them all with the one staffer he was assigned when he headed up Sporting's newly formed Youth Recruitment and Training Department in 1987. So Pereira did what any top executive does when presented with insufficient resources and an impossible workload. He outsourced it.

Not long after taking up his new position, Pereira wrote to every one of Sporting's 90,000 members, or *socios*, asking them to recommend the sharpest young prospects in their local area. The missive proved to be a masterstroke. He was tapping into every soccer fan's deeply held belief that they possessed a cultured nose for talent. Within a few days replies were flooding in, and within a few weeks Pereira and his thoroughly overworked assistant began collecting and categorizing the tips, organizing them by age and location. Within a few months Pereira had assembled the most comprehensive database of young talent that Portuguese soccer had ever seen.

What started as an improvised workaround quickly turned into an invaluable resource. Over the next 10 years, Pereira's network of wannabe scouts established recruiting pipelines that stretched the length of the country. The socios would bring Pereira the best players from their region, and he would bring the best of those players to Sporting. No recommendation was too obscure or too remote. He once made a 300-mile drive to the mountain town of Bragança, on the northeast border with Spain, to follow up on a young player. It took Pereira three minutes to decide whether the boy would make it. He had seen enough and got straight back in his car to drive the 300 miles home.

So Aurélio Pereira thought nothing about taking a cold call on a cold February afternoon from someone claiming to have a tip for him, a man named João Marques de Freitas, who had been a lifelong Sporting diehard despite living 600 miles away on the island of Madeira.

"Mestre Aurélio, I have one for you," de Freitas said. "There's a kid who they say is extremely talented."

Pereira got dozens of tips like this every week, but he still considered each one carefully. Sporting's youth academy had gotten very successful in the last 10 years, but it had also gotten very expensive. The best youth players required the best youth setup, and with all the upgrades to the pitches and training facilities, running the academy now cost more than $1 million each season. Pereira knew he couldn't afford to ignore clues about a possible talent. Besides, if word about a kid had reached him, even a kid as far away as Madeira, it wouldn't be long before the scouts at Benfica and Porto found out about him too.

"How old is he?" Pereira asked, already envisaging a new entry in the database.

"He's 11."

Pereira grimaced. "That's very young."

"He's small—very slight and fragile," de Freitas added.

Pereira wasn't worried about how big the boy was. In fact, smaller was better. At that age, bigger kids could rely on their physical superiority to stand out. Pereira preferred to recruit the ones who hadn't developed physically yet. Once they caught up, their skill would shine through. Of much greater concern was *where* the boy was. Pereira was wary of kids from Madeira. He'd seen it happen too many times: the transition to the mainland proved too tough, and the distance made everything more complicated. At the first sign of difficulty, they always ran back home to the middle of the Atlantic.

"He's with Nacional," de Freitas continued. "The coaches say he's very good."

Pereira paused. Nacional made for an interesting wrinkle. The Madeira club owed Sporting some €20,000 after recently signing a defender named Franco—a kid Pereira had recruited as a teenager almost a decade earlier. He turned it over in his mind. Maybe they could come to some sort of arrangement if this kid was as good as they said.

Pereira reluctantly agreed. He told de Freitas that he'd have one of the "Pereira Army" scouts stop by to take a look. If the boy showed promise, he would come to Lisbon for a short trial. And if things went as he expected, Cristiano Ronaldo would be back home on Madeira within a day or two. The only cost to Sporting would be the price of his airfare.

It didn't take Aurélio Pereira much to work out if Cristiano Ronaldo had what it took—and this time it had nothing to do with the way he tied his laces.

On the second day of the trial, Pereira left his office and wandered down to the training ground next to the club's Alvalade stadium to lay eyes on the boy himself. Ronaldo's technique was immediately apparent. He could play with both feet, and he was a natural athlete. Pereira noted how quickly he moved in possession, as though the ball were an extension of his body. But more than the way he controlled the ball, what caught Pereira's eye was the way he controlled the other kids. Ronaldo was already directing them on where to run and where to pass the ball—which was usually directly back to the feet of Cristiano Ronaldo. *He's coaching his teammates through the game*, Pereira thought. The boy was fearless, totally unfazed. Nothing like the shy, introverted island kids from Madeira he'd known before.

Pereira always said there were good players, great players, and pure talents. With the right training and the right attitude, a good player could be transformed into a great player. But no amount of training could turn a great player into a pure talent. That required something else—a certain strength of character, an inner confidence. It required charisma. As Pereira watched Ronaldo, it was like marveling at a matinee idol. Not for the last time, a bunch of guys who had just been humiliated by Cristiano Ronaldo immediately began clamoring for their coach to sign him up.

"The older kids all felt that he was there," Pereira recalls, "that he was different, extraordinary."

That night he drafted a memo to Sporting's senior executives urging them to bring Ronaldo on board, even if it meant waiving the debt they were owed by Nacional. He knew it was an unusual request. Sporting was not accustomed to paying transfer fees for kids fresh out of elementary school, let alone a fee that amounted to tens of thousands of euros. But Pereira was insistent. "It may seem absurd to pay so much for a 12-year-old boy, but he has enormous talent," Pereira wrote. "It would be a great investment for the future."

Two days later, Pereira received word that the deal had been approved. The club's finance director told him he was crazy.

IN CRISTIANO RONALDO'S mind, he was already on the way to living the life of a professional soccer player. Sporting, though, reminded him that he was 12.

As an academy prospect, he was expected to attend classes every morning and was required to stay on top of his schoolwork. Anyone who fell behind had to stay down and repeat the year. Youngsters were expected to show respect and courtesy at all times. Unfortunately for Sporting, educating Cristiano Ronaldo proved to be even harder than defending him one-on-one.

The transition to life in Lisbon was rough. He was only 600 miles from home, but it felt like a different planet. The other boys teased him mercilessly for his heavy Madeiran accent, and he got into a series of bust-ups and scrapes in the schoolyard. When Ronaldo felt that a teacher was making fun of the way he spoke in class, he threw a chair at her.

He was lonely and homesick. He cried every day for months. Bad marks and improvised absences began to add up, and the Sporting directors threatened to send him home if his attitude didn't improve. Ronaldo thought about quitting. The situation dragged on like this for almost a year before eventually resolving itself in the age-old way that difficulties for gifted athletes usually do. The club and player came to an agreement, and Ronaldo was quietly allowed to drop his studies. "I always felt that I wasn't cut out for school," Ronaldo explained later. "So what was the point?"

With schoolwork out of the way, Ronaldo used the time he would've spent daydreaming through math or chemistry to work on something he felt a genuine passion for: himself.

Still slender as a goalpost at age 14, he understood that anyone bigger than he was could easily knock him off the ball. He also noticed that pretty much everyone was bigger than he was. But Ronaldo had picked up enough biology to know that the solution to his problem was straightforward enough.

"I was skinny. I had no muscle. So I made a decision," Ronaldo wrote. "I was going to stop acting like a kid. I was going to train like I could be the best in the world."

If only Sporting would let him. The club's academy had strict limits on the amount of time young players were allowed to work out. It was one of the golden rules passed down by Aurélio Pereira himself. "We never put children in gyms," he said. "That's one of the secrets behind our players' long careers. It's important to let them grow naturally."

Only Ronaldo had spent 14 years growing naturally, and it wasn't having the desired effect. He started sneaking out of the dormitory at night to lift in the gym. When the Sporting coaches caught him, they punished him with detention. When he kept sneaking out, they started to padlock the gym every evening. Still Ronaldo wouldn't listen. He took buckets into the showers after training, filled them with water, and used them as weights for squats and push-ups. When they took the buckets away, he began strapping weights to his ankles and racing cars away from stoplights on the street. And when the coaches even took the balls away after training to stop him from overdoing it, he found a bowl of fruit in the cafeteria and practiced ball juggling with oranges.

"He always wanted more and more and more," says Carlos Bruno, Sporting's fitness coach. "Most players, when the training goes on too long, they say, 'Hey, Coach, too much water kills the plant, you know?' Cristiano was a guy who always wanted more water in the plant."

Ronaldo's physique soon blossomed into something closer to what he was going for. No one outmuscled him on the field anymore, and the snickers he once heard from opposing players about his size had stopped. "Now they would be looking at me like it was the end of the world," Ronaldo wrote. Usually it was. Ronaldo's improvement alerted the national team, and he made his debut for Portugal's under-15s in early 2001, scoring in a 2–1 win over South Africa. He played 11 more games for his country that year, bagging nine goals, and returned to Sporting convinced that he was firmly on his way. Ronaldo told his teammates, "I'll be the best in the world one day."

The coaches at the academy had reached that conclusion months earlier. Aurélio Pereira was so sure of it, he had even informed the top brass. "He told me, 'We have the best 15-year-old player in the world,'" says Carlos Freitas, the former general manager. "Of course, I thought maybe he was just a little excited."

In the summer of 2001, Ronaldo's rapid ascent hit a roadblock. The team that finally slowed him down was a squad of physiologists in the Human Kinetics Department at the Technical University of Lisbon. They put him through the tests that Sporting required of any under-18 player to assess his readiness for senior football. Measuring bone density, growth rate, and physical maturity, they concluded that playing regularly against grown men might stifle his physical development. The physiologists recommended that Ronaldo stay with the youth team for another season to make more natural progress.

In order to fast-track nature, Sporting devised a special strength and coordination regime to make Ronaldo more explosive—not like the haphazard weight training he'd been sneaking off to do on his own. The first-team coach, László Bölöni, wanted him as strong, versatile, and dangerous as possible before he put him in the lineup. "He was going to very quickly come up against very strong defenders who were going to try and kick him to Brazil," Bölöni says. "He understood that what's important isn't just the technical prowess that the Portuguese love so much and overemphasize sometimes."

In the summer of 2002, the poindexters at the university could no longer hold him back. His time at the academy was over.

RONALDO WASN'T THE finished article quite yet. That much was apparent when he joined up with Sporting's senior team for preseason in the summer of 2002. He was so anxious during his initial training session that the first time someone passed him the ball he did something utterly out of character: he passed it straight back. "I was really nervous because I was playing alongside some of my heroes," Ronaldo recalled later. If that experience wasn't intimidating enough, Ronaldo also had reason to feel a little sheepish around the club's star striker, Mário Jardel. Just a few weeks earlier, Ronaldo had started dating Jardel's little sister.

The spark between Ronaldo and László Bölöni took a little longer to materialize. Bölöni, a gruff Romanian in thick glasses, had joined Sporting the year before, leading the club to the league and cup double in his first season in charge. Now he had set his sights on making a run in the Champions League, and he was far from convinced that another one of old Aurélio's academy kids was going to make that happen.

A few days into preseason, he was even more skeptical. By then, Ronaldo had overcome his nervous habit of passing the ball as soon as he received it. The problem was that he no longer passed the ball much at all. "He has no tactical awareness as an individual or team player," Bölöni wrote in an early coaching report on Ronaldo, bemoaning the youngster's excessive reliance on dribbling and penchant for stepovers. Bölöni signed off the report with a single word, underlined twice: "Selfish."

At that stage, it looked as though Cristiano Ronaldo would face a longer road to regular first-team football than his academy teammates Hugo Viana and Ricardo Quaresma, who had gone straight from the youth team into Bölöni's starting lineup a year earlier. But two circumstances that summer conspired to clear a path for Ronaldo. First, Sporting's star striker, João Pinto, punched a referee during Portugal's World Cup defeat by South Korea and was banned for four months by FIFA. Second, when Bölöni asked Carlos Freitas how much he could spend on a replacement, he was told in no uncertain terms that there was no money for one. The club was broke.

So Bölöni set to work on incorporating Ronaldo, his replacement for a replacement. The first thing he did was move him from center forward to the wing, where his dribbling and stepovers would be more effective. The second thing he did was instruct him to cut down on the dribbling and stepovers. He knew better, however, than to have Ronaldo eliminate them completely. "My task was to tell him that dribbling past one or two players is fine," Bölöni said. "But five was too many."

It wasn't long before Ronaldo was back doing what he did best. His first senior goal for Sporting came in an exhibition game against Real Betis, when he was still so unknown that the TV station broadcasting the match credited the strike to someone called Custodio Ronaldo. They managed to get it right for his first Primeira Liga appearance though, off the bench on September 29, 2002. Eight days later, Ronaldo made his first start and scored twice. The first goal was a spectacular strike after a couple of stepovers.

Up in the stands, his mother nearly fainted.

DOLORES AVEIRO WASN'T the only person in the stadium feeling a little overcome. Les Kershaw, Manchester United's chief scout, was also present that day, on his latest mission to Lisbon to check in on Cristiano Ronaldo and his teammate Ricardo Quaresma.

United had been tracking the duo for two years already but had stepped up their interest lately. That was largely at the behest of Carlos Queiroz, a former Sporting manager born in Portuguese Mozambique who had joined Manchester United as Alex Ferguson's assistant manager that summer. One of Queiroz's early conversations with the new boss concerned the best young talent in Portugal, and in particular the pair of teenage prodigies at his old club. Queiroz responded with a full-throated endorsement of Ronaldo and Quaresma. Pressed on which of them United should sign, he was unequivocal: "There is no doubt," he said. "Both."

Kershaw felt sure they both had the talent to make it at Old Trafford.

He was less sure about each player's temperament. Quaresma was outrageously skillful but appeared tactically ill disciplined and was constantly winding up opponents. In the derby match against Benfica that season, he'd lasted just nine minutes before he was sent off for stamping on a defender and then making his point by headbutting him too. Ronaldo was more disciplined on the pitch, but had a habit of drifting out of the game when things went against him.

As Kershaw followed Ronaldo over the course of the 2002–2003 season, those concerns slowly disappeared. Ronaldo became a regular with Sporting, and that summer Kershaw watched him light up the Toulon tournament, leading Portugal to the title despite being the youngest player on the field. (In what would become a theme of his career, Ronaldo narrowly missed out on the best player award to a diminutive midfielder from Argentina. This one was named Javier Mascherano.)

Kershaw's final scouting report on Ronaldo was plain. It was time for United to act. Now 18, he was entering the last year of his contract, and in light of its precarious financial position, Sporting was determined to cash in. Quaresma had already been offloaded to Barcelona earlier that summer, and Barça had since joined the long list of clubs interested in Ronaldo. Txiki Begiristain, Barcelona's director of football, had even made arrangements to scout Ronaldo in person by attending one of Sporting's exhibition games that summer, a red-letter preseason showdown to mark the opening of Sporting's new stadium. The opposition would be Manchester United.

IT WAS A little after 4:00 a.m. when Manchester United touched down in Lisbon on a red-eye from Philadelphia.

The Sporting match was 40 hours away, though United's players hardly knew what day it was as they trooped off the plane. They had been on the road for nearly three weeks now and were about to play their fifth match in a third different time zone. Alex Ferguson sent his players straight to the hotel and told them to rest up. There would be no team activities that day. Everyone was far too exhausted for training. And besides, Ferguson had plans of his own.

The United manager, a gruff Scotsman from the shipyards of Glasgow, hadn't turned himself into the most dominant manager in English soccer by being a brilliant tactician in the dugout. Instead, he had gone from former hard-nosed striker and onetime pub landlord to the top of the Premier League thanks to two fundamental qualities. The first was his irresistible power of motivation, which he sometimes supplemented with a shouting treatment known as The Hairdryer. The second was his uncanny ability to know exactly when his squad needed a shake-up. Landing in Portugal was one of those moments.

Ferguson just had time for a change of clothes before heading out to Cascais, a small beach town west of Lisbon. He wasn't looking for a suntan. He was there to meet with Jorge Mendes for what seemed like the first time. Though there had, in fact, been a previous encounter, it had proved more memorable for one man than the other.

One year earlier, Mendes had gotten word that Carlos Queiroz was looking for a backup goalkeeper. Mendes didn't have any clients who fit the bill at that time, but in the world of European soccer agents that counted as only a minor inconvenience. He wasn't about to miss out on a chance to make inroads with Ferguson. So Mendes made a few calls, and soon he had inserted himself as an intermediary in the proposed transfer of a keeper named Ricardo from Real Valladolid to Old Trafford. Crucially, Mendes was among the party of agents and advisers who would travel to Manchester to close the deal.

At least, that was the plan. The night before the trip, Mendes was making the long drive back to Porto from Madrid with his girlfriend when the rear axle came loose from the truck in front of them. Mendes swerved to avoid a collision and lost control of his Porsche. The car spun 90 degrees and smashed into the guardrail on the side of the road. Airbags saved their lives, but Mendes's face was covered in blood. When paramedics arrived on the scene, they found that the skin around his ear had been completely torn off.

As soon as an ambulance delivered him to the emergency room, Mendes informed the staff that he had no time to be examined by doctors. Instead, he ran to the nearest pharmacy, grabbed four rolls of gauze bandages, and ordered a car to take him to the airport. There was a flight to Manchester that morning, and Mendes was aboard, stuffing a wad of gauze into his ear to stop the blood from dripping on his suit.

The journey was excruciating, but Mendes made it. He even positioned himself at the table in such a way that Ferguson wouldn't see the unsightly mess that used to be his ear. It was a heroic effort, but to no avail. Mendes, his ear throbbing and heavily bandaged, uttered no more than four words the entire meeting. One year later, Ferguson had no recollection of him being there at all.

This time Jorge Mendes had more to say.

He knew that Manchester United needed a marquee signing. The club was flush with cash and in the market for attacking options. Unlike in US sports, where players are traded, international soccer talent is bought and sold during two set periods in the calendar. That summer's transfer window was due to close in three weeks, and even the senior United players were itching for Ferguson to make a move.

Mendes was also under pressure. He'd convinced Ronaldo—and Ronaldo's mother—that he was the right man to mastermind his career. Now he needed to deliver. After all, this was the pitch he had used to poach Ronaldo away from another agent named José Veiga, whose client list included everyone who was anyone in a Portugal shirt. When Sporting had three youngsters tipped for stardom—Hugo Viana, Ricardo Quaresma, and Ronaldo—Veiga snapped them all up. But Veiga was too old school to care about looking after teenagers. He had superstars moving between Barcelona and Real Madrid to worry about. So when Ronaldo complained about Sporting taking too long to pay him or for not arranging extra comp tickets for his mom, Veiga passed him off to an assistant.

Mendes sensed an opening. He took Ronaldo out to dinner and spent the whole time putting on the doting son-in-law act for Dolores. He knew he'd made the right impression a few weeks later when Ronaldo split with Veiga via fax.

The challenge for Mendes wasn't drumming up interest in Ronaldo. It was securing the right offer. Mendes understood that a wrong move could jeopardize his entire career—and would probably hurt Cristiano's too. Man United was the right offer.

Like any good agent, Mendes opened the negotiations with a completely ridiculous proposal. Ronaldo would sign for United if Ferguson could guarantee he would play in 50 percent of the club's first-team games that season. Some clubs might have accepted. But Manchester United was categorically not one of them. When it came to negotiating, Ferguson wouldn't guarantee that Wednesday came after Tuesday. The training ground was the place to decide who played and how often. In a managerial career that seemed like it began in the early Cretaceous period, Ferguson had never once promised playing time to a new recruit. And he certainly wasn't about to start with an 18-year-old with less than one season of senior football under his belt.

With anyone else, Ferguson might have walked away then and there. But he could see that times were changing, that a new breed of agents like Jorge Mendes controlled the future of the game and United's chances of staying relevant in the transfer market. So he played along. If Ronaldo signed, Ferguson guaranteed he would play six Premier League matches.

Six matches. Mendes thought it over. This was some way short of 50 percent. In fact, it was some way short of 20 percent. But it was also Manchester United. Six games there were worth entire seasons elsewhere. The 61-year-old Scot and the 37-year-old Portuguese shook hands. Small matters like the transfer fee, a world record for a teenager, would be left to Carlos Freitas and Peter Kenyon, United's chief executive. The important business was done.

Later that night, Mendes visited Ronaldo's Lisbon apartment to deliver the news. Cristiano was ecstatic about moving to the team he'd admired since it scooped up three trophies in the same season in 1999. "Let's go celebrate!" he told Mendes.

But Mendes demurred. His mind had already moved on, gears whirring on the next deal. Besides, he told the 18-year-old, there was a match the next day to prepare for. Cristiano Ronaldo needed to show his new teammates who he was.

TWO

The Farm System

AMID THE CHATTER of agents, Lisbon executives, and his own players, there was one more thing nagging away at Alex Ferguson on the night he signed Cristiano Ronaldo. It had been bothering him for more than two weeks now. Even as he pulled off one transfer coup, Ferguson was still upset about missing out on a different one. Right before United took off on its preseason tour, the club had been snubbed by a different Portuguese-speaker with a taste for stepovers and male jewelry. His name was Ronaldinho, the Brazilian World Cup winner and Paris Saint-Germain star who had run rings around every soccer club in France and seemingly closed down every nightclub in Paris.

Ferguson had wanted him to be United's new icon, someone to make Old Trafford forget the ugliness of David Beckham's 2003 exit, which followed the bizarre incident of Ferguson kicking a stray boot in the dressing room and hitting Beckham above the eye. But the Ronaldinho saga kept dragging. Ferguson even made a trip to Paris to close the deal himself when he felt PSG was dithering. PSG felt instead like he'd come to bully them. Both sides were probably right. While this dance went on, Spanish giant Barcelona saw an opportunity to cut in. "In many ways I think the player would prefer to come to Barcelona for the weather and other factors," a smug club spokesman said at the time. "It's closer in culture to the Brazilian way of life."

Barcelona, as a club, was also closer in culture to the Brazilian way of chaotic financial management. It was carrying more debt than at any point in its 104-year history and staring down the barrel of possible bankruptcy. For an institution that viewed itself as a pillar of Catalonia as much as an organization that fielded 11 soccer players in *blaugrana* stripes on a Saturday—along with teams in basketball, handball, and roller hockey—this went way beyond an economic crunch. Barcelona was facing an existential crisis. Again. (The club seemed to stumble into one every 20 years or so.) Ronaldinho's arrival was supposed to herald a reset right when the club needed it most.

Barcelona had gone four consecutive seasons without a trophy of any sort, but that was only the tip of the iceberg. Much more troublesome was the sense that the club, one of the charter members of La Liga in 1929 and one of only two genuine superpowers in Spanish soccer, was growing stale and dusty. It boasted the largest stadium in Europe, but the club's members, known as *socis*, who'd been born into fandom and received their membership cards as ritually as first communion, simply weren't coming anymore. The club had 95,000 seats and no one to fill them.

The indifferent members had a point. Even if no Catalan worth his *pan amb tomaquet* would ever admit it, a second-place finish behind Real Madrid was at least digestible. It had happened more than a dozen times in the past, and it would happen again. At least the general order of the universe still made sense. In the 72 seasons since La Liga's foundation, one or the other had been Spanish champion 45 times, with Real racking up 29 titles to Barça's 16. No one else had won more than eight. But what Barcelona fans couldn't tolerate was the depressing slide behind the likes of Mallorca, Celta Vigo, and Deportivo La Coruña. Between 2000 and 2003, Barça finished fourth, fourth, and sixth. That last indignity cost the club its spot in the pan-European Champions League, where a deep run was worth more than €30 million.

The Barça Dream Team of the early 1990s—which had lifted its name from the gold medal–winning US basketball team at the 1992 Olympics in the city—now seemed a long way away too. No one felt it more than Johan Cruyff, the Dutch master and architect of that team who had shaped every notion about how the club should play soccer and elevated it to a near-religious experience in Barcelona. A silky play-maker who epitomized Dutch cool—despite his ability to pick a fight with nearly anyone—he'd arrived at Barcelona from Ajax in 1973 after falling out with the boyhood team that had nurtured his gift and turned him into a world-beater. The reason was a dispute over the captain's armband. Cruyff's teammates, fed up with his ego and exhausted by his constant nagging, had voted him out of the role.

In the Barcelona locker room, he found a more receptive audience. Comfortably the best player anyone there had ever seen, Cruyff often acted as if he were the team's coach. And by 1988 he actually was, after trading in his short-shorts for an oversized trench coat. During his eight-year stint in the dugout, Cruyff led the club to four straight Liga titles and its first European Cup, preaching a playing philosophy that Barcelona took as gospel. As his player Pep Guardiola would say later, Cruyff "built the cathedral."

Now, in the early 2000s, Cruyff spent his time outside the congregation, sniping at new management from his newspaper column. Fans echoed his complaints about uninspiring players and Barça's high crime of fielding a team without a discernible style. Where was the swagger? Why were they so dull on the pitch?

What the fans should have been more worried about was the brewing disaster on the club's books. In 2003, Barcelona was carrying debt of €186 million, which accounted for 151 percent of the club's annual income. "FC Barcelona was in an untenable situation and at serious risk of missing the train to globalization being taken by the world's main clubs," wrote Ferran Soriano, who took over as Barcelona's chief financial officer in 2003. "The club was almost bankrupt. The team, *the product*, we were selling was neither attractive nor did it offer any guarantee of success."

Any other company would have turfed out the directors and begun begging for mercy from creditors. Only Barcelona isn't structured like any other company. The club is run as a nonprofit and owned by the dues-paying members. Decisions are made by a board of 20 or so directors and a president elected every six years. The men who vie for the top job—and they are always men—manage their campaigns as if they're running for the US Senate in a midsized state. They glad-hand around town, agree to every interview, and use that platform to make outrageous promises.

For a fast-talking lawyer named Joan Laporta, the crazy pledge in 2003 was to put Barça back on track. He was going to address both of the club's pressing issues—its lack of style and money—the same way most soccer problems are solved: by burning more cash.

As Laporta's campaign gained momentum, he had trained his sights first on an English pop icon who sometimes played soccer, David Beckham—except it was already too late: one of the summer's hottest targets was already on his way to Real Madrid. These things happen when a disturbance ripples through the Spanish transfer market—one club inevitably messes with the other's plans. Laporta brushed it off. Without hesitation, he pushed all of his chips onto Ronaldinho. If anyone was worth digging deeper into debt for, he figured, it was the Brazilian who seemed to control the ball with his mind.

This was going to be Barça's return to relevance. Cruyff was long gone, and so was the squad of brilliant soloists he had turned into European champions a decade before. But now the socis had their game-changer, a player worth the price of admission. He could put the Celtas and Deportivos of the world back in their place and light up the cathedrals of European soccer. Barcelona finally had a new genius to be excited about.

Deep inside the club, the men preaching the gospel of Cruyff at the youth academy agreed.

They just knew that Barça's new genius wasn't named Ronaldinho.

AT THAT POINT, the boy who would save Barcelona was barely 16 years old, growing too slowly, and still rage-quitting at PlayStation. His Argentine passport read Lionel Andres Messi Cuccitini, but around Barcelona's youth academy, known as La Masia, he introduced himself as Leo—that is, when he spoke at all. The kids who met him back then remember thinking he might be mute as he sat in the corner of the dressing room taping his ankles. Once they discovered he wasn't, they mocked him for unleashing an Argentine accent thicker than *dulce de leche*. They mostly heard all those "sh" sounds and dropped consonants when he came out of his shell during marathon video game sessions on the road. After that, what time they didn't spend talking to him, they spent talking *about* him. "How can I forget? He was a very tiny boy, very shy," says Cesc Fàbregas, who played alongside Messi in the youth ranks. "You could feel that he was coming from somewhere very different to where he arrived. The first training session already, you could see that he was special."

Fàbregas, born and raised in Catalonia, was the archetype of a Masia kid. Surrounded by a family of socis, everything about his soccer career was geared toward FC Barcelona from the time he first kicked a ball. He became a card-carrying member of the club as a child and joined the youth academy before his 10th birthday. Camp Nou, the site of all his wildest dreams, stood about 35 miles from his house. If FC Barcelona could plant seeds in the Catalan soil and water them till they grew into footballers, they would look like Cesc Fàbregas.

Founded by the Barça president who would one day hire Cruyff as manager and on another day fire half the team, La Masia opened its doors in 1979 with the mission of melding the local talent with as many boys from around Spain as it could recruit. La Masia itself, originally an 18th-century farmhouse, was co-opted to serve as a dormitory and the center of a boarding school that grew into a Catalan Eton for soccer. The philosophy behind La Masia evolved over the years, but as with everything else at the club, it was heavily shaped by Cruyff, who, being a Dutch soccer person, had strongly held opinions on anything and everything. When it came to La Masia, he happened to be right.

Having grown up in the football hothouse that was Ajax in Amsterdam, Cruyff knew that a soccer academy needed to be less like the boot camps that were being run in England and more like a music conservatory. Players needed to evolve inside a structure that shaped them as humans first, so that school would not be compromised. Students would attend classes every weekday morning and have supervised study time in the afternoons. They also needed a framework to understand the game. It wasn't enough to drill fitness and individual skills—students had to develop a sense for where each player should be on the pitch. With his chesslike understanding of space and consequence, Cruyff was famous as a player for shifting teammates around by as little as a yard or two. He wanted to make sure this kind of awareness was instilled in kids before they realized what they were learning. It was Cruyff who'd insisted that every Barcelona team at every age group play the same 4-3-3 formation. That style full of short, sharp passes would be seared into the soccer mind of any kid who came through the system. "When you have possession you make the field big, and when you lose it you make it small again," was the simplest way Cruyff could think to describe it. His more abstract term was *juego de posicion*.

But as easy as it is to picture La Masia as soccer's Dead Poets Society, the academy's purpose is not the pursuit of some aesthetic goal for the sake of aesthetics. The primary reason La Masia exists is to save Barcelona money.

A homegrown talent will always be cheaper than a camera-ready player signed on the open market. When Harvard Business School published a case study of the club in 2015, it found that 530 boys had passed through La Masia's residential program. Some 14 percent of them went on to play at least one game for the senior team, a staggering return considering just how much can go wrong in the development of a young athlete.

Barcelona itself had conducted a similar analysis when Ferran Soriano arrived in the club's finance department in 2003. The question he asked himself was simple: Was running the academy worth it? The club's number crunchers took the global costs of running La Masia over the previous decade—everything from coaching to housing to breakfast cereal—and divided it by the number of players who reached the first team. They found that the club's average investment in every kid who made it was roughly €2 million (which might buy you a third-string goalkeeper on the European transfer market today).

All this development happens, Barça will tell you, without turning these children into soccer robots. "Among other top European clubs, we have the highest rate—50 percent—of our 18- and 19-year-old players studying at the university level," La Masia director Carles Folguera told the Harvard researcher. "Unlike most other clubs, we are happy with more hours spent studying rather than in the gym."

Neither a natural student nor a gifted athlete, Messi was happy to ignore both. The classroom and the gym were not where he chose to spend his time.

THAT MESSI WAS in Spain at all to be a soccer prodigy and a mediocre student was entirely a matter of timing.

First, it required his skeleton to be extremely behind schedule. At age nine, he was just four-foot-one. And everywhere he went during his mesmerizing early days tearing up youth soccer in his native Rosario, Argentina, the question was always the same: Will he grow? Messi joined his local team, Newell's Old Boys, and did what any player with even half his talent does at that age. With preternatural control of the ball and an innate sense of rhythm in his runs, Messi made other kids look like toddlers.

Stories about the childhoods of brilliant soccer players who reach the pinnacle of the game are all pretty much paint-by-numbers at this point. Like Ronaldo, Messi always had a soccer ball at his feet. Like Ronaldo, he loved to play with his friends in the street. All his teammates had to do was pass him the ball and they would win. Messi checked all those boxes, complete with the backdrop of a crowded South American city, three hours north of Buenos Aires. Where his story diverged was that his body wouldn't seem to catch up. His nickname was El Enano. The Dwarf.

Height—or lack of it—isn't necessarily a deal-breaker in soccer, one of the few sports in the world that accommodates all body types, provided you can run for 90 minutes. Argentina knew this better than most: the greatest player it had ever seen, Diego Maradona, was only five-foot-five. But Messi's lack of growth seemed so abnormal that his club suggested that his family consult a local professional to find out whether something was wrong with the boy in the billowing jersey. The answer came from a Rosario endocrinologist and Newell's fan named Diego Schwarzstein. He suggested that little Leo could be treated with a growth hormone. Even if years of regular injections seemed a radical treatment for an 11-year-old, the family was prepared to sign off on it to give Messi a chance to reach his full height.

"I don't know if you will be better than Maradona," Schwarzstein told him. "But you will be taller."

It would take years for Dr. Schwarzstein to be proven right. In the meantime, the Messi family needed to keep finding ways to pay for the shots amid a collapse of the Argentine health insurance system. Newell's did its best to help out. Throughout the year 2000, it was kicking the Messi family $100 to $200 a month for a treatment that cost nearly a grand. The strain on the family was growing, but so was Messi's reputation. A video circulated of him juggling an orange off the ground with his feet 113 times without exploding it. He repeated the trick with a tennis ball 140 times. Rosario's local newspaper, *La Capital*, also featured him in a Q&A in early September in which he revealed that his favorite book was the Bible, that his second-favorite sport was handball, and that if he had to pick a job he would like to be a phys ed teacher.

A web of agents and talent-spotters were now taking an interest and writing checks for the hormone injections too. Their bet was that, young and undersized as Messi was, someone in Europe would at least want to take a look. Barcelona was that someone. In September of 2000, the club invited Messi, his fledgling agent, and his father to Spain for a tryout. Leo had never been on a plane.

The trio flew overnight through rocky turbulence and landed in Barcelona, only to learn that they'd traveled more than 6,000 miles to see a man who, at that precise moment, was on the other side of the world. Club sporting director Charly Rexach, who would make the call on whether or not to sign him, was scouting players at the Summer Olympics in Sydney. "Charly, this is a phenomenon," the Argentine agent Horacio Gaggioli had told him. "You have to see him." Rexach assumed he was talking about some promising 17-year-old. When he learned that Messi was 13, he decided that he very much did not have to see him—at least not immediately. Rexach knew that the logistics of signing a 13-year-old were made infinitely more complicated by rules that prevented clubs from acquiring the rights to players from outside their immediate areas unless their parents were moving to the city for work. (The idea was to regulate an industry that sometimes had too much in common with human trafficking.)

Still, Messi had made the trip now—he was here. So the coaches who had heard vague rumors about the kid sent him out to a practice field for some close-control drills. He nailed every one like there were magnets in his ankles. Then they plugged him into some training sessions with La Masia boys, and there, too, Messi did his thing so stunningly that word spread throughout the academy to come watch him. Everyone wanted a look at the shrimpy dribbler from Argentina.

All told, Messi kicked around Barcelona training sessions for 11 days before Rexach came home to watch him. The final test was a game against kids two years older than Messi—and so much bigger that the gap might as well have been a decade. Strolling in with the match already in progress, Rexach walked from the corner of the pitch to the bench. He watched for all of five minutes and saw "a boy who was transformed on the field," he wrote. "Outside he was shy, very quiet. But when he played, he was another, a born winner, brave, never abandoning a play."

"You have to sign him," Rexach told his bosses.

Messi may have turned up with Rexach on the other side of the globe and been stuck in Catalonia for nearly two weeks, but he couldn't have picked a better window to land there. When he arrived for good later that year—his first contract famously drawn up on a paper napkin—a unique set of circumstances had come together without Messi ever realizing it.

It turned out that Barcelona in the early 2000s was the perfect place and time to be a young athlete who was also a genius. A rare confluence of culture, teachers, and political forces was brewing in Catalonia to create a moment in history not unlike 1860s Paris for painters or 1980s

Silicon Valley for computer geeks—only this one was for tiny soccer players.

One major catalyst was Barcelona besting Paris and Brisbane to host the 1992 Summer Olympics, the impact of which stretched long after the closing ceremony. Fàbregas can't quite explain what was in the air in the years that followed the Games, but he felt it. "It brought these sports vibes," he says. "And also being a great city next to the beach, next to the sea, it's a fantastic place to be when you want to do sports and grow into a talent."

The Olympic organizers made it easy. The Barcelona Games are widely regarded as the most successful ever for creating a useful legacy. Any kid with even a passing interest in sports had a wild array of new infrastructure to choose from. One program called Campus Olimpia opened Olympic venues to kids during their summer vacations. Another, created by the School Sports Council of Barcelona, organized competitions in the venues for some 40,000 children. And all over the city, neighborhoods were reinvigorated expressly with sports in mind. The disused Estació del Nord railway station, which had sat empty for 20 years, became a multi-use sports hall that far exceeded its purpose as the Olympic table tennis venue. Even sports that no Catalan would ever care about were reshaping the city's soccer scene. The main stadium for the Olympic baseball tournament—which saw Spain lose its first six games by a combined score of 79–8—was converted into the home ground for one of Barcelona's well-supported lower-division teams, CE L'Hospitalet. From 1999 onward, the 7,000-capacity park enabled perennially mid-table Hospi to boast what one local councilor called "undoubtedly the best football field in Segunda B."

Something less tangible was also happening: the city of Barcelona was rediscovering how to be itself. The Catalan language and flag had been officially banned during the dictatorship of Francisco Franco until his death in 1975. Seventeen years later, Catalan was one of the Games' four official languages, along with Spanish, English, and French. Some 35,000 Catalan *senyeras*—the red-and-yellow-striped flags of the region—appeared around the city, according to the local government. The 1992

Olympics were a global event that somehow belonged to a single region of northeast Spain. "It invited people to understand more the Catalan culture and what Barcelona really is," Fàbregas says.

For the soccer team, this was long-awaited validation. FC Barcelona, one of the staunchest defenders of Catalan identity through the Franco years, had been constantly at odds with the regime in Madrid. Now, at the dawn of soccer's global and commercial age, the club's Catalan slogans, "Visça Barça" and "Mes que un club," were primed for a worldwide audience. And any kid who played under its colors wasn't just representing a team. Barcelona was a nation.

It helped, too, that during those Olympics the Spanish team that won its first soccer medal since a silver in 1920 had a strong Catalan accent. The best player on Spain's road to gold at Camp Nou was the busy young local midfielder Pep Guardiola, who played for Barça. Despite a lack of flashy technical gifts, he embodied Cruyffian soccer with a metronomic understanding of the simple yet devastating mantra: get the ball, pass the ball. "Pep in the field was the conductor, everything happened through him," his Barcelona teammate Albert Ferrer said later. "The passes that nobody sees, he saw."

Guardiola, who was being coached at Barça by Johan Cruyff himself, was demonstrating what players molded by Cruyff's system at La Masia might look like. He was just 21 and had won the European Cup and Olympic gold in the space of a few months. What would happen if Barcelona could assemble a whole team of Masia graduates?

By 2000, the club was just starting to find out. The boys who had never known anything but the Cruyff method—the lessons that he had instilled at the academy—were beginning to reach maturity. Growing up with the Dream Team, they'd been raised on a diet of successful Barcelona sides, a club that played beautiful, aspirational soccer with a style burned into their collective consciousness. A kid like Fàbregas had heard "get the ball, pass the ball" ever since he could run.

Not all of Cruyff's teachings, however, were being applied perfectly. At the senior level, he had instilled in the club a strange obsession with Dutch players. That was all well and good when the Dutch player was

Ronald Koeman, the swashbuckling defensive midfielder of the 1992 Dream Team, but not so useful by the end of the decade when Barça seemed to leap on any international player wearing an orange jersey. That obsession was another factor in the deepening malaise. The stale team needed to be turned over, and major signings, like Ronaldinho, were necessarily short-term solutions. The long-term answer had to come from within.

They needed to tap the Masia pipeline.

JUST WHAT WAS in the *rioja* during the summer of 1986 may never be known, but the crop of Spanish players born in 1987 that converged on Barcelona at the same time as Messi would be talked about for a decade. The team was known as Generación 87, which sounded a lot like the nickname of Messi's utterly dominant side at Newell's, "The Machine of 87." The difference in Barcelona was that Messi was surrounded by other world-beaters in the making. Three kids in that lineup stood out already: future World Cup winner Cesc Fàbregas, future Barcelona captain Gerard Piqué, and the striker who was just as deadly in front of the goal as Messi, a local boy named Víctor Vázquez. All four were clearly bound for the big time. Only Vázquez fell somewhat short, his career waylaid by a catastrophic knee injury at 18.

What was so remarkable about them together is that they understood as preteens what many never grasp even after a decade at the top level. Without thinking, they knew how to circulate the ball in complex patterns, move into open passing lanes, and create numerical superiority on the pitch. They seemed to keep the ball for eons, won it back quickly on the rare occasions they lost it, and seemed never to have heard of a header. These undersized kids were tidy enough on the ball to operate in the tightest spaces, yet they used that ability, counterintuitively, to make the field as big as possible. You didn't need to be huge if your opponent couldn't get near you.

From the earliest practice sessions, the Barça boys could see that Messi had been raised on a completely different version of soccer. The ping-ping-ping of short passes, known as *tiki-taka*, was not what made heroes in Argentina. Kids from Buenos Aires to Messi's Rosario grew up worshiping close control and mazy dribbling. If Brazil could claim that its soccer was flavored by samba, Argentina's answer was a tango designed to seduce the defender, then step on his ankle. Diego Maradona's second goal against England in the quarterfinal of the 1986 World Cup became the epitome of it. Four minutes after deceiving the referee by punching home Argentina's opening goal—the Hand of God moment—he danced away from four Englishmen and beat the goalkeeper. Messi spent his formative years re-creating this before moving to Catalonia.

"In Barcelona, we are more like collective players—passing the ball, moving the ball around, playing for each other," Vázquez says. But Messi could do it on his own. "The first time you were, like, in shock."

Even the youth team's coach at the time, a veteran named Rodolfo Borrell, couldn't quite believe what he was seeing. So in one session he assigned Fàbregas an impossible task: "Try to stop him. Even if you have to [kick] his legs." Following orders, Cesc eventually swept Messi's little legs out from under him. Messi got up without a word, because he had already made his point. "We thought we were amazing players, we were doing so well," Vázquez says. "But this guy had something different than we had."

Around the club, kids in various age groups were always checking in on each other. Messi and his friends would spend their entire weekends watching other Barça sides play their matches, from the youngest juniors to the senior team at Camp Nou. And pretty soon, Generación 87 was drawing crowds too. Word was spreading fast around the club— and beyond—that coaches, parents, and even the parents of opponents needed to see what was happening here.

The Generación 87 *cadetes* knew they were also being watched as they began traveling around Europe for high-profile tournaments. They were La Masia. No one played like them—and no one could live with them. With misdirection and subtle feints, Messi turned every run into a fleeting display of close-up magic at speeds that opponents could never hope to process. When they inevitably gave up, they would change tactics and start pummeling Messi instead. Even then, his low center of gravity usually allowed him to twist away before some clumsy boot made contact with his ankle. Though this was only youth soccer, opponents tried what many hopeless senior sides would do in years to come against the great Barcelona teams in La Liga and the Champions League. They dropped back on defense, packed the edge of the penalty area, and prayed for a glimmer of hope on the counterattack. And still, Vázquez says, "we were destroying them. We were super good. We were moving the ball so fast. And at that age it makes a lot of difference." No youth team had the physical conditioning to give chase.

"We were dominant," Fàbregas says. "People say we were the best team in history in La Masia. I don't know if that's true or not. All I remember is that you become a winner. You are obsessed with winning."

Once the Generación 87 boys took the lead, they tended to pile on fast. In fact, this was mandatory. "If you can score 10, score 10," coaches told them. "But if you can go to 12, score 12. Never stop. Because if you stop, you're showing them disrespect."

If the twin philosophies of having fun playing soccer with your friends while pounding opponents into the ground seem incompatible, it's because they were. Messi and his teammates were not insensitive to the damage they were inflicting. Vázquez remembers one match on the road when Barcelona went up 15–0 in the first half, only to be told in the dressing room, "Go for 15 more." But as the players toddled back to the field, they realized they didn't have the heart to do it. "You can see the faces of the poor guys in front of you," Vázquez says. "They're like, 'We don't want to play anymore.'" The boys agreed that they would tack on a few more goals for appearances and then take their foot off the gas. *Tranquilo.*

The game finished 20–0. The team's only reward was a stern talking-to about commitment, winning mentalities, and why it's sometimes okay to make other children cry.

Messi didn't have to be told twice. Any of the Generación 87 boys who had faced him on PlayStation knew that inside his miniature frame breathed a frothing, snarling competitive monster. In one of their many blowout victories, Vázquez remembers racking up 10 goals. Messi had nine. And as the minutes ticked away, after more than 20 goals, everyone in a Barcelona shirt knew the score. On the pitch, Messi's teammates could see him simmering. "Look, look, he's going to score one more."

He scored two. Messi finished with 11.

SOMEHOW, THAT 11-GOAL performance doesn't come close to being Messi's most memorable game at La Masia. That would be the Catalan Cup final that lives on in Barcelona lore with a name like a movie title: El Partido de la Máscara. The Mask Game.

Inevitably, the opponent was Espanyol, Barcelona's other, slightly less historic club. The team felt like it played Espanyol every week. And in this case, it had. Eight days before the Cup final, Barça and Espanyol had met in the final league game of the season. Barcelona won easily, but victory came at the cost of Messi's cheekbone. He had fallen victim to yet another boy who couldn't follow his twists and turns and decided it was easier just to crash into him so forcefully that Messi was briefly knocked unconscious. Espanyol had seen enough. "We felt really, really, really bad because we were killing them since more than seven years," Vázquez says. "We were winning always, always, always." On the one occasion Espanyol eked out a victory, he adds, they "celebrated like they'd won the Champions League."

The Catalan Cup final was going to give them a chance to repeat the upset—especially if Barcelona's best player was now injured.

Messi was supposed to be sidelined for at least 15 days with the broken cheekbone. He sat out practice all week and spent the time silently fuming instead. By the Friday before the match, Messi couldn't stand it anymore. He told the team's coach at the time, Álex García, that he wanted in. García asked him if he was sure—because if he wasn't scared of getting hurt again, there might be a way to get him on the pitch. García already knew the answer: given the chance to play, Messi would take it every time.

By complete coincidence, another graduate of La Masia, defender Carles Puyol, had suffered a facial injury earlier in the season. He'd been able to keep playing for the senior team thanks to a plastic face mask that looked like an unpainted prop from the Zorro movies. Luckily for Messi, that mask was still knocking around somewhere. The only hitch was that Puyol's head was enormous and Messi was, well, Messi. On the day of the game, he fitted the plastic contraption to his face and realized he might as well have pulled on a blindfold.

Messi was fiddling with it right from kickoff. He complained to his teammates that he couldn't see—the damn thing kept slipping. And it was making him sweat too. Before the 10-minute mark, Messi was fed up and ripped off the mask entirely. He tossed it over to the bench and immediately normal service resumed. When his coaches finally saw some sense and subbed him out at halftime for his own safety, Barcelona was winning 3–1. Messi had scored two goals and assisted the third. To this day, those who saw the crowning match of Generación 87 believe they witnessed a miracle.

"This is another kind of player," says Vázquez, who was on the pitch. "This is not normal."

THE SOCCER-INDUSTRIAL COMPLEX knew this too.

One by one, scouts descended on Barcelona to pick off the stars of Generación 87. The boys understood that at some point in the past couple of years they had slid into a game for much higher stakes. They'd survived every cut and were closing in on adulthood. Suddenly, reaching the first team felt possible. And the kids who'd been their childhood friends were now their rivals. Coaches ramped up the intensity. Some of the players were told that this was the end of the road. "Maybe you get there, maybe not. But they have to prepare you to be there," Vázquez says. "And when you get the chance, you have to be ready because once you get in the first team, then it's no fun anymore. You have to win, you have to win and you have to win."

The closer they got, the more apparent it became that for all the brilliance of Generación 87, not all of them were going to make it. Fàbregas looked around and could see that players like Mikel Arteta and Andrés Iniesta were ahead of him at his position and a few years his senior.

"There are hundreds and hundreds of very talented kids in La Masia, and how many make it? Very, very few," Fàbregas says. "They would get their chances before me."

If the right offer came, Fàbregas was open to it. That's when Arsène Wenger's Arsenal swooped in. Having just missed out on Ronaldo, Wenger wasn't about to whiff on Fàbregas. So weeks after the Mask Game, Fàbregas made the heart-wrenching decision to leave the only club he'd ever known and move to England. A year later, Piqué would do the same. Sensing a bottleneck among central defenders, he leapt at the chance to join Manchester United to work under Alex Ferguson. The surprise wasn't so much that these players wanted to leave. It was that Barcelona let them.

The sharks were circling around Messi too, but the club knew enough to keep them away from him. And unlike Piqué or Fàbregas, he had no reason to look elsewhere. There was no one else like Messi in the pipeline. His road to the first team was completely unobstructed.

Barely six months after the Mask Game, Barcelona was playing a midseason exhibition on the road in Portugal against a Porto side coached by a former Barça assistant named José Mourinho. The match itself was entirely forgettable. The only moment worth remembering was the 71st minute, when the visitors waved Messi onto the field for his Barcelona first-team debut.

He was 16 years, four months, and 23 days old. Barcelona had signed him effectively for free, then raised him as one of its own.

THREE

The Two Jorges

THE TWO JORGES who steered Ronaldo and Messi out of their boyhood clubs and into the cathedrals of European soccer could not have been more different. Though neither Jorge set out to become a soccer agent or to plunge into negotiations with hundreds of millions of dollars on the table, one of them had always dreamed of fame and fortune—and it wasn't Jorge Messi.

If Jorge Mendes had always been a creature of pure ambition, Messi Sr. spent the first half of his life chasing more modest goals. He was an unremarkable player who made his living as a supervisor in a metallurgy plant to feed his family of four children. He coached the youth section of his local club in Rosario, a team called Grandoli, and more or less made it up as he went along. Life was organized around work, football, and family. Jorge only began to consider what might lie beyond Rosario in the wide world of professional soccer because Grandoli's best player happened to be his own offspring.

So when Jorge Messi the dad became Jorge Messi the improvised soccer agent, the plan was only ever to have one client. Just because he lacked experience, though, didn't mean Messi Sr. wasn't a shark. Even as he begged Newell's to help pay for Leo's hormone treatments—and with interest from Barcelona still in the early stages—Jorge organized a tryout for his son at River Plate, one of Argentina's two preeminent clubs based in Buenos Aires. The audition didn't come to much—although another future Argentine national team player, Gonzalo Higuaín, was present—but it was enough to alert Barcelona that interest was growing in the boy from Rosario. Messi's pressure tactic had succeeded.

It wouldn't be the last time. Once the entire Messi family was settled in Barcelona so Leo could progress through the ranks at La Masia, it seemed that the boy was the only member of the clan who was happy. He played football in the sunshine with his friends all day. The rest, bored and homesick, sat around watching television 6,500 miles from Rosario. Once again, Jorge wanted guarantees that all of this was going to be worth it. When he felt that his son wasn't being treated properly by Barcelona—which was usually a question of improving his contract—his favorite threat always boiled down to two simple words: Real Madrid. Look after my son, or that other club will. It was a blunt instrument, but for the dad figuring out that the agent business was all about leverage, it worked every time.

OVER IN PORTUGAL, Jorge Mendes learned that there was a little more art to this whole thing. A more natural salesman, it didn't matter whether he was dealing in footballer contracts or endorsement deals. To him, it was all the same skill that he had learned hawking sun hats and beach toys on the Portuguese coast as a kid. The boy who was nicknamed Cabanas and came from a modest Lisbon neighborhood harbored dreams of playing pro soccer—or at least being as close to the game as possible. What Mendes lacked in God-given talent he made up for in hustle.

Chasing work shortly after high school, he moved to Viana in the north of the country where, leaning on a loan from his brother, Mendes launched into another business that involved shuffling around assets and identifying superstars. But unlike being a soccer agent, this one also involved a lot of rewinding: Mendes was opening a video store. Named after a dreamy island off the coast of Thailand, Samui Video would have a crucial advantage over the competition, as far as Mendes was concerned. The business had to come with convenient parking. And it was a good thing customers weren't walking home, his partner recalled, because Mendes loaded up customers with more VHS tapes than they could carry or conceivably watch. "He had something in the way he spoke to them," Antonio Alberto says in Mendes's memoir. "Most people came to rent one movie and left with five! And they'd have to return them 24 hours later!"

At the same time, Mendes was playing fullback for a small semipro club called UD Lanheses in the Portuguese third tier. While his teammates earned €150 to €200 a month, Mendes had wangled himself a deal in which he pulled down more than €1,000. His extra pay came not for his abilities on the pitch but for his skill at selling advertising on the boards that surrounded it. Naturally, the list of local sponsors included Samui Video.

Mendes was just getting started. Everywhere he looked there were new customers to capture. With the video store, he'd grabbed folks who were happy to spend evenings sitting at home. His next venture was for people who wanted to go out. This time Mendes invested in a little complex by the beach and opened the Alfândega nightclub. That's where he met his first true soccer client, a square-jawed young goalkeeper by the name of Nuno Espírito Santo.

Nuno was hoping to secure a transfer away from Guimarães to some bigger club, and he hoped that his new friend, often seen directing evenings from behind the Alfândega bar, could get him there. And so, in the summer of 1996, Jorge Mendes the video-store owner, nightclub manager, and third-division fullback, also became a soccer agent. It didn't take him long to grasp that this was a business where the rules were made up on the fly and an agent was only as good as his nerve and his gas tank. Mendes seemed to spend his life on the highways up and down Portugal and across to Spain to meet with teams in person. But when he thought he'd struck a deal for Nuno with FC Porto, Guimarães got in the way. The club president insisted that Nuno wasn't going anywhere.

Mendes kept hunting for another, higher offer and soon secured it from Deportivo La Coruña. All it took was driving the 400-mile round trip between his home and northern Spain on a nearly daily basis to close it. Still, Guimarães wouldn't budge. It was time for drastic action: Mendes and Nuno agreed that the solution was simply to disappear

Nuno after the 1996 Olympics in Atlanta. Not only did he fail to show up to preseason training at Guimarães, he failed to show up anywhere anyone could find him. As far as the club could tell, its goalkeeper had fallen off the face of the Earth.

Where he landed was between Mendes's relatives in Lisbon and a secret location in La Coruña. For three months, Nuno kept himself in shape away from professional soccer, waiting for the clubs to strike a deal. He ran daily. He worked out on the beach. Mendes even learned to become a stand-in goalkeeping coach to put Nuno through his drills. The Iberian press kept asking, "Where is Nuno?" Mendes was happy to leave the papers hanging. The whole soap opera came to an end in October, well into the new season, when Guimarães agreed to sell, if only to rid itself of these pests, Nuno and Jorge.

It had taken three months, hundreds of gallons of gas, and some light kidnapping, but Mendes had finally completed a transfer.

The next few wouldn't require quite as much spycraft. By sweeping up promising local talent and understanding the skewed incentives of Europe's transfer market, he was able to create his own Portuguese soccer diaspora. Mendes could see that international soccer's reliance on transfers meant the real money wasn't in securing huge salaries for his clients. It was in having them move as often as possible and collecting a percentage of each transfer fee. The whole thing was a game of trust. Players had to believe that they could become superstars, and club presidents had to be convinced that they weren't just plugging a hole in their lineups but setting up a conveyor belt of talent for years to come. In the years after he moved Ronaldo to Manchester United, Mendes would ship two more players from the Portuguese league to Alex Ferguson: Nani, a winger who had also grown up at Sporting Lisbon; and Anderson, a Brazilian midfielder so thrilled by his rich new contract that he began wearing gaudy watches on both wrists. With all those repeat customers, Mendes was reinventing the job, sliding from agent as intermediary to agent as general manager. From the time cell phones became widely available in the late 1990s, Mendes always carried at least two. And when Bluetooth technology made it possible for every client and every club to be literally inside his ear canal at all times, he leapt at that too.

"You cannot imagine my life," Mendes liked to tell people.

Even as Mendes's stable of players and coaches ballooned in the early 2000s, Ronaldo remained the clear favorite. Mendes had promised stardom and delivered him to one of the biggest clubs on the planet. The next item on the agenda now was building him a commercial empire. The only problem was that in matters of major brand endorsements, Mendes had about as much know-how as Jorge Messi. They weren't in video stores or metallurgy plants anymore—not that it would stop either of them from trying to figure things out. What they both knew was that all soccer empires were built on the same foundation: it started with getting their boys a boot deal.

FOR AS LONG as anyone could remember, the market for the soccer boot had been controlled by a pair of warring families—who were actually the same family—from a sleepy Bavarian town called Herzogenaurach. On one side of the river that runs through the center sat the clan led by Adolf "Adi" Dassler, the revolutionary cobbler who named Adidas after himself and slapped the name on his game-changing experiments with athletic shoes. On the other was the brood of nieces and nephews guided by Adi's brother Rudolf, who named his rival outfit Puma when the two split in 1948.

The pair had begun in the 1920s, peacefully enough, manufacturing track spikes and soccer boots that looked more suited to plowing the fields than dribbling. From his glue-soaked workshop, the obsessive Adi spent years refining and fiddling with ever lighter, ever sturdier designs that improved quickly once he took some actual shoemaking lessons. Among athletes, the rumor was that the Dassler brothers' spikes might be a kind of secret weapon. They didn't advertise much—and in 1936 an American sprinter from Ohio State made sure they didn't need to. When Jesse Owens lit up the Berlin Olympics and enraged Adolf Hitler, he wore the Dasslers' German handiwork on his feet.

They understood earlier than most that the shoes spoke for themselves.

It was just a matter of getting enough athletes to lace them up. They groomed distributors all over the world and plied them with stock, followed by instructions to do whatever was necessary to get it out there. The Olympics were still run under the supreme code of amateurism, but the world of shoe endorsements had about as many rules then as it does now, which is to say almost none. Sneakers were handed out from duffel bags and the trunks of cars, and payments came in wads of cash. When the sports world was ready to resume after World War II, the brothers were in prime position to take over.

Only then did they venture seriously into soccer. Rudolf's Puma had an early edge in expertise after the split in the late 1940s, but the newly dubbed Adidas company had a connection to the West German national team and an all-important new invention: adjustable studs. And had the skies over the Wankdorf Stadium in Bern not opened up one afternoon in 1954, Adi Dassler might have never had the chance to show them off. The day that changed the course of soccer boot history was the World Cup final between the unfavored Germans and a virtuosic team of Hungarians known as the Magical Magyars. They were faster, more nimble, and more sophisticated than the Germans—at least until the rain drenched the pitch in the hours before the game. That's when West German coach Sepp Herberger instructed Dassler to switch his team's boots to the longer studs, according to Barbara Smit's history of the company.

"Adi, screw them in!" Herberger told him.

By then, having also grasped that his shoes needed to be more distinctive to pop clearly in photographs of sporting triumph, Adi was painting the strips of leather built into the shoes for structural support a different color. So, as the Germans kept their footing and upset Hungary 3–2 to win the World Cup, their Adidas boots not only featured new technology on the bottom but also sported three crisp white stripes on the side.

Much of the soccer world soon fell into two camps. The brothers, their respective branches of the family tree, and their legions of reps entered into an arms race that spread across continents and reached a fever pitch every four years around the World Cup. They signed up entire squads just to put their boots on a single superstar. They expanded into apparel, balls, and jerseys. The world's most popular sport was also becoming the world's most popular billboard. When Puma picked up Johan Cruyff, Adidas signed Germany's Franz Beckenbauer, both at great expense. Prices spiraled so far out of control through the 1960s that the Dasslers even agreed (some might say colluded) to make one particular player off-limits, because an all-out bidding war would have been too counterproductive. In a temporary truce, the two families, now led by first cousins Horst and Armin Dassler, came to a rare compromise: they wouldn't bid at all. Their deal became known as the Pelé Pact.

But a single handshake was nothing compared to a decades-long feud. Leaning on a German journalist and his relationship to the Brazilian national team in the lead-up to the 1970 World Cup, Puma took a chance. It offered Pelé, the most famous player on the planet, $25,000 to wear its boots for the tournament, plus another $25,000 a year for the next four years. On top of all that, it promised him a 10 percent royalty on all Pelé signature boots, sleek black numbers with Puma's wide leather strip along the side. The entire payment was made in cash, which Pelé tossed casually into a safe.

As far as pitchmen went, there was no bigger star in the sport. Yet around that time Adidas had a realization that would secure its place in the fiber of soccer in a way Puma could never match. The company figured out that beyond any individual team or player, what it really needed was an institution. And in a small office in Zurich in the 1970s it found a willing partner: Adidas began trading in marketing rights for FIFA and the World Cup. Its biggest advocate in the building was a former Longines executive with thinning hair and a cloying sense of humor named Sepp Blatter. He was on a path to the pinnacle of world soccer and would always make sure that Adidas went along for the ride. In one of its many long-term deals, the company manufactured the ball for the 1970 World Cup. Adidas hasn't stopped making them since. For players growing up in the 1980s and 1990s, there was only one brand that became synonymous with the game's most prestigious tournament.

The Dassler brothers, meanwhile, never reconciled. Rudolf died in 1974, and Adi passed away four years later. They were buried in the Herzogenaurach cemetery, in opposite corners.

WHAT NEITHER OF the Dassler brothers lived long enough to see was the serious emergence of a new rival more than 5,000 miles from Bavaria. Founded by track coach Bill Bowerman and his former student Phil Knight, who started out selling sneakers out of a van, Nike quickly became a force to be reckoned with in running, American football, basketball, and tennis. But other spheres still felt safe to the Dasslers' descendants. Even as Nike dominated the US pro leagues and revolutionized sports marketing with the launch of Air Jordan in 1984, soccer remained an esoteric pursuit. Nike wasn't going looking for it.

In 1994 soccer came looking for Nike. The World Cup landed on North American shores for the first time, and with matches scattered across nine US cities, the country's leading sportswear manufacturer could no longer afford to keep the world's favorite sport on the back burner. While it was too late to get in on making jerseys for teams at the tournament, the plan was to make a splash immediately afterward. Adidas had outfitted 10 of the 24 teams, with Diadora, Lotto, Umbro, and a few national brands kitting out the rest. Nike could only sit back and wait for its moment to surge out of seventh place in the global soccer market. "The feeling was that people didn't really take us seriously as a soccer brand," one Nike executive recalls.

That summer smashed records for attendance and ticket revenue. Now excitement was building for the inaugural kickoff of the newly formed Major League Soccer. Two centuries after the laws of the game were first written down in a London pub, it finally looked as though soccer was establishing a foothold in America. Nike's job was to make sure that foothold had a Swoosh on the side. Changing the perception that Nike knew nothing about the world's most popular sport was the remit of a young ad man named Jelly Helm and a few coworkers as they huddled in an office block in Oregon late in 1995. True, they knew next to nothing about soccer. But they knew a lot about selling shoes. And so they resolved to crack the soccer market by turning to the one group of pitchmen who had sold more shoes over the years than anyone else: all-star teams. "We had seen the '92 Dream Team play in Portland," Helm says, "with Jordan, Bird, and Magic, and we knew if we could assemble a team of all-star footballers, European kids would fucking freak out."

There was just one minor hiccup: European soccer doesn't actually have all-star teams. It would take more than that to stop Nike.

To make its vision of a soccer all-star team a reality, the company agreed to bankroll the most expensive commercial in its history. Soon, some of the biggest names in world soccer were jumping on chartered jets and pulling on Nike cleats, including the Portuguese winger Luís Figo, Italian national team captain Paolo Maldini, Mexican goalkeeper Jorge Campos, and, oddly, Tomas Brolin, a squat Swedish midfielder who would retire from the game within two years and go on to become a prize-winning vacuum cleaner salesman. In the absence of an opposing team of all-stars to play against, Nike hired the special-effects crew from *Apollo 13* to create an army of undead soccer demons, with Satan as their player-manager. The ad would be called "Good vs. Evil."

The reaction to Nike's blockbuster ad bordered on hysterical. The spot was denounced by FIFA, banned from movie theaters in Denmark, and later honored at the Cannes Film Festival. Within six months of the ad's debut, Nike had inked a deal to become the official sponsor of the Brazil national team, thanks to a 10-year, $400 million contract. It was the soccer industry's disruptor before anyone knew what "disruptor" meant.

They did, however, have a sense of what it might look like. If Adidas revolved around soccer heritage, Nike was going to put the brightest, hottest stars at the center of its universe—even if some of them threatened to blow up. The first major name was a supernova named Eric Cantona. Outrageously gifted and impossibly Gallic, he arrived in England in 1992 and taught a nation that collars on soccer jerseys were for popping. Cantona had been wearing Nike boots since before the Brazil deal. He wore them on the Man United training pitch, where he inspired a young generation of boys with names like Neville, Beckham, and Scholes to train harder. He was still wearing them as he won four Premier League titles, lifted the FA Cup twice, and drilled home the winning penalty in the "Good vs. Evil" ad. And on the January day in 1995 when Cantona launched a kung-fu kick at a heckling Crystal Palace fan, the last thing the supporter saw before impact was a Swoosh flying at his face.

So it was less than ideal for Nike's growing football department when Cantona fell out of love with football and went into sudden retirement in 1997—especially as Nike's market share across all sports abruptly declined and the company posted a $40 million loss for the year. Luckily on the soccer front, the company's roster of swaggering forwards had plenty of backup. It wanted edgy stars who crackled on-screen, and it ran around the soccer world signing them up as fast as possible. The company's market, one senior executive says, was evolving from what Nike called the FCK to the FOT—the "football-crazy kid" to the "football-obsessed teen." And that teen didn't care about anything that came before. Boots didn't have to be plain black, and jerseys didn't need to fit like garbage bags.

In the United States, Nike had a women's national soccer team that played in jerseys actually cut to women's bodies—the team looked slicker and more professional than anyone else before even kicking a ball. In North London, Nike recruited striker Ian Wright, who exuded irreverent cool as he banged in goals for Arsenal. And out of Brazil, it handpicked a gap-toothed striker who moved like lightning. Ronaldo Luís Nazário de Lima was the original Ronaldo, the one they knew in Rio as O Fenomeno. Since leaving South America, the Brazilian Ronaldo had lit up leagues in the Netherlands, Spain, and Italy at a rate of 34 goals per season between 1994 and 1998. He was also a figure Nike could build around, using the tried-and-true tactic it had used for its US sports empire but never yet deployed in soccer: the signature shoe. Cantona, for all his eccentricities, had mostly worn the classic black boots with a logo stitched into the side. Ronaldo would take the field at the 1998 World Cup in a silver-and-blue number known as the R9

Mercurial. Those were Ronaldo's keys to a small club of Nike athletes that had opened with Michael Jordan and his Air Jordan 1s in 1984 and most recently had expanded to promote a smooth young golfer with a name made for billboards, Tiger Woods. More than confirming Ronaldo's status as a worldwide sports icon, a signature boot also carried major financial implications. Players weren't giving away their name for free; they were earning a royalty on every single pair. In those days, according to one Nike executive, the going rate was around 7 percent. Combined with Ronaldo's salary at Internazionale, it was enough to make him the highest-paid soccer player on the planet.

Gaining fast was Adidas's own poster boy of the moment, David Beckham, whose marketing potential was changing the game over at the German company—not only through his rising profile but also his relationship-slash-merger with one Victoria Adams, better known as Posh Spice. "Beckham was really the one who set everything off," says Adidas's head of football at the time, Thierry Weil.

Still, it was safe to say that Nike's late entry into the game had been a success. What took getting used to was having to scour the entire world for potential pitch men and women. This was no longer a question of keeping an eye on a few dozen college basketball and football programs and handing out sneakers at Olympic trials. The next superstar could just as easily come from a village in Brazil as from a council estate in Liverpool. The same way soccer clubs were figuring out how to cast a wider net than ever before, Nike relied on its own network of scouts, friendly coaches, agents, and anyone else who might funnel it information in exchange for a few free tracksuits and a finder's fee.

Portugal was an especially happy hunting ground for Nike. It had a long-standing relationship with the national team and, just as importantly, with soccer-watchers around the country. Those connections had already delivered the signatures of midfielder Manuel Rui Costa and Figo. Now, as half of Europe vied for Cristiano Ronaldo's attention during his final season at Sporting, he joined the one team he would stay with longer than any club. After a brief flirtation and a few dozen pairs of boots, Ronaldo partnered with Nike in 2003. By then, Messi was on board with Nike too, as his father began to figure out that their last name might soon be worth something.

Less than a decade after it decided to care about soccer, Nike had two long-term bets on the table that would put it in position to conquer the sport once and for all. Through shrewd judgment, canny timing, and a bit of dumb luck, it had spotted two players who might define an entire era and tied them to the Swoosh at the dawn of their superstar careers. The same way it would later endorse Roger Federer and Rafael Nadal in tennis, or LeBron James and Kevin Durant in the NBA, the company had managed to secure both sides of a brewing argument, only this time it was happening in the world's number-one sport. Billions of eyeballs would be watching, and Messi and Ronaldo were somehow both Nike guys.

Then Nike lost one.

THERE NEVER WAS an official answer inside Nike's Beaverton headquarters as to how Messi slipped through the net. "Success has many fathers," one former executive says of the incident, "but failure is a bastard."

In this case, the problem was one father in particular. For the first couple of years, Jorge Messi had been perfectly content to let his boy trot around in the same Nike gear that Barça had always supplied. The company was building entire campaigns around Ronaldinho. And leading into the 2006 World Cup, Nike decided that Leo was on that trajectory too. In 2005, it produced an ad cutting together footage of kids doing tricks on the streets of Barcelona—here's two juggling on the beach, here's another making a nuisance of himself in the market, and here's one in a field oddly bending a free kick onto the head of a scarecrow. A few were budding talents from La Masia; others never got quite as far. During the 60-second spot, each kid turns to the camera and says their name. Jonathan dos Santos, a future Mexican national team player, pops up from a balcony to announce himself, but most of the players were forgotten by the time the thing ever aired.

Then, just as the ad appears to end, a shaggy-haired teenager on a dark practice field sweeps a free kick over some dummies and into the net from 25 yards. He stares straight down the lens and puts the soccer world on notice.

"Recuerda mi nombre," he says. *Remember my name.* "Leo Messi."
He's wearing Nike from head to toe.

That was the year Messi turned 18. It was also the year that anyone who was anyone in football learned that he could no longer be ignored. In the summer of 2005, he dazzled at the FIFA World Youth Championship, a World Cup for under-20s. Not only did Argentina lift the trophy, but Messi scored in every knockout round game and twice from the penalty spot in the 2–1 victory over Nigeria in the final. For lighting up the tournament around the Netherlands, he took home a golden clog. And by bringing Argentina some silverware, he sent Diego Maradona into hysterics—not that it took much for the most excitable man in soccer. "Lionel Messi will be my successor," he proclaimed, having previously anointed successors from Ariel Ortega to Andrés d'Alessandro. "He will be the new Golden Boy."

The difference this time was that knowledgeable people concurred with El Diego's grand pronouncement. Everyone from Barcelona to Beaverton knew that Messi's next stage needed to be the senior World Cup in Germany. Though he would be wearing an Adidas jersey there with the Argentine national team, Nike was all in on the tournament. For the first time since breaking into soccer, it would outfit more teams at a World Cup than its German rival. (Puma was also making a major national-team play at the time, but never attempted a serious run at Messi or Ronaldo.) The campaign Nike cooked up was built around the slogan "Joga Bonito," Portuguese for "Play Beautifully." With its stable of otherworldly dribblers, led by the swaying, sashaying Ronaldinho, the approach made perfect sense. The summer of 2006 was going to be all about flair—and the ads were once again going to be freakout-inducing.

So, all over Europe, Nike began getting its stars in order more than a year ahead of time. The company arranged a photo shoot with Messi in Barcelona and had him perform all the tricks in his repertoire, over and over, from every angle. It wasn't clear precisely what Nike would do with all of this, but the creative teams that had gained a clear edge over Adidas with a string of classic spots—from the Brazilian national team frolicking around an airport to superstars duking it out in a soccer cage match—knew they could put all this Messi content to good use. That is, until Nike received a call in early 2006 telling them to scrap all of it.

Messi was not to appear in any promotional materials, because Messi was no longer sponsored by Nike. He was an Adidas player now.

Nike couldn't believe what it was hearing. The company had been shipping boots to him since he was 14 years old, and it sponsored the only pro club he had ever turned out for. If ever there was a natural candidate for a lifelong bond with the Swoosh, Messi was it.

There are competing versions of just what triggered the switch. The truth is that it was a combination of factors, all linked by the single thread of Jorge Messi deciding that Nike wasn't treating his son properly. In one telling among former Nike executives, Adidas had stepped up its game with ever-increasing offers to the Messi camp, and the money men in Oregon decided not to go to war over a teenager. The easily distracted Nike crowd in the United States was always ringing the team in Europe after catching any glimpse of talent on TV—"We gotta get this guy." But at a time when players in Messi's and Ronaldo's positions were earning low six figures annually from the company, a tenfold increase to keep up with Adidas's million-dollar bid didn't seem worth it. Besides, Jorge Messi wasn't exactly in a receptive mood. Another person familiar with the Messi account remembers Leo's father losing his mind over a seemingly innocuous request for more kit. Neither Nike Iberia nor Nike South America had responded in time, and that had been enough to sour the relationship.

In any event, the minds of the Messis, father and son, were made up. But Nike wasn't going down without a fight. Years of investment in Leo had been on the verge of paying dividends as he broke into the Barcelona first team. As far as the company was concerned, there was a deal in place for many more years to come. "Nike has got a binding agreement with Lionel Messi," a company spokesman told reporters at the time.

The company was prepared to take "whatever measures necessary" to enforce it.

Jorge Messi's reply was, essentially, *bring it*. The dispute would be settled "wherever it has to be settled," he said, meaning the Spanish courts, but not seeming to rule out a fistfight in a back alley either.

The biggest problem for Nike was that there was no contract. A legally binding agreement had never (or no longer) existed. What the company had in place with the Messi camp was more of a heads-of-terms letter, which Spanish judges ruled over the course of several months wasn't worth the fax paper it was printed on. On February 1, 2006, Messi trotted onto the Camp Nou pitch for a Copa del Rey match against Real Zaragoza in a pair of Adidas F50s. Although he scored that day, his first Adidas-branded strike would have to wait—the goal against Zaragoza was a header.

Over at Adidas HQ in Herzogenaurach, executives were ecstatic—or at least most of them were. A few inside the building privately worried that while they had acquired the rights to one of the most talented soccer players in the world, they had also picked up a pitchman with all the charisma of a silent film star. The nearly mute kid teammates had known at La Masia was now a nearly mute 18-year-old who barely looked like an athlete. Left to his own devices, he fed himself with pizza and Coca-Cola. His kit billowed around him like he'd borrowed it. Messi hardly knew where the Barcelona weight room was.

But at the top levels in Herzo, poaching Messi was momentous enough that Adidas CEO Herbert Hainer had to highlight it in the middle of the company's first-quarter earnings call that May. "I wanted just to mention some additional positives we've seen in our football activities," he said. Top of the list—ahead of mind-boggling figures for a new soccer ball (15 million sold) and the latest Adidas football boots (750,000 pairs in the first year alone)—was "the signing of the world's top-ranked footballer under 21 from Argentina . . . who many claim has the potential to be the next Maradona."

• • •

ALL OVER EUROPE, people were catching on to this fast—especially in Spain, where the last thing any other club needed was an ascendant Barça. The most audacious effort to mess with the next Maradona came from Deportivo La Coruña. During Barcelona's down years in the early 2000s, Depor had carved out a place in the upper reaches of the league table and won its first Spanish championship in nearly a century of trying. Now it quibbled that Messi had been registered for the 2005–2006 season after the August 31 deadline, when rosters were supposed to be set in stone. Not by coincidence, Barcelona's crosstown rival Espanyol joined in the complaint. Club president Joan Laporta suspected someone else of pulling the strings—namely, Real Madrid. "Everyone is against Barcelona," he fumed.

Everyone, that is, except the Royal Spanish Football Federation, which ruled that Messi was registered legally and declined to suspend him. But by then, Laporta was used to fending off trouble. In 2005, as La Liga enforced strict limits on how many non-European Union players a club could carry, he arranged for Messi and his father to obtain Spanish passports. Had he failed, Espanyol was ready to take Messi on loan for a season while Barcelona reshuffled its roster to free up a non-EU player spot for him. PSV Eindhoven in the Netherlands tried the trick as well, as did Italian giant Juventus. After being torn apart by Messi in a preseason friendly, the Turin-based club had caught wind that Spanish bureaucracy might create an opportunity for them. Just 25 minutes after laying eyes on him, Juve manager Fabio Capello tried in vain to sign Messi on loan. But the most serious bid came from Internazionale. The Milanese club run by Italian oil magnate Massimo Moratti, who never met a left-footed player he didn't love, fell head over heels for this little genius. "I'd spend crazy money if I could buy Messi," he told the Italian press.

All of which became a source of extreme headaches for Laporta, whose phone was ringing off the hook with urgent calls from immigration lawyers, potential suitors for Messi, and as always, Messi's dad. The offers for his son had been music to Jorge's ears. Only three months after securing a new contract for Leo in the summer of 2005, he sensed another chance to sweeten it. Jorge let Laporta know as much: Leo was prepared to pack his bags for Milan.

Laporta had to move quickly. Over the course of two emergency meetings, he did his best to appease the Messis and assure them that Leo's home was in Barcelona. The Spanish passports, when they finally came through, just about did the trick. So did a third contract improvement in the space of a year and a half.

"It all happened very quickly," said the now Spanish Messi, who turned down the chance to play for Spain's national team in the process. "I signed, I swore allegiance, and it was all over."

Laporta's administrative two-step had been enough to keep Leo in the squad. Putting him on the field was up to someone else, a supremely talented former Dutch midfielder named Frank Rijkaard. He had been appointed manager in 2003 as part of Laporta's grand effort to reconnect Barcelona to its glorious Cruyffian past.

As a player, Rijkaard saw the pitch like Cruyff, he moved the ball like Cruyff, and he even argued like Cruyff—occasionally with Cruyff himself. Rijkaard had played for his fellow Dutchman at Ajax for most of the 1980s until losing his temper for good at a training session one day in 1987. Rijkaard, fed up with the constant needling, stormed off the pitch and vowed never to play for Ajax again—a promise Cruyff was happy to help him keep. Rijkaard was loaned out to Sporting Lisbon and Real Zaragoza before landing at AC Milan.

Now, in his first major management role, Rijkaard's job was to pick up where Cruyff left off. Gradually, he integrated boys from La Masia into the team and started the process of giving Barcelona its identity back. Midfielders like Xavi and Andrés Iniesta, along with defender Carles Puyol and goalkeeper Víctor Valdés, were pure Barça, dyed in the blue-and-red wool. And since the 2004–2005 season, Rijkaard had been blending them with the more worldly experience of players such as Ronaldinho, Samuel Eto'o, and Deco as the club built a serious challenge for a first Liga title since 1999. Back then, Messi was still spending his weeks training with the first team and playing matches for the youth team. In fact, over the entire league campaign, Messi was on the pitch for Barça for a grand total of 84 minutes, and most of them were completely forgettable—short run-outs at the tail end of comfortable victories. Messi's final four-minute stint of the season was the one that stood out. Barcelona was leading 1–0 at Camp Nou against lowly Albacete, and Messi, subbed in for Eto'o, quickly broke free of the defense. With a flick of his left foot, he notched his first official goal for the Barcelona senior team and became the club's youngest ever goalscorer a couple of months shy of his 18th birthday. When the goal was chalked off for offside, he only had to score it again a few minutes later—a delicate lob over the goalkeeper, followed by a leap into Ronaldinho's arms. Rijkaard saw it as little more than proof that he'd once again made a correct decision.

"It was the right moment to bring on a young kid like Messi," he told reporters.

The Barcelona sports press was a little more effusive. In the dozens of pages it devotes to every match, it reserved a special place to gush over Messi, the kid they had already been writing about for years but rarely seen up close. "Messi now feels that the Liga title, which in all likelihood, Barça will win, will be his own," *Mundo Deportivo* wrote the next day.

Yet Leo didn't see it that way. Nor did Jorge, who routinely complained that his son wasn't playing enough. Rijkaard upped Messi's minutes the following season, in 2005–2006, using him in more than 20 games as he figured out precisely where he could be most useful. Messi had been an offensive Swiss Army knife as he sliced apart opponents in youth team matches, where the tactics hardly mattered. The lineup in the first team was a little more crowded. The chief playmaking role fell to Ronaldinho through the middle, and Eto'o was the immovable striker. So Rijkaard mostly tried Messi on the right wing, where he spent the bulk of his time getting kicked by clumsy defenders. And when it came to the biggest matches on the calendar, Rijkaard still felt that Messi's best position was on the bench. The one exception was a Champions League round-of-16 match against Chelsea at Stamford Bridge in London in February 2006. Messi had appeared in the opponents' scouting report as "very left-footed." On that night, a 2-1 win for

Barça, he ran Chelsea's fullback ragged and drew a furious rant from manager José Mourinho, who accused Messi of getting the defender sent off with relentless flopping.

"How do you say cheating in Catalan?" asked Mourinho. (Mourinho spoke Catalan fluently.)

Messi started out just as dangerously two weeks later during the return leg in Barcelona, where the club punched its ticket to the quarter-finals. The trouble was that he lasted just 25 minutes that night: Messi discovered that he was carrying a two-inch tear in his hamstring and had to be replaced by Swedish forward Henrik Larsson. The second Chelsea game, which he left in tears, would be his last of the season.

Over the following weeks, Barcelona went on to win La Liga and advance to the 2006 Champions League final against Arsenal in Paris without Messi, who sulked and counted the days until he could play again. In Messi's mind, nothing that happened on the pitch belonged to him if he wasn't out there as well. Even inside the Stade de France on the night Barcelona became European champions for the second time in the club's history—and for the first time since the Dream Team—Messi felt like just another spectator. He sat on the bench watching Larsson take over his position in the second half to tee up both Barça goals in the 2–1 victory. At the final whistle, Messi decided that he'd seen enough and his night was over. He stalked off down the tunnel before the trophy presentation.

While his teammates collected their medals, he was already aiming bigger, at the things he could control, like the 2006 World Cup and beyond. Messi could sense his moment coming—before Rijkaard knew it, before Argentina knew it, and certainly before Nike knew it. He felt he was about to explode. And when he did, there would be only one consolation for those who'd stayed on the fence about him a little too long.

"We always said," recalls one Nike executive, "Imagine how much trouble we'd have been in if Messi had a personality."

FOUR

PlayStation Footballers

WHEN ARGENTINA'S NATIONAL team arrived in Germany for the 2006 World Cup, the red carpet was waiting for them in a place nearly no player could pronounce. In early June, they pulled up to the Adidas campus in Bavaria to find freshly renovated rooms, manicured training pitches, and a full staff of hotel workers, including at least 20 who had learned to speak Spanish for the express purpose of making the squad comfortable. They had even replaced the German duvets with Argentine bedsheets and added three Spanish-language channels to the television menu. Welcome to Herzogenaurach, Messi's home away from home for the tournament.

Adidas had revamped the facility at a cost of €30 million, all with an eye to serving as the base camp for one of the 16 teams it was kitting out at the 2006 World Cup—a list that included France, Spain, and the host nation Germany. But Argentina expressed interest first, officials said, and secured the five-star HerzogsPark for the latest poster boy in the Adidas stable, along with his national-team amigos. That the head of the Argentine Football Association, Julio Grondona, was also the finance chief of FIFA, one of Adidas's most significant partners, was mere coincidence.

A tournament base is usually little more than a glorified summer camp inside a luxury resort. Sports in the morning, meals at long refectory tables, and all the pastimes that growing boys might need to stay out of trouble between the most important matches of their lives. Pool, table tennis, and a "time room" that played new-age music and had soothing lights—anything to break up the monotony between sessions on Adi Dassler Field. Inside the halls of HerzogsPark, as Argentina counted the days till its opener against Côte d'Ivoire, Carlos Tevez blasted cumbia music and Hernán Crespo ran the card game. Juan Román Riquelme's quarters, meanwhile, were pressed into service as a café where the veterans lounged around drinking maté, the bitter, caffeinated tea that Argentine players can't function without. That's also where the older players gossiped and made fun of Messi for spending so much time in his room on his PlayStation. Sometimes, they thought, he had more in common with their kids than he did with them.

If that sounds like jealousy talking, it's because that was part of it. Messi had taken up more than his fair share of the headlines in the buildup. He'd only made his Argentina debut in 2005—when he was sent off after just 25 seconds for elbowing a Hungarian defender—yet Messi was somehow the team's main source of intrigue. Between his obvious talent and the lingering injury, all anyone in the traveling press pack wanted to know was, would Leo be fit enough to play?

Messi himself was unequivocal. He'd committed his entire spring to nursing his hamstring between Barcelona and Rosario with the sole intention of being ready for the World Cup. Now, he told reporters, he felt "a la perfección."

Argentina's silver-haired manager, José Pékerman, wasn't so sure. The grandson of Ukrainian-Jewish immigrants to South America, he had once been a taxi driver before maturing into one of the country's most important stewards of young talent. As the longtime coach of Argentina's under-20 World Cup side, he had won the biennial tournament three times between 1995 and 2001 as he tended to an entire generation of national team players. Those former kids now formed the core of his squad in Germany as maté-sipping veterans. And the way they saw it, the teenager with all the Adidas commercials, healthy or not, needed to wait his turn. When Argentina beat Côte d'Ivoire 2-1, Messi watched from the bench.

This being the Argentine national team, the threat of complete bedlam was never far away—especially once Diego Maradona threatened to drop in on the camp. He had already made a spectacle of himself in the stands during the first match in Hamburg, and he intended to repeat his theatrics during the second game against Serbia and Montenegro in Gelsenkirchen, complete with a screaming visit to the dressing room beforehand. Above all, El Diego wanted to see Messi on the pitch.

The pressure to comply was soon growing on Pékerman from all sides. Maradona might have been easy enough to ignore—he was always raving about something or other. But Jorge Messi talking to the media was more irksome. In his backhanded way, Jorge was making it plain that Leo wasn't pleased with the way this World Cup was going.

"Lionel is well, fit to play," Jorge said. "Whenever he plays, Lionel is happy."

Making matters worse were the rumors that Adidas had joined the calls to get its prized investment some more playing time and was leaning directly on Pékerman, insisting that he put Leo in the lineup. The gossip became so persistent that the company had to address it to preserve what little peace was left around the camp. "Argentina have one of the best coaches in the world, and it is his job to pick the team," company spokesman Thomas van Schaik told reporters. And by the way, he added, the players who were starting ahead of Messi, forwards Hernán Crespo and Javier Saviola, were also sponsored by the company. Both had worn the Three Stripes to score against Côte d'Ivoire.

Pékerman finally caved the following week—a little. By the time he called Messi's number 19 in the second game, Argentina was already up 3–0 against Serbia and Montenegro in the 75th minute. Maradona, overweight and drenched in sweat, marked the occasion by freaking out like he was sitting in the front pew of a revivalist church. Messi rewarded his faith by notching a goal and an assist as Argentina closed out the 6–0 romp.

That was enough to send the clamor into overdrive. Any time Pékerman appeared before a bank of microphones, he had to answer the Messi question. Yes, he would start the final group match against the Netherlands with Argentina already qualified for the round of 16. And no, he didn't know how the team would line up for the game after that against Mexico. As it turned out, Pékerman brought Messi into that one six minutes from the end of regulation as a pair of short, fresh legs for extra-time. Leo got to work immediately on the right flank, cutting into Mexican traffic to open up the play on the opposite side of the pitch. Within seven minutes, he'd involved himself in the buildup to Argentina's winning goal—although truthfully, he had about as much to do with Maxi Rodríguez's bending masterpiece as Michelangelo's pigment crushers had to do with the Sistine Chapel. Still, Messi's string of touches early in the move to dance away from three defenders were all anyone needed to see to be convinced that he belonged in the side for the quarterfinal against Germany. Anyone, that is, except Pékerman.

From the moment Argentina unveiled the starting 11 for the game, Messi again became the main topic of conversation. The team had celebrated his 19th birthday along with Juan Román Riquelme's 28th the night after the Mexico victory with steaks imported from home. Leo was just starting to fit in with the older crowd, and the older crowd was just starting to understand how important he could be. But when it came to Germany, the manager prioritized experience above anything else. Messi sat on the bench.

For about 80 minutes, Pékerman's call seemed to be the right one. Argentina took a 1–0 lead early in the second half and decided the best thing it could do was focus on protecting it. Pékerman's first substitution of the match was forced, when he had to replace his injured goalkeeper. His second was switching Riquelme for the more defensive-minded Esteban Cambiasso. And with his third and final change, 10 minutes from full-time, he figured it was finally time to replace an attacker. That's when Pékerman yanked Crespo and replaced him with someone who was distinctly not Messi.

Messi sat in the dugout disgusted. Though he said nothing, cameras caught him kicking off his Adidas F50 boots. That told Argentina fans everything they needed to know.

A minute after Crespo came out, Argentina conceded an equalizer before going on to lose in a penalty shoot-out. The Messi debate followed

Argentina all the way home. Pékerman ducked out of it by resigning his post before the team even boarded the bus, but the inquest continued in the South American press for days. What message was Messi sending by sitting barefoot on the bench? Was Argentina already wasting his talent? And who could bring Argentina back—was it finally time for Maradona? Could demigods teach tactics?

In Germany, the World Cup was moving too fast to linger on a single country's postmortem. Twenty-four hours after Argentina's exit, the spotlight was already on the quarterfinal between England and Portugal. And as far as controversies went, Portugal's biggest talent was about to do something far more outrageous than taking off his shoes.

CRISTIANO RONALDO WAS way past worrying about playing time.

In the three years since moving to Manchester United, he had established himself as a vital presence for both his club and his country. If Ronaldo was healthy, he was starting. The question in the hours leading up to the England game, however, was, how healthy? Barely seven minutes into Portugal's round-of-16 win over the Netherlands, a Dutch defender named Khalid Bouhlarouz had caught him with a vicious, raking tackle that started somewhere near his chest and ended at his knee. In soccer, this sort of challenge is known as a "reducer," an act of premeditated aggression against the opposing team's best player, designed to intimidate and lessen their impact on the game. In other walks of life, it's known as first-degree assault. It worked out just as Bouhlarouz had planned. When Ronaldo eventually uncrumpled himself on the turf, he discovered a three-inch gash on his thigh and was subbed out of the game. The scar would remain visible nearly two years later.

Bouhlarouz's act of grievous bodily harm had turned out to be merely an *amuse-bouche* in one of the most flagrantly violent matches in World Cup history, one that produced 16 yellow cards, four reds, and a pair of touchline brawls. Victory in the Battle of Nuremberg, as the match came to be known, had come at a cost. Deco and Costinha were banned for the quarterfinal following their ejections, and with Ronaldo injured,

Portugal faced the very real prospect of taking on England without three-quarters of its starting midfield.

But Cristiano Ronaldo had no intention of sitting on the bench. He wasn't about to let a flesh wound keep him out of a World Cup quarterfinal. This was his opportunity to remind the world just how good Cristiano Ronaldo really was.

He'd been hammering that point ever since his first half hour in English soccer back in August 2003. Making his debut against Bolton Wanderers as a second-half substitute just days after moving to Manchester, Ronaldo won a penalty, set up another goal, and generally caused such mayhem in 29 minutes that United legend George Best pronounced it the most exciting cameo he'd ever seen. By the time Ronaldo left the field at the final whistle, the Old Trafford crowd was already chanting his name.

The year leading up to the 2006 World Cup was markedly less triumphant. In fact, it had been the hardest of Ronaldo's life. In September, his father, Dinis Aveiro, died of liver failure at the age of 51, on the eve of a Portugal World Cup qualifying match in Moscow. Portugal's coach, Luiz Felipe Scolari, delivered the news at the team hotel, telling Ronaldo that a car was waiting to take him to the airport so he could return home. Ronaldo informed Scolari that he wasn't going anywhere. "I wanted to play, that's all I knew," he said later. "I wanted to show everybody that I was a great professional and took my job seriously." He flew back to Madeira for the funeral after the match. And three days later, Ronaldo was back in training. Still only 20 years old, he missed just a single game for Manchester United.

The following month Ronaldo was questioned by British police over allegations that he sexually assaulted a woman at a London hotel. No charges were filed, but news of his arrest had been splashed on front pages across the world.

Before long there were more unwanted headlines for less serious offenses. First, Ronaldo was caught flipping off the crowd at Benfica, Sporting's great rival, after an ugly loss knocked Manchester United out of the Champions League. Weeks later, he was involved in a training ground dustup with United teammate Ruud van Nistelrooy, who took issue with Ronaldo's infatuation with stepovers—and did so a lot less gently than László Bölöni had done in the past.

"He should be in the circus! He shouldn't be on the pitch!" van Nistelrooy screamed before storming off the practice field.

Relations between the pair deteriorated over the rest of the season, and though United offloaded van Nistelrooy to Real Madrid that summer, the dressing-room disharmony weighed on Ronaldo.

It had all added up to an erratic 2005–2006 campaign for the club, and a nagging sense that Ronaldo's career was beginning to stall. There was no question he remained one of the most exciting young players in the world. But there was now a doubt over whether he remained the most exciting young player in his own dressing room. That was down to the arrival in 2004 of another precocious teenager who had been coveted by Europe's top clubs since before he was old enough to drive. His name was Wayne Rooney.

Just eight months younger than Ronaldo, Rooney looked as if he belonged to a different era—when soccer was a considerably rougher and more violent enterprise. With a square jaw, a squat frame, and a perpetual snarl on his face, Rooney came off more like a boxer than a footballer. And he played like one too. His game was built on brute force, unbridled aggression, and a backside that could keep a rhinoceros at bay. While Ronaldo glided past defenders with the grace and speed of an Olympic speed skater, Rooney barreled straight through them—and often trod on them for good measure. In the first four years of his career, his spectacular shooting and spectacularly short fuse combined to deliver 42 goals, 32 yellow cards, and one red. At times Rooney looked like he could get himself booked taking his dog for a walk.

Despite their differences, Rooney and Ronaldo—the single entity known as Roonaldo—were united by a maniacally competitive spirit that stretched from the practice field to the ping-pong table and made them firm friends around Carrington. They were the first two into training every morning, where Alex Ferguson and Carlos Queiroz marveled over breakfast at their ability to entertain themselves with their "kingdom of activities."

That friendship also made them a nightmare for defenders. On the pitch, it showed up in an understanding that produced irresistible sequences of attacking play. The apparent mind meld allowed Rooney and Ronaldo to pull off intricate moves, exchanging passes and switching positions at such devastating speeds that defenders could barely keep track of the ball.

Increasingly, though, it was Rooney finishing off those moves and emerging as Manchester United's true star. While Ronaldo struggled through a season of personal traumas, Rooney flourished, scoring a career-high 16 goals. Weeks before the World Cup, he was named English soccer's young player of the year. Ronaldo, who had been shortlisted too, was annoyed to discover he had lost out on a prestigious award—not least because, he discovered, he couldn't even count on his own teammate for support. Rooney had cast his vote for Arsenal's Cesc Fàbregas.

The World Cup would be Ronaldo's chance to put things right. "There are several players who can end up with the label of best player at the World Cup, and I am going to try to be one of them," he announced before the tournament. "I want to show everyone what I am worth."

And what better stage than a loser-go-home meeting with England and Rooney?

THE WORLD CUP quarterfinal was a little more than an hour old, and the Arena AufSchalke jangled with nervous tension. The 54,000 fans inside—and the 40,000 more watching on a giant screen at a nearby racecourse—had not been treated to a barn burner.

Right from the start, England and Portugal were locked in a tight, scrappy game of anxious mistakes and frequent stoppages. The longer it went on the less likely it seemed that anyone would score. It was one of those cagey international soccer games crying out for a superstar to make something happen.

Wayne Rooney felt it too. He had recovered from a broken foot in just eight weeks to make the World Cup. Powering through his recovery and defying medical advice, he enraged his manager, Alex Ferguson, who told him to skip the tournament and rest up. But once Rooney arrived in Germany, he realized he wasn't match fit. Worse, he was pretty sure he'd torn his groin in training 10 days earlier, but was afraid to tell the team doctors in case they sent him home.

Now, in the biggest game of his career, Rooney was playing a lot like someone with a sore foot and a torn groin. Pressed into an unfamiliar role as the lone striker, he had been marooned upfield for 61 minutes, huffing and puffing to little effect. He'd lost possession half a dozen times, and when a shooting chance finally came his way, he whiffed, missing the ball completely. In the humidity under the arena's closed roof, sweat poured off Rooney like lunch meat in the sun. He was hot, tired, and frustrated. It was time to do something about it—which usually meant someone was about to get clobbered.

Rooney dropped back to receive the ball just beyond the halfway line, but as he tried to turn upfield, he was caught by Portuguese defender Ricardo Carvalho, causing him to stumble. He regained his balance in time to prod the ball away from another defender, but Carvalho was back snapping at his ankles right away. Rooney fell and recovered again, and now Carvalho was tugging on his arm, trying to pull him to the ground. Rooney couldn't shake him loose. At that precise moment, in the fury of a World Cup quarterfinal, Rooney's hair-trigger temper clicked. He stomped on Carvalho's nuts.

It was an act of senseless violence. But for millions of viewers around the world—and the entire population of England—the most egregious act committed that afternoon was what happened next.

Cristiano Ronaldo was some 30 yards away from Rooney's tangle with Carvalho. He'd been on the edge of the action all night. Scolari had entrusted him with a free role, explaining, "I don't think that a footballer should be a tame cow from a Nativity scene, a Mary who only says 'yes' and 'amen.' I like them to participate and say some things." But Ronaldo had yet to heed that instruction. When he finally stopped acting like a tame cow, it was not quite what Scolari had in mind. Cristiano raced to the scene of Rooney's crime and loudly ordered the referee to take action.

That Ronaldo was working the officials to get his Man United teammate sent off was tantamount to treason for the match commentators calling the game on the BBC. "Ronaldo's there straight away, chirping at the referee to do something," sighed Mark Lawrenson. It also dismayed Rooney, who gave Ronaldo a hard shove to the chest. Their disappointment turned to disgust when the Argentinian referee, a former gym teacher and amateur poet named Horacio Elizondo, brandished a red card, ending Rooney's involvement and all but killing England's chances of reaching the semifinals.

Rooney marched off the field, giving a water bottle an almighty boot before disappearing down the tunnel. It was at this point that the TV cameras zeroed in on Ronaldo as he stepped away from the melee. He glanced toward the Portuguese dugout, a smile playing across his lips.

Then he winked.

It was a gesture that said nothing and everything. And it sent the commentators in the BBC studio completely over the edge.

"Look at that!" spluttered Ian Wright, a man whose nonchalant cool had once made him so appealing to Nike. "Has he just winked there?"

"Please tell me no," Alan Hansen groaned in a deep Scottish brogue.

When Ronaldo later buried the winning penalty in the shoot-out, having planted a kiss on the ball before blasting it into the top corner to send Portugal into the semifinals, it seemed as though he had carved out a permanent place in the annals of British infamy, alongside Jack the Ripper, the Sheriff of Nottingham, and Wet Wet Wet.

Naturally, the British press treated the entire episode with a due sense of gravity and proportion. "Do not let this man into our country anymore," screamed the *Daily Mirror*. "Give Ron One in the Eye," was the headline splashed across the front of the *Sun*, above an image of "Portuguese nancy boy Cristiano Ronaldo," whose face was superimposed onto a dartboard. Even the usually staid *Times of London* was caught up in the hysteria, suggesting that Ronaldo's wink could negatively impact Portugal's $15 billion tourism industry. Ronaldo was blamed for everything but the English weather.

The outrage wasn't confined to the British Isles. During Portugal's semifinal loss to France, Ronaldo was booed every time he touched the ball. (The *Sun* and *Mirror* both came up with the same headline for the game: "You're Not Winking Anymore.") And in an early sign of his divisiveness online, he was the target of an internet voting campaign to stop him from winning the FIFA award for the World Cup's best young player. When that honor was given to Germany's Lukas Podolski instead, the panel responsible for choosing the winner acknowledged that the wink had been a key consideration. "He may have accumulated a couple of minus points due to his gesture with Rooney," said former Germany captain Lothar Matthäus.

For Ronaldo, who values individual awards so highly that he maintains a collection of every childhood trophy he ever won from the age of six, this was the final straw. Being mercilessly booed was one thing. Depriving him of personal recognition was something else entirely. If English soccer didn't appreciate him, then it was time to say *adeus* to English soccer. In an interview after Portugal's loss to Germany in the third-place match, Ronaldo revealed that he had set his sights on a move to Spain.

Jorge Mendes jumped on the case. He held informal discussions with Barcelona and Real Madrid and even got so far as to agree on a contract with Valencia. "I'm not going to stay at Manchester United," Ronaldo said. "After what happened with Rooney, I can't remain there. In a couple of days I will have my future sorted out."

The only person who wasn't totally outraged was Wayne Rooney.

Even before Ronaldo had sealed England's elimination in the shootout, Rooney made the decision while sitting alone in the dressing room, staring at the furniture he'd just smashed up, to let the incident go. "I put myself in Ronaldo's shoes. Would I do the same? Probably," Rooney wrote. "Would I be in the ref's face to make sure he got sent off? If he deserved the red, if it would help us win—yes, no question." He admitted privately that he'd tried to get Ronaldo booked in the first half for diving.

Rooney made an initial attempt to smooth things over in the tunnel after the match. "I've got no issues with you," Rooney told him. "Enjoy your tournament and good luck. I'll see you in a few weeks—and let's go try and win the league." Weeks later, Alex Ferguson made a personal trip to Portugal's Algarve region to assure Ronaldo that the hostility back home wouldn't last forever. He'd been through this with David Beckham after his temper-tantrum red card contributed to England's elimination from the 1998 World Cup. At United, villains could be rehabilitated.

When Ronaldo returned to Manchester for the first day of preseason training, Rooney greeted him with a wink.

FOR ONCE, FERGUSON was wrong. More than a year on, Ronaldo was still getting booed at stadiums around the country.

As the abuse rained down on him on an August Wednesday night in Portsmouth, he tried to ignore the hailstorm of jeers and whistles while trudging off the field. He even managed a weary smile as he reached the tunnel that led to the visiting team's locker room. Everywhere he went with Manchester United, Ronaldo was showered with insults, expletives, and a sublimely offensive song comparing him to a one-eyed rat. English soccer fans have never knowingly passed up an opportunity to roast someone, and now, 13 months on from the World Cup, Ronaldo was still their favorite target.

On this occasion, though, the vitriol wasn't solely about that wink. It was also about the fact that Ronaldo had just headbutted someone.

In reality, it wasn't much of a headbutt. With Manchester United pushing for a late winner in an early-season game at Portsmouth, Ronaldo collided with a Scottish midfielder named Richard Hughes before a corner kick. The two players squared up to each other, there was some light shoving, and then Ronaldo appeared to catch Hughes on the side of the head. Like any good professional soccer player, Hughes reacted like he had been struck by a cruise missile.

Years later, Hughes would describe the incident with Ronaldo as one of the highlights of his career. "I'm not someone who scored loads of goals, so I have to remember other landmarks," he said. "I can always say one of the game's greats headbutted me."

Not everyone felt so magnanimous. Ronaldo was shown a straight red card by the referee and suspended for three matches by the Football Association for violent conduct. After the game, Alex Ferguson experienced what can only be described as a meltdown, raging at Hughes, the referee, and even Ronaldo himself. "He was provoked and he fell for it," the United manager fumed.

Ferguson's team had ended a three-year championship drought a few months earlier. With their World Cup beef behind them, Ronaldo and Rooney plundered 41 goals across all competitions in 2006–2007 as Ferguson's decision to rebuild around a pair of teenagers was finally, thrillingly rewarded. But Cristiano's momentary loss of cool had thrown a wrench into the club's title defense. With the draw at Portsmouth, United had failed to win either of its opening two games of the season for the first time in nearly a decade. Rooney was already out injured. And now there was a ban coming for Ronaldo, who described the three-game ban as "absurd and unjust."

That exceptionally harsh punishment changed the course of Ronaldo's career. His suspension coincided with a break in the regular season for national-team play, which would keep him away from the United first team for an entire calendar month. In soccer's era of manic overscheduling, when the game's stars routinely play three times a week and more than 60 games a year, a monthlong break amounted to a sabbatical. He didn't travel to road games and was excused from tactical drills and recovery sessions. For the first time in what felt like forever, Ronaldo was basically free to do what he wanted.

Bored at his home in the Manchester countryside—"A big farmhouse, with cows and stuff," he said in an interview with *Vogue*—Ronaldo chose to indulge in his favorite pastime: some extra training. That proved to be a lucky decision, because it led him to spend a lot of time in the company of a man named René Meulensteen.

THERE'S NO GETTING away from it: nothing about René Meulensteen's coaching career suggested he would one day help unlock the greatness from one of the greatest players in history.

Born and raised in the Netherlands, Meulensteen was a pedestrian defender who turned out for a handful of semipro clubs. When it became clear he wasn't going to reach the top as a player, he retired and went into coaching at the age of 26.

After a few years of that, it looked like he wasn't going to reach the top as a coach either. His CV highlights were working as an assistant for two clubs in Saudi Arabia and a stint coaching Qatar's under-18 squad. He was as far away from the big leagues as Qatar is from Manchester.

Things started to look up when a chance meeting with Les Kershaw, the Manchester United scout, led to a job offer. It was a job coaching United's seven- and eight-year-olds—equal parts teaching fundamentals and babysitting—but it was a start. Over the next five years, Meulensteen progressed to coaching roles with the club's academy and reserve teams. And in 2006, he parlayed that experience into his first job as a manager, joining the Danish club Brondby on a three-year deal. He lasted less than half a season. Brondby won just six of 18 Superliga games during Meulensteen's tenure, a spell remembered mostly for a bizarre prematch team talk in which he demanded that each of his players adopt an animal alter ego and then named a starting lineup that included an elephant, a fox, a giraffe, and a tiger, among other creatures. "We're sending an entire zoo on the field today," Brondby captain Per Nielsen thought. An actual menagerie could scarcely have performed worse than the human lineup. Brondby lost 4–0 and finished with nine players.

It was the sort of catastrophic career move that might have ended Meulensteen's aspiration to become an elite coach. Instead, it resulted in a promotion. Six months later, he was back at Old Trafford, this time as one of Alex Ferguson's assistants.

How Meulensteen's zoological brain fart led him to shepherding the likes of Wayne Rooney, Ryan Giggs, and Cristiano Ronaldo was down to Ferguson's latest innovation. These days the United coach is mostly remembered as a fierce disciplinarian itching for a blustery halftime rant. But behind the drill sergeant exterior beat the heart of a progressive, deep-thinking CEO. He had been an early adopter of squad rotation and load management. He'd also taken up the "split-striker" system, in which one of the center forwards dropped back to link up with the midfield. His latest preoccupations were optimizing his coaching staff and the art of delegation. Ferguson was taking a page from the NFL's playbook and assembling a staff of specialists.

The idea was to turn his newly crowned Premier League champions into champions of Europe by embracing the "marginal gains" philosophy that was revolutionizing other sports in Britain, from rugby to track cycling. No detail was too small to focus on if it could deliver a small improvement, because all those small improvements soon added up. Carlos Queiroz, now in his second spell as Ferguson's assistant manager, had become United's de facto tactical coach. Tony Strudwick was hired as performance coach to ensure the players were in peak physical condition, and Meulensteen returned to Old Trafford as technical skills coach. By the start of the 2007–2008 season, Ferguson's staff had swelled to such an extent that they needed to reconfigure the Old Trafford dugout.

If Meulensteen's return to Manchester United had seemed unlikely, his first major assignment seemed completely ludicrous. Trying to improve Cristiano Ronaldo's repertoire of technical skills is on par with offering Dale Earnhardt Jr. driving lessons.

Fortunately, Ronaldo didn't see it that way.

In his mind, the thing that had set him apart from everyone else on a soccer field all these years wasn't natural talent. It was his work ethic. Even now, the kid who raced cars away from stoplights in Lisbon could be seen dribbling in and out of the trees that lined the edge of

Manchester United's training ground long after the other senior players had called it a day. The red card at Portsmouth was his cue, not to take a break, but to spend even more time working on his game. And as it happened, his new technical skills coach felt Ronaldo could use some work on one skill in particular, the oldest and most fundamental trick in the sport: sticking the ball in the net.

Ronaldo had always scored goals, just never as many as his coaches expected. He knew that because Ferguson never stopped reminding him. Ever since Ronaldo joined the club, he and Ferguson had had a rolling £100 wager on how many goals he would score each season. The first season, the over/under was set at 10. Ronaldo lost. The next year, it was 15. He lost again, and then again the season after that. Finally, in his fourth year at the club, with the pot at £400, Ronaldo made the breakthrough: his 15th goal arrived in February, with three months of the season left to run. Ferguson did his best to weasel out of the bet—"Penalties don't count!" he groused in a postgame interview—but by the end of the campaign he had no choice but to pay up. Ronaldo scored 23 goals in all and felt like he had figured out that part of the game.

Meulensteen disagreed. In one of their early sessions during the suspension, he pressed Ronaldo on his targets for 2007–2008. How many goals did Cristiano think he could score this time around?

"Thirty goals," Ronaldo replied. "Seven more than last time."

"Okay, that's better," Meulensteen agreed.

"How many do you think?" Ronaldo asked.

"I think you should go for 40."

"But that's nearly double!"

"Yes," Meulensteen countered, "but you've never even practiced finishing before."

Meulensteen's biggest influence as a young coach had been a fellow Dutchman named Wiel Coerver, remembered by history as the coach who believed that skill didn't come from innate talent but had to be taught. In other words, he was the anti-Cruyff. Meulensteen decided that over the next four weeks he was going to teach Cristiano how to really score goals.

The first step was to reconfigure Ronaldo's entire approach to putting the ball on target. The way Meulensteen saw it, Ronaldo had never been a great goalscorer because he was far too concerned with scoring great goals. "Look at me! Top corner!" Meulensteen chided. "You always want to blast the ball through the net, when a little tap-in would have done the trick."

To reinforce the point, they studied videos of the great Manchester United strikers who had played under Ferguson—like Eric Cantona, Ruud van Nistelrooy, Mark Hughes, and Andy Cole. Hundreds of goals flew in, one after another: headers, volleys, tap-ins, overhead kicks. When the highlight reel was over, Meulensteen turned to Ronaldo and asked what he had seen. "I saw lots of goals," he said. So they rewound the video and watched it again. This time the idea took hold. "I see it now," Ronaldo said. "Most of the goals are one or two touches, and most of them are scored from inside the box, at different angles."

Now that he understood, Meulensteen got down to brass tacks. He designed a series of shooting drills to make Ronaldo aware of his positioning on the field and show him how to score from different angles inside the box. He devised a map of the pitch and goal to categorize every type of finish. Focusing on three distinct locations—directly in front of goal (zone 1), either side (zone 2), and out wide (zone 3)—and nine different areas of the goal, they worked on identifying the best approach from each area. "Lace kick, inside foot, one touch or two," Meulensteen recalls. "You need to make scoring a habit, that is why we did the sessions."

To say that Ronaldo completed the sessions is to undersell things pretty significantly. He completely devoured them. Every morning Meulensteen would arrive at United's Carrington headquarters to find Ronaldo waiting outside his office. He barely had time to gulp down a cup of tea before he was hustled out to the field, where Ronaldo would go through the finishing drills over and over. Then Meulensteen would hustle back to his office and download the footage so Ronaldo could study it later. They spent so many hours out on the training pitches that Meulensteen estimates Ronaldo scored 5,000 goals during those four weeks.

Once they were done with finishing, Ronaldo would jog over to "The Cage": a small astroturf pitch enclosed within a chain-link fence, where United's players went to work on adding new skills to their arsenals. Ronaldo stripped his game down to the bare essentials. *Touch, turn, shoot. Touch, turn, shoot.* The pimply stepover merchant from Sporting would never have recognized him.

"His whole mindset towards finishing had changed," Meulensteen says. "It went from 'I want to score the goal of the season' to 'I want to be a goal machine.' He was on a mission."

Operation Goal Machine didn't take long to produce results. Ronaldo was held scoreless in his first two games back from suspension, but netted the winner in the third. In his next 15 Premier League games, Ronaldo scored 18 goals—17 of them from inside the box, and with one or two touches.

When Ronaldo netted his 30th goal in March, with two months of the season left to run, it became clear this was no ordinary purple patch. He had leveled up. There was no doubt about who was the best player in the United dressing room now. Ferguson had redesigned the team's entire setup to allow Ronaldo to inflict maximum damage. He didn't have a set position, but a license to go wherever his instincts took him. "He finds the weakness in the back four," United defender Gary Neville wrote in a newspaper column. "If he's not getting the left back in the first 15 minutes, he'll switch to the right back. If he's not getting the right back, he'll switch to the left center back. He'll find someone in your back four who is weak and doesn't like defending one-on-one and against pace and power." Wayne Rooney and Carlos Tevez, world-class forwards in their own right, were expected to take their cues from Ronaldo and fill in the gaps.

Ronaldo had undergone similar transformations before. Early in his career, United's coaches determined that he needed to toughen up. He hit the deck too easily and spent too much time rolling around on the floor looking for fouls. Walter Smith, one of Ferguson's assistant coaches from outside Glasgow, devised a solution for that one. He stopped calling fouls in training altogether. No matter the infraction—late hits, high tackles, dangerous challenges—it was open season. Before long, Ronaldo swung open the door of Ferguson's office, demanding an answer. "Boss, do they not have fouls in Scotland?" Ferguson recalls him asking. "He came with all the tricks in the world and wanted to beat all the players, but he learned. He learned how to pass the ball, no question."

He also bulked up like never before in his career. In the space of a few seasons, he went from the body of a wiry teenager to that of a super-middleweight boxer. Large sections of him seemed chiseled directly from granite, which was appropriate enough since no one had any more doubts that he had his place on the Mount Rushmore of Man United players. Ronaldo had carved out a place on his own in the long line of stellar occupants of the number 7 jersey.

Never mind that he had asked for 28, the number he wore as a teenager at Sporting. That request was dismissed by Ferguson out of hand. At Manchester United, the number 7 shirt meant something, Ferguson explained. It was the number of George Best, of Denis Law, of Eric Cantona, and of David Beckham. The number 28 jersey? That was the number of Danny Higginbotham.

Ronaldo warmed to the new number so quickly that it wasn't long before he had co-opted a piece of United history into his own personal brand. In 2006, Ronaldo opened his first CR7 clothing boutique in Madeira. He had the number 7 inscribed on the cupboards, sofa, and bed at his Cheshire mansion and tiled on the bottom of his swimming pool. And in 2007, he agreed to pay £150,000 to buy the CR7 vanity license plate from a Scottish insurance broker—Ronaldo was eyeing it for his silver Bentley.

Even as Ronaldo reached new heights, he strove to expand his game even further. The finishing exercises with Meulensteen were now an established part of his daily routine, alongside ab crunches, ice baths, and several hours spent applying hair gel. But he also spent time with Carlos Queiroz and Mike Phelan learning to read opposition defenses and make the sort of anticipatory runs that led to chances. He had proven he could score goals. Now he had to think like a goalscorer.

One morning in the spring of 2008, during a training session at

Carrington, Meulensteen called Ronaldo over to test him on that mindset. Instead of asking for the ball to be played directly into his feet so he could take off and dribble, he wanted Cristiano to see more of the field. There was so much more room out there for him to do damage.

"Cris, tell me: are you quick or slow?" Meulensteen asked.

Ronaldo looked as if he'd just been asked whether Portugal was close to Spain. "I'm quick," he shot back.

"How quick?" Meulensteen continued. "Compared to your teammates, do you think you're the quickest of the lot?"

"I think so," Ronaldo answered.

"And who do you think is the best passer on the team?"

Again Ronaldo looked puzzled. Anyone who'd seen United play in the past 10 years knew that Paul Scholes could hit the pointy end of a toothpick from 50 yards away. "Scholes," he said.

"Do you think Scholes can put the ball wherever you want it?"

Ronaldo nodded.

"So let me ask you something: why do you always want the ball into feet?" Meulensteen asked, stiffening his tone like an angry schoolteacher. "You just told me you're the quickest one on the pitch. He's Paul Scholes! He can put the ball anywhere you want. So when the opposition squeezes up, why would you want it into feet and try to outplay players when you can get it in behind and just go straight for goal?"

This was another lesson that didn't take long to sink in. Days later, in the first leg of a crucial Champions League quarterfinal against AS Roma, Scholes lofted a pass into the penalty area from the right edge of the box. On the TV broadcast, Ronaldo wasn't even in shot when the ball left Scholes's boot. But he timed his run perfectly, tearing into the box to send a blistering header into the bottom corner. It was a classic striker's goal.

"Again and again and again," gasped the English TV announcer Clive Tyldesley as Ronaldo was swamped by his United teammates. "Same man, same old story."

Ronaldo was the biggest fish in the biggest pond. The Premier League was basically wrapped up, and now United turned its eyes to an even shinier prize.

EPIC SPORTS RIVALRIES have a tendency to sneak up on us. The initial encounters often occur far from the spotlight and with little fanfare, their significance recognizable only in hindsight.

When Roger Federer lost to a 17-year-old Spaniard named Rafa Nadal in the third round of something called the Nasdaq-100 Open in Miami in 2004, it received barely a mention in the next day's newspapers. The first time Tiger Woods and Phil Mickelson played in a pro golf tournament together, neither of them made the cut.

But when Cristiano Ronaldo and Lionel Messi shared a football pitch for the first time in the spring of 2008, the soccer world already knew it was witnessing the start of something monumental. As soon as the meeting was confirmed, the Barcelona papers dubbed it "a match the world will stop for." This being a Champions League semifinal, they were set to play twice in the space of six days.

The focus on their individual matchup was so intense that Messi actually had to remind the international press that there would be 20 other pairs of legs on the pitch. "It's not a game between Cristiano and me," he said.

Messi was supposed to be part of a Fantastic Four. At least, that was the way Barcelona had envisioned it. But Ronaldinho was washed up. Thierry Henry, another United rival from his eight years at Arsenal, took time to adapt. And Samuel Eto'o was sidelined for three months after an early-season injury. In the end, the Fantastic Four was only ever seen in training. Ronaldinho, Henry, Eto'o, and Messi never played a single minute together on the field as a foursome. Johan Cruyff was withering in his column: "If you want to see the 'Fantastic Four' then go to the cinema."

Everything was about Messi. More than just another talented Barça youngster, he'd become the player who could produce miracles. And nothing had made that clearer than what he had done on an April evening in 2007 against a Madrid-based club called Getafe.

For the better part of a quarter-century, Maradona comparisons had been attached to every undersized Argentinian footballer who could beat a defender off the dribble. But no one had produced anything close to El Diego's "Goal of the 20th Century" against England in the 1986 World Cup, a moment etched into Argentine lore and resurrected at least every four years as a cultural touchstone of near-religious nostalgia. So when Leo Messi conjured his own version of it for Barcelona, it sent the football-watching world into raptures.

Just like Maradona, Messi ran half the length of the pitch with the ball. Just like Maradona, he beat five players. Just like Maradona, he dumbfounded the keeper and finished from a tight angle.

It began with a five-yard pass from Xavi inside the Barcelona half that had no business becoming an assist. Messi received the ball on his right foot, then took three quick touches with his left to escape two defenders in the blink of an eye. Even at full speed and without breaking stride, he kept the ball mere inches from his feet in the close-dribbling style that Maradona had elevated to high art. On Radio Catalunya, Joaquim Maria Puyal calling the game burst into hysterics: "Deco to Xavi, Xavi to Messi. Messi, Messi, Messi, and still Messi, Messi, Messi . . ." In all, there were 18 consecutive Messis before the inevitable: "Gol! Gol! Goooooooool!"

Between Xavi's pass and the ball hitting the net, Messi traveled some 60 yards in 16 seconds, touching the ball just 13 times.

A few years earlier, a goal against Getafe in a Copa del Rey semifinal would have been the kind of highlight that could easily be lost to history. But within a few hours, the entire soccer world seemed to be drooling over it thanks to a two-year-old video-sharing platform called YouTube—back when "viral" was still a medical term.

The Catalan press immediately labeled it "the Goal of the 21st Century." And though there were still 93 years left, it didn't seem like much of an exaggeration. Messi and Maradona were now connected by much more than a passport and a shirt number. As if to prove the point, Messi scored another goal eerily reminiscent of Maradona just a few months later. In a match against Espanyol, he punched in an equalizer with his left hand. So as he prepared to share a pitch with Ronaldo for the first time, fans had every right to expect a heavyweight showdown.

In the end, the decisive figure turned out to be Manchester United's Portuguese schemer. Just not the one everyone expected.

Carlos Queiroz led the team's preparations all week with the sole objective of stopping Messi. During interminable tactical sessions, he laid out gym mats on the training pitch to mark the exact positions he wanted his defenders to be. The message was: Don't worry about possession. Let Barça have the ball. This game would be won or lost on how Manchester United took up space on the field. "Stay compact and when you win the ball go forward as quickly as possible," Queiroz told them. Then get it to Ronaldo.

"We'd never seen such attention to detail," Gary Neville remembers. "We rehearsed time and again, walking through the tactics slowly with the ball in our hands."

Over the course of 180 minutes of soccer during the two legs, there was only one goal scored. It came from Paul Scholes, United's pinpoint passer, who picked out the top corner of Barça's net in the return match at Old Trafford. And that was it. Messi caused trouble but couldn't find a way through the United barricade. Defender Wes Brown stayed so close to him that it was a wonder he didn't end up in the Barcelona dressing room at halftime.

Ronaldo was unusually quiet over the two legs, and no one could really dispute that Messi edged their individual showdown. Ronaldo didn't care—or at least acted like he didn't. United was heading to the final in Rome, where it beat Chelsea in a penalty shoot-out.

In Ronaldo's mind at least, that outcome settled it. He finished the season with a Champions League medal around his neck and swept up every available award in England after 31 goals in 31 Premier League games. A few months later, he won his first Ballon d'Or. He had no doubt that he was the best player in the world.

As if he needed any more proof, Real Madrid was now trying to buy him.

REAL MADRID'S PLAYBOOK for acquiring superstars was always the same. It started with a campaign in the friendly sports press and continued with enough leaks to fill the Bernabéu Stadium. The club president would declare that the deal was done, or close, or imminent, and for weeks one of the football-driven dailies would keep up a drumbeat of stories until the player was holding up the white jersey at his formal unveiling. The approach did two things at once. When it worked, it turned up the pressure on selling clubs to get a deal done quickly, if only to make the circus go away. And when it didn't, it still sort of worked by turning a player's head enough that his sole objective in life became joining Real Madrid, even if it took another season or two to push the deal over the line.

In Ronaldo's case, the campaign picked up steam over the course of 2007–2008. Leading it was Ramón Calderón, a Madrid-based white-shoe lawyer who had risen to the Real presidency in 2006 in the depths of a mini–ice age for the club—it hadn't won La Liga for three seasons before his arrival, nor had it reached a Champions League final in four. This qualified as a crisis. Calderón presented himself as the man to move Real past its first Galácticos era and build on a new foundation of players who were in it for the long haul. The problem was that he kept whiffing on major transfers. He'd tried to sign Kaká from AC Milan and Cesc Fàbregas from Arsenal, but neither took the bait. Still, that wasn't nearly as embarrassing as the time in 2008 when he thought he was bringing the actor Nicolas Cage into Real's locker room at the Bernabéu, only to discover that he'd been duped by someone who was more con man than Con Air. The not-very-convincing lookalike was in fact an Italian television presenter running a prank.

So by the spring of that season, the club president was looking for some credibility. He was prepared to do whatever it took to bring the fans back onside and put Cristiano Ronaldo in a white jersey.

Calderón had firmly believed for at least a year that Ronaldo might be open to a move. He knew, because Jorge Mendes had told him so. Calderón had struck a deal with Mendes that summer to acquire Ronaldo's old Sporting teammate, the Portuguese defender Pepe. And it was during those talks that Mendes mentioned in passing that, by the way, Ronaldo had always very much admired the club. "He would like to leave," the agent said bluntly. "And Madrid would be a good opportunity." Calderón took careful note.

That a player of Ronaldo's stature would leave the world's preeminent sports competition and move to La Liga might have seemed like a head-scratcher, considering the global economics of the sport. The English Premier League wasn't just the most powerful on the pitch, sending at least one club to every Champions League final between 2005 and 2009—even its last-place team took home more prize money than a club in La Liga's top three.

But Real Madrid and Barcelona weren't like the rest of the fractured Spanish league. And Ronaldo wasn't there to think about balance sheets anyway. What Real offered him was a connection to a ready-baked European legacy and the next step in a career he'd been plotting since the dorms at Sporting.

The possibility of Ronaldo's exit from United had been weighing on Alex Ferguson and his assistant Carlos Queiroz for a while. They acknowledged between them that holding on to Ronaldo for as long as they had—a full five years—was already a pretty good return. But in public Ferguson was every bit the Glasgow brawler any time the subject of Real Madrid came up. "You don't think we'd get into a contract with that mob, do you? Jesus Christ," he huffed. "I wouldn't sell them a virus."

He had, however, sold them an Argentine defender by the name of Gabi Heinze the previous summer. Privately, Ferguson knew that transaction had only whetted Real Madrid's appetite by letting the suits in Spain know that Manchester was open for business. Then, in December, Real sacked its German manager, Bernd Schuster, after just 17 months in charge. Ferguson turned to his longtime boss-slash-consigliere, United chief executive David Gill, and told him that the firing would somehow turn up the temperature on Ronaldo stories. The way he saw it, Real had only two answers in a tight spot: canning coaches or signing superstars—and they were all out of coaches.

"We have to ignore it because we can't keep worrying about them," Ferguson said. "We need to concentrate on our own publicity and our own form. There can be anger in this situation and we can get annoyed. But there's no point. We know their game and it won't affect us."

That wouldn't stop Madrid from seeing the game to its logical conclusion. The best Ferguson could do to sabotage the club's plans was to orchestrate a last-minute counterdeal, according to a person familiar with the talks: he and Mendes worked on offering Ronaldo to Barcelona. As much as it pained Ferguson to lose Ronaldo, selling to a Spanish club—any Spanish club—was still more palatable than possibly losing him to a Premier League rival.

The Barça plan didn't get anywhere, because Ronaldo himself was already set on a move to Madrid. And once that much was out in the open, Calderón knew the drill. "In my experience, when you approach those players and they really want to leave and come to your team, that's a point of money," Calderón says. "What you need to do is to decide how much and to get an agreement with the club for that."

The saga played out in full view on the front page of *MARCA*, a Madrid-based daily sports newspaper that is often accused of reporting on Real Madrid with as much objectivity as *Pravda* covering the Politburo. Stories had been ramping up for months, but in mid-May, as Ronaldo headed for the Champions League final, the volume was deafening.

It kicked off in earnest with a news splash on May 16 that quoted Ronaldo as saying, "I'd love to play in Spain." A week of front pages later, an affection for Spain had evolved into "My dream is to play for Madrid." By then, Ferguson was openly accusing Real of trying to rattle Ronaldo again, which was true of course. Day after day, week after week, *MARCA* moved papers by finding different ways to tell readers that the transfer was just around the corner. Only on June 2 did it first admit the possibility that this might not be an entirely done deal—at least not right away. That morning's front page featured Calderón saying, "If Cristiano does not come, it will not be a failure." The next day *MARCA* was already touting possible plan B signings before moving back to plan A just 72 hours later. By June 6, the headline was "Acuerdo Total"—Total Agreement.

Over the 19 days between May 20 and June 8, Cristiano was on the front page of *MARCA* 17 times. It took Rafa Nadal manhandling Roger Federer for his fourth straight Roland-Garros final and Spain kicking off its Euro 2008 campaign to put an end to the run. And after all that, it turned out that the agreement was distinctly not total.

Alex Ferguson wasn't letting Cristiano go anywhere. *MARCA* branded him a "little General Franco."

That was far from the end of it. Ronaldo found an unlikely ally in a Swiss bureaucrat who expressed genuine sympathy for him in the most inappropriate terms. FIFA president Sepp Blatter, an honorary socio of Real Madrid, examined the situation and declared that there was "too much modern slavery" in soccer—a big claim to make about a man with more than one Ferrari parked at home. More shocking was that Ronaldo agreed. "What the president of FIFA said is correct," he said in an interview on Portuguese television that July. Ronaldo was making over $10 million a year at the time.

Whether it was Spanish tabloid headlines or spurious claims about indentured servitude, Ferguson was fed up with the noise. By midsummer, he decided that the only people who needed to do any more talking were him and Cristiano. So he had Carlos Queiroz broker a meeting at his family home on the outskirts of Lisbon. Though Ronaldo tried to bail out at the last minute, claiming he had to undergo some physical treatment, Queiroz leaned on him to handle the conversation like a man—Queiroz calls it his "fatherly coaching authority."

"When you finish this meeting," he instructed Ronaldo, "you need to have a solution for both sides."

Ferguson and Gill flew in for United, while Mendes attended to back up his client. But when they got down to brass tacks, everyone except Ferguson and Cristiano waited outside. Queiroz closed the door of his sitting room for over an hour.

Not one to mince words, Ferguson cut straight to the point: Real Madrid were a bunch of amateurs. He explained that Calderón and the club had behaved unspeakably in their pursuit and that this was not how the game was played. Ferguson, Cristiano needed to understand, simply couldn't be seen caving to those types of tactics. "If I do that, all my honor's gone, everything's gone for me, and I don't care if you have to sit in the stands," Ferguson said. "I know it won't come to that, but I just have to tell you that I will not let you leave this year."

Ronaldo didn't do much talking—then again, it didn't need to be said. Ferguson understood that he had his heart set on Real Madrid. "But," the boss added, "I'd rather shoot you than sell you to that guy now. If you perform, don't mess us about, and someone comes up and offers us a world-record fee, then we will let you go."

For Ronaldo, that was good enough. Spain would still be there in a year. This solution allowed him to get to Real Madrid eventually and avoid disappointing Ferguson, the man he viewed as a father figure. They shook hands on it and planned to regroup in Manchester for preseason training.

After the summit, Ronaldo felt he needed to break the news to Real personally. He rang Calderón in Bogota, Colombia, where the club was playing an exhibition against Santa Fe. "Mr. President," Ronaldo told him, "I would like to stay here for one more year. There's an agreement with United for leaving the club in 2009."

Calderón paused to think about it. It wasn't what he wanted to hear, but this was undoubtedly good news. The first of the next Galácticos was on his way—even if Calderón would be voted out of office before Cristiano actually landed in Spain. In 2008, Real Madrid could now begin plotting its future around Ronaldo, precisely as its greatest rival felt itself slipping backward. Years ahead of schedule, Barcelona was back in hand-wringing mode and preparing to consign the Ronaldinho era to history.

IN THE GAME of dueling crises played every so often by Real Madrid and Barcelona, this was the Catalan club's bid at the end of the 2007–2008 season: it had been two years since the Champions League title in Paris, and there had been exactly zero major trophies since. Frank Rijkaard, in the midst of a divorce, seemed distracted. And Ronaldinho's reacquaintance with constant partying had contributed to his worst season at the club. He missed half the year through injury and scored just eight goals. "He needs a new challenge," club president Joan Laporta said in a quietly scathing interview on Catalan television. "When a cycle finishes, it is normal that the most emblematic pieces also come to an end."

Laporta was feeling the end-of-empire pressure more than most. While he pointed Ronaldinho and Rijkaard toward the exit in May, Barcelona's own board was moving to do the same to Laporta. The angry politicking culminated in a confidence vote against him that July. The socis were invited to the polls for a straight up or down poll on Laporta, his board, and his entire era in charge. FC Barcelona is proud to say it's a democracy, but for its leaders, the power of the people when those people are football supporters can be a distinct inconvenience. Around 40,000 members cast ballots at polling places around Camp Nou in a process that needed hundreds of staffers and cost the club some €500,000. Laporta narrowly survived. A two-thirds majority was required to oust him, and his opponents had garnered only 61 percent of the electorate. Now he just had to face up to that majority of fans who had made it clear they wanted him gone. "The reaction of the Barça environment was, in my opinion, not proportional," Laporta said later.

But that spring was no time for proportion. Momentous decisions seemed to be happening all the time. The confidence vote was, in fact, the board's second era-defining decision in the space of two months.

The previous one had been appointing a new manager. And many members of the Barcelona board believed they had the ideal candidate for that position right under their noses. He was young, he was ambitious, and he'd proven himself adept at turning homegrown players into world-beaters. Not only that, the candidate they had in mind had already spent his formative years at Barcelona. He knew the culture of the club intimately. He'd worked with the kids from La Masia. He even understood Catalan.

The prospective manager was perfect. His name was José Mourinho.

Eight years after Mourinho had left his role as an assistant coach, a large chunk of the board felt it was time to bring the club's adopted Portuguese son home. His years in Barcelona had begun as a right-hand man to the English manager Bobby Robson when the pair arrived to succeed Johan Cruyff in 1996. Mourinho had previously been Robson's interpreter in Portugal, and the sharp young thing from Setúbal had proven to be a quick study. He soon graduated from finding the right words for "It was a game of two halves" in press conferences to drawing up practice sessions. (Not that it impressed the Barcelona president at the time, Josep Lluís Núñez, who insisted on referring to José as "The Translator.") After he outlasted Robson's tenure in Spain, Mourinho stuck around to work under Louis van Gaal and was so well regarded internally that Barcelona let him coach the Barça B squad too. That turned into the launchpad for his return to Portugal as a head coach in 2000. In quick succession, he took charge of Benfica, União de Leiria, and a Champions League–winning team in Porto, before making the "Special One" leap in 2004 to Chelsea, where he broke up the Premier League duopoly of Alex Ferguson's Manchester United and Arsène Wenger's Arsenal. Mourinho may have left Barcelona as The Translator, but he'd be coming back as the hottest, cockiest, most sought-after manager in Europe.

Not everyone at Barcelona was sold on him. There was another internal candidate who boasted many of the same qualities with the added advantages of having worn the Barcelona shirt and *actually being* Catalan. On any résumé sent to Camp Nou, those were worth at least a decade's experience—which is handy, since Pep Guardiola had next to no experience at all.

Pep, the balding former midfield maestro of the Barça Dream Team of the early '90s, was in charge of Barça B in the Spanish fourth tier at the time. With a squad of La Masia products—including Messi's old pal Víctor Vázquez and future top-tier pros Sergio Busquets, Pedro, and Thiago Alcântara—Guardiola played a high-purity form of Barça-ball. The pass-and-move style was hardwired into him. After all, Guardiola had spent his entire footballing life at Barcelona, aside from a five-year interlude that took him to Italy, Mexico, the Gulf, and Wenger's North London kitchen, where he'd asked to play for Arsenal only to be told he was too old for what the club was cooking. Now all of the lessons he'd learned by steeping in the culture of the club for more than two decades were allowing his team to use beautiful soccer to beat up on local teams like Castelldefels and Rapitenca. No one outside of Catalonia had ever heard of them.

Crucially, though, one man in Catalonia had. And as Barça B marched toward promotion to the third tier, Barça's Dutch prophet had given Guardiola his blessing. "Pep knows," Johan Cruyff said on Catalan radio in April 2008. "And he's very clever. He has amply proved that he has the ability to coach the first team." Rijkaard hadn't even been dismissed yet.

Around the offices at Camp Nou, the choice between Mourinho and Guardiola became a daily debate that spilled into the sports newspapers. Laporta was known to favor Pep. His finance chief, Ferran Soriano, the man who had steered the club's books back from the brink in 2003, was pro-Mourinho, according to one board member. But in the end, Barcelona's obsession with hiring disciples of Cruyff won out. Anything that could bring the club closer to the great man by drawing a direct line of succession was a gamble worth taking. Never mind that Guardiola was about to go from coaching in the fourth tier to the Champions League.

"From our point of view, it was not as risky as people said," Laporta said later with a thinly veiled drive-by on Real Madrid. "It is much riskier to create a team by paying a lot of money to buy names."

NOT WINNING SOCCER matches is a pretty risky strategy too. Which is exactly what happened in Guardiola's first league game in charge of Barcelona in August 2008. In front of fewer than 10,000 people on the road in central Spain, the team lost 1-0 to Numancia. Then the next week Barça drew 1-1 at home against lowly Racing de Santander. This did not mix well with the ambient hysteria that tends to surround the club. The wild vibes had permeated Barcelona for so long that Cruyff even had a shorthand word for them: *el entorno*. The environment.

But just as a cloud of panic began to settle over Camp Nou, Guardiola received two key endorsements. The first came from up on high. In his regular Monday column in the *Periódico de Catalunya* newspaper, Cruyff launched an "I'm-right-you're-wrong" broadside at all the doubters after the Racing match. "I don't know what game you saw," he wrote in typically belligerent style. "The one I saw had not happened at Camp Nou for a long time." Barcelona had lacked a few goals, sure, but the fundamental elements were there. Cruyff saw the intricate passing again, as well as players like Messi and Andrés Iniesta, who got what all of this was supposed to be about. He described Guardiola as "neither inexperienced nor suicidal" (this counts as praise, by the way) and commended him for his ideas (which, coincidentally, were adapted from Cruyff's ideas). "What was drawn on the blackboard," Cruyff beamed, "became flesh, boot, and ball on the grass."

The second proclamation of faith came from the players. It didn't bother them that they were off to Barcelona's worst start to a league campaign since the Franco era. They were enjoying themselves again, in the matches and in the endless possession games at practice. Iniesta, the 24-year-old playmaker, made sure to let Guardiola know in person. He popped into the manager's basement office after the Santander game with a brief message: "Don't worry, boss. We'll win it all. We're on the right path. . . . Please, don't change anything." On his way out, Iniesta lobbed back a "¡Vamos de puta madre!" *We're going fucking great!*

Messi was less enthused. Some of the coach's new rules concerned him directly—soda was now banned at team meals, and players were forbidden from getting intimate with their partners after midnight. Guardiola also urged Messi to give up pizza and bulk up in the gym a little to hold his own against all of the men constantly trying to kick him. But for the most part, Messi and Guardiola barely spoke. As one former Barça teammate put it, "They had more of a silent conversation."

• • •

ON THE RARE occasions they did chat, they made it count in history-shaping ways.

One particular conversation has slipped into the canon of Messi stories, retold as a flash of sudden inspiration every bit as significant as Isaac Newton getting bopped on the head by an apple. (Even Pep tells it this way.) It's the night before Barcelona travels to Real Madrid late in the 2008–2009 season. The team has recovered from its shaky start and taken a commanding lead in the Liga standings. Guardiola, as he always does before big matches, is sitting in his office watching game tape. Classical music plays softly in the background. Guardiola knows that a good result in the 90,000-capacity bear pit that is the Estádio Santiago Bernabéu would all but seal the league championship for Barça. He's watching for something he hasn't seen before, letting his mind float to see if it might form some new connections. He's looking at movement and spaces and most of all the places on the pitch where Real might do something stupid. Around 10:00 p.m., he finds it. Guardiola rings Messi. "Leo, it's Pep. I've just seen something important," he says, as described in the book *Pep Confidential*. "Really important."

Messi is summoned to the office. Guardiola explains that instead of playing on the right side of midfield, he will switch midgame into a more central position just behind the strikers, where he can torment the Real Madrid center backs who are too reluctant to step up that far from the goal. If he does the job correctly, in the withdrawn forward position known as the False 9, Messi should find himself in acres of space to create all sorts of lovely problems.

Messi adores the idea. Guardiola fills in his staff, and even though they aren't convinced, they agree to move forward with the plan anyway. "If this goes wrong, we're going to lose the league," assistant coach Domènec Torrent thinks to himself. "And he'll get slaughtered."

The next day the only ones getting slaughtered are Real Madrid. Messi scores twice, Barcelona wins 6–2 on the road, and the Madrid meltdown begins. In one fell swoop, Guardiola has not only embarrassed his most important rival to effectively clinch La Liga in his first season at the club—he's also solved the problem that Rijkaard couldn't crack. Pep now knows the most effective way to employ Messi.

As an apple-on-the-head episode, it couldn't be tidier—a eureka moment, a secret weapon, and a crushing victory. But the truth is that Real Madrid might have seen it coming if they had paid attention to a lower-profile match seven months earlier. That's when Barcelona really deployed Messi in the False 9 role for the first time, late in a 6–1 September blowout against Sporting Gijón. It was Guardiola's first league win as Barça manager after the loss and the draw in the opening two games—and somehow the stakes had been even higher than in the Clásico. Guardiola felt that anything less than a victory meant he might as well start packing his bags. "If we lose," he told Torrent, "it could be the first time in Barcelona's history that we find ourselves at the bottom of the table."

Few people noticed the tactical innovation that saved Guardiola's job that day. But when he used it to dismantle Real Madrid, it became impossible to miss.

Surrounded by the boys he'd admired as a kid at La Masia, in a system he'd been drilled in for close to a decade, Messi thrived in the Guardiola team. For the first time since the academy days, Messi cleared 20 goals in a league season and 30 in all competitions. The campaign that had begun with so much uncertainty was turning into a procession for Guardiola's Barça. In the space of a few weeks in May, the team clinched the league and picked up the Copa del Rey by stomping Athletic Bilbao in the final. There was no doubt that this was the best team in Spain. But to become the best team in Europe, it would also have to overcome the best teams in England. In the spring of 2009, those were still Chelsea and Manchester United.

Built on the riches of pay television, the English Premier League had matured from its foundation in 1992 into the wealthiest soccer competition on Earth. Its clubs had turned into magnets for global talent by paying the highest transfer fees and the highest salaries. The money ran so deep that any given season produced multiple would-be champions of Europe. Since Barça last won the Champions League in 2006, nine of the 12 spots in the semis had been occupied by English teams. In fact, between 2006 and 2009, AC Milan was the only non-English side besides Barcelona to reach the final four. If Guardiola's version of the team was going to complete the treble of major titles, then a meeting with some Brits seemed inevitable. So did another meeting with Cristiano.

Before that, though, there had to be the most nail-biting semifinal anyone in Barcelona could remember: two brutal legs against Chelsea. Messi encountered a level of physicality that he hadn't been prepared for. After all, he hadn't been through the same North-of-England vulcanizing process as Ronaldo. While Cristiano spent his formative years at United being mercilessly stepped on by teammates at practice and opponents in games, Messi had found that most Spanish defenders couldn't get near him—and his Spanish teammates weren't crazy enough to go in with their studs up at practice. "No one would risk tackling him," says one. "We knew he was going to make us win."

Not only that, but anyone foolish enough to go in too hard on Messi instantly became the focus of Leo's revenge for the rest of the session. He would unleash his bag of tricks with the sole purpose of embarrassing that person. Needless to say, Messi usually emerged from training without a scratch.

The Chelsea games were a different story. The English club came to Camp Nou determined to break up Barcelona's flowing buildup play by any means necessary. In the first leg alone, Chelsea committed 20 fouls, an average of one for every 110 seconds that Barça had the ball in play. Messi and Iniesta alone were elbowed, hacked down, and pulled back by the jersey seven times. "Barcelona was the only team who wanted to play," an irate Gerard Piqué said that night.

Barça came out swinging for the second leg in London. And still it took more than 90 minutes of manhandling before Messi found a breakthrough. With his team reduced to 10 men after a red card and needing a single goal to advance, Messi shook off the mob of defenders that had trailed him all night and teed up Iniesta in the 94th minute to put

Barcelona in the final. Now it was Chelsea's turn to fume at the referee. (One player pointedly shouted into a TV microphone that his performance had been a "fucking disgrace.")

The Barça bench didn't care. It spilled onto the field to celebrate the ugliest win of its most beautiful era. Messi was back in a Champions League final. And defending champion Manchester United was there waiting.

On a warm spring night in Rome, Ronaldo and his teammates arrived at the Stadio Olimpico as favorites to become the first team to retain the title since the European Cup morphed into the modern Champions League in 1992. They combined drive and skill with the kind of power that Barcelona's side of diminutive geniuses viewed as a foreign language. Barça generated its speed through short, crisp passing, the death-by-a-thousand-cuts approach that was widely dubbed tiki-taka, even though Guardiola hated the term. Pep saw tiki-taka as passing for passing's sake. What his team did was pass to probe and prod and create numerical advantages. It had more in common with chess opening theory than with Man United's approach to overwhelming opponents. And if the bookmakers couldn't see that, Alex Ferguson could. He warned before the game that Barça's midfield wizards, Andrés Iniesta and Xavi, along with Messi drifting around the final third of the field, could easily put teams "on a carousel."

It didn't take long for Ferguson's worst fears to come true. The Barcelona passing machine cranked into gear and began finding space around, through, and even under United defenders. The twin pillars of Rio Ferdinand and Nemanja Vidić in the back line—a combined 12.5 feet of defensive muscle—found they could barely keep track of where these five-foot-seven nuisances were moving. Barça's first goal, after just 10 minutes, came from a move that went from Iniesta to Messi to Iniesta to Samuel Eto'o. Even when Ferdinand tried to cut Messi down, he discovered that Messi changed direction so quickly that he practically ducked beneath him. Arsenal manager Arsène Wenger would later call Messi a "PlayStation footballer," the kind of player who seemed controlled by a joystick and all the cheat codes. Wenger also believed it was a shame that Messi wasn't *even shorter*, imagining what he could do even closer to the ground.

So it was especially galling to United when Messi scored the second goal in the 2–0 win with a header. One of the smallest players on the pitch leapt backward and, without craning his neck, guided the ball over United's goalkeeper.

Ronaldo failed to have the same effect. Although he claimed half of United's 10 shots in the game, four of them missed the target entirely. One year after sobbing tears of joy into the turf in Moscow, he finished the night staring off into space in Rome. He stuck around for the trophy ceremony only to remember how it felt.

This time, Messi stuck around too. Unlike Paris in 2006, here was a Champions League title that he felt he'd earned.

To Guardiola and the high priests of Cruyffism, including the prophet himself, this season was pure, unadulterated validation. Within hours of the final whistle, Cruyff had said as much in his column, calling out the believers in "resultism" who cared only about outcomes instead of process. "Style wins," Cruyff wrote. "The best style wins."

"This Barça has imposed a style of play that has provoked millions of praises in every corner of the world," he added. "And it has written, in large golden letters, the most widely read text message of 2009: you can win by playing beautifully, by putting on a show. Copy this proposal. If you dare."

But there was one resultist not buying any of this—and who definitely did not read "resultism" as a dirty word. To Cristiano Ronaldo, trophies were the only recognized method for keeping track of success. The score was the score. Wasn't this the whole point of every sport from tiddlywinks to the Champions League final?

For once, though, he had to recognize he was beaten. More than that, he felt that Manchester United had taken him as far as it could in his quest to be the greatest player on the planet. He understood that the stage was now elsewhere, in Spain, on his rival's adopted turf—and he was determined to make that turf his own. It was time to go.

The next time Ronaldo met Messi, it would be in Barcelona.

PART 2

Greatest(s) of All Time

FIVE

Galáctico Brain

CRISTIANO RONALDO STRODE onto the pitch at the Estádio Santiago Bernabéu and soaked in the adulation of nearly 80,000 white-clad supporters. As usual, he thought about how all those people had come solely to watch him. Only this time, he was right.

There was no game that day. Still, fans had lined up outside for seven hours for a chance to get in the building. Those who didn't make it would have to settle for a giant screen outside. More royal wedding than glorified press conference, Cristiano's official unveiling as a Real Madrid player was the hottest ticket in the Spanish capital and, as far as Real Madrid president Florentino Pérez was concerned, anywhere in the soccer universe.

It was, in fact, the second time Pérez had thrown a party like this one in the space of a week. A few days earlier, Real Madrid had welcomed Kaká as the most expensive player in soccer history. Only he didn't quite get the full treatment—the club limited the number of supporters allowed inside the stadium because the pitch was being relaid. Besides, Pérez knew that Kaká's days as soccer's most expensive player would be short-lived. Real Madrid's protracted chase for Ronaldo was coming to an end with an agreement for yet another record fee.

"I'm happy to be the most expensive player in the history of football," Ronaldo said afterward, as if it were only natural.

The long list of official duties that come with a player unveiling in

Madrid is not dissimilar to the requirements of a state visit to Spain—except for the moment when the dignitary is photographed with his shirt off at the club-mandated physical exam. This was the part Ronaldo was born for. The club doctor, Carlos Díez, spoke about him as if he were the Six Million Dollar Man. "The cardiac and lung capacity is extraordinary," he said. "Everything is in perfect condition."

There was a tour of the Bernabéu, a formal lunch with club legends, and finally his emergence onto the pitch with the Real Madrid badge on his chest and the number 9 on his back. (The club icon Raúl owned the number 7, so in a show of magnanimity Cristiano agreed to switch for a year—but only after trademarking "CR9" in Spain.)

Pérez had been picturing this moment for months. There were only a couple of details he had hoped would turn out differently. For one, he didn't want "Ronaldo" written across the back of Cristiano's jersey—he preferred "C. Ronaldo." Real Madrid, Pérez explained to him, had recently fielded a Ronaldo, the Brazilian one, and sold boatloads of his shirts. Fans already had their "Ronaldo 9" kits at home. Cristiano didn't care.

The other blemish on the day was the big orange Swoosh on the T-shirt Ronaldo had worn all morning. With Real Madrid being an Adidas club, Pérez wasn't keen on his shiny new prize parading around in Nike gear. But minor complaints notwithstanding, it was a relief to finally see Ronaldo in a Real Madrid jersey—and not just because it had taken two and a half years to come about.

Ronaldo was feeling unusually settled too. His restlessness had reached an end in Madrid. Twelve years after his ambition to become the world's best footballer had taken him from Madeira to Sporting Lisbon, six years after he made the step up to Manchester United, and 12 months after the transfer saga threatened to derail his move to Spain, Ronaldo was finally where he felt he belonged: at a club as certain of his status as the world's best player as he was.

Pérez just wondered whether Ronaldo quite understood the order of things. Though the club had spent a soccer eternity courting him, Ronaldo needed to remember that Real had been around for a century before him and would still be around a century after him. As Pérez watched Ronaldo play to the crowd, this aggressively low-key bureaucrat was on his way to becoming the most powerful executive in European soccer. Over the course of two decades, he would do more to reshape the world's most popular game than anyone else on the planet.

And Ronaldo was part of Pérez's master plan, not the other way round.

FLORENTINO PÉREZ WAS four years old when he attended his first Real Madrid game at what would become known as the Estadio Santiago Bernabéu. The experience left a mark. He had spent most of the match fooling around by the handrail, but when Madrid scored, he raced back toward his parents and slipped on the stadium steps, splitting open his lip. "They patched me up there and then," he recalled later, "but I was left with a scar. A war wound from the stadium."

It would take more than a busted lip to put him off. Over the next 70 years, Pérez estimates, he missed barely a handful of Real Madrid home games. The son of a drugstore owner, he grew up in a middle-class home a short walk from the stadium, and trips to the Bernabéu were part of the family routine. At one point, Pérez held 29 season tickets in the Tribuna Preferencia for various family members, close friends, slightly less close friends, and business associates. And on the day of his wedding he presented his bride with what he considered the truest expression of lifelong devotion: her own Real Madrid membership card.

Pérez's formative years, when he fell head over heels for Real Madrid, coincided with its emergence as one of the most seductive teams in the game. The Real side of the 1950s and 1960s was European football's first dynasty, the ultimate winning machine, reeling off five European Cups in a row. The run began in 1956 with the inaugural tournament—which threw together the champions of Europe's major leagues—and reached its pinnacle with a 7–3 dismantling of Eintracht Frankfurt in the 1960 final. Real added a sixth title in 1966 on top of 12 Liga championships in two decades. No one had left Spain and done this much damage abroad since the conquistadors. For those like Pérez, who came of age in the era of Alfredo Di Stéfano, Ferenc Puskás, Paco Gento, and the rest, it was an established fact of life that soccer's greatest talents wore white jerseys.

"That's what made it different and gave it a certain place in the world," Pérez says.

But by the 1990s, that place was a lot lower down the table than Pérez and the 28 friends sitting alongside him were accustomed to. The name Real Madrid was no longer feared across Europe. After a stretch of four years without a title, it was barely feared across Spain.

Fortunately, Pérez was now in a position to do something about it. Because in the rare parts of his life that he didn't devote to watching Real Madrid, he had carved out just enough time to become the billionaire head of a multinational corporate empire. It was a remarkable achievement, not least because Pérez never especially intended to go into business. His true calling was politics. After graduating from Madrid's School of Civil Engineering, Pérez talked his way into a job at a lobby group for the construction industry, a position that allowed him to mine valuable contacts in the city's business community and labor unions. Those connections paid off when, at age 29, he was tapped by the mayor of Madrid to run the city's sanitation department. That same year he became the youngest city councilor in Spanish history. And in the early 1980s, Pérez was a rising star in the centrist party led by Adolfo Suárez, the prime minister appointed by the Spanish king in 1976 to oversee the transition to democracy following the death of Francisco Franco. He occupied a position at the Ministry of Agriculture and was seemingly headed for a long career in central government—until his upward trajectory was interrupted by something that a lifetime of rooting for Real Madrid had not adequately prepared him for: a spectacularly terrible defeat.

In the 1982 general election, Pérez's political party was all but wiped off the map, losing 93 percent of its seats as the Socialist Party won in a landslide. It remains the heaviest loss suffered by a ruling party in modern European history. Never much good at shaking off a setback, Pérez quickly came to the decision that if he was going to rebuild an organization from the ground up, he might as well be compensated for it properly. In 1983, he moved into the private sector, acquiring a small, bankrupt construction firm named ACS for the price of just one peseta.

He would spend decades building the company into one of the world's largest engineering conglomerates. Exactly how he managed to do it is usually credited to three things: his political touch, his meticulous approach (his favorite expression is "every screw in its right box"), and what the Spanish call *enchufe*, or friends in high places. ACS grew to more than 25,000 employees and an annual turnover of half a billion pesetas, thanks in no small part to its knack for winning lucrative public works contracts awarded by government officials from Pérez's past.

By 1995, Florentino Pérez, head of one of Spain's biggest companies, a trusted adviser to the prime minister, and the country's 40th richest man, finally felt qualified to apply for the only job he had ever really wanted. That summer he announced his candidacy for president of Real Madrid.

With his glasses, neatly parted hair, and quiet demeanor, Pérez doesn't look like a bombastic sports executive. He doesn't own a car, he loathes fancy restaurants, and the closest he gets to extravagance are the rare occasions he switches out his customary pale blue shirt for something a little racier—like a slightly darker shade of blue. But between his business chops, his social and political connections, and half a lifetime of attending matches at the Bernabéu, Pérez was confident that his fellow *Madridistas* would view him as a natural choice.

THE FIRST EVER president of Real Madrid had definitely not been a natural choice.

For starters, he came from Barcelona. Yet it didn't take Juan Padrós long to nail down the requirements of the job. Shortly after he was chosen to lead the newly formed board of directors of the Madrid Foot Ball Club in 1902, he set up a new national soccer tournament in honor of

King Alfonso XIII. Madrid proceeded to do what it does best and take home its first ever championship.

Padrós was succeeded in 1904 by his brother Carlos, but his brief tenure as president neatly encapsulated how the role is supposed to work in the eyes of Real Madrid followers. The club's members are responsible for electing a president every four years, and the victorious candidate is expected to repay the socios with a bunch of trophies.

What matters to Real Madrid more than anything else is glory. Unlike other clubs that see soccer as a form of artistic expression and feel it's their duty to elevate the act of advancing a ball downfield, Real Madrid has no such pretensions. It doesn't want to be universally loved and admired for its distinctive style of play. The club's sole purpose is to be the best. Events on the field constitute the means, but winning is the point. Real's philosophy is captured in its trophy room at the Bernabéu, which is open to visitors seven days a week as a permanent and prodigious tribute to the club's greatness. In 2015, Pérez called it "the most illustrious trophy cabinet of all time." The dozens of pots, plates, and cups—from a record 35 Liga titles to something called La Pequeña Copa del Mundo (won twice)—make the point more forcefully than an airhorn in a library: this is the winningest team in soccer history. A special place is reserved for each of its 14 triumphs in the European Cup, a trophy Madrid has lifted so many times that it literally started using numbered nicknames for each of those victories—la Septima, la Decima, etc.—so that fans could distinguish one triumph from the next.

In case you hadn't picked up on this already, Madrid's towering record of success is matched only by its towering self-regard. Absolute greatness goes hand in hand with absolute grandiosity. On the occasion of its centenary in 2002, Real staged a four-team summer tournament with AC Milan, Bayern Munich, and Liverpool by way of celebration. The club also paid a visit to the pope, invited itself to the United Nations General Assembly in New York, and in December of that year staged a special anniversary match against a one-night-only team of FIFA all-stars. Because you only turn 100 once, Real requested that all other official games on the planet be stopped on its birthday. FIFA, led by honorary socio Sepp Blatter, happily obliged. This was, after all, FIFA's "Club of the 20th Century." Real is still working on the 21st.

IF SUCCESS WAS what distinguished Real Madrid from everybody else, the structure of the club increasingly set it apart too. For most of the 130 years since a pair of Scottish doctors founded Spain's first soccer club as a way to get their employees some regular exercise, teams were run by the same fans who turned up to watch them every weekend. Club members would elect a president and board of directors, whose job was to oversee the day-to-day administration of the club and carry out important functions like hobnobbing with dignitaries and posing for photos with new signings. Managing the finances didn't require much work because, for the most part, there weren't any. What little money Spanish clubs brought in came from ticket sales, membership fees, and whatever the local business had stumped up to put its name on the front of the jerseys or the pitchside boards. Television revenue made no impact for decades, since Spanish television had only two stations until 1982 and no private channels until 1990. Even the glory years of Di Stéfano and Co. were funded largely through the simple fact that Real Madrid boasted the biggest stadium of any team in the European Cup.

This model of fan ownership served Spain well for the better part of a century. But by the 1980s, the business of running a soccer club had become an increasingly costly proposition. After the European Community established freedom of movement for soccer players, Barcelona paid a world-record transfer fee of $7.6 million to sign Diego Maradona in 1982, and La Liga's top players now commanded annual salaries in excess of $100,000. With next to nothing in the way of TV or commercial income, Spanish clubs became increasingly reliant on another source of revenue: bank loans.

Almost every professional club in Spain soon sank heavily into the red, although that alone wasn't anything out of the ordinary. Sky-high debt is as much a part of modern European soccer as the halftime break and obscene chanting. But Spanish football's ownership structure presented a problem. Some teams were in such trouble that there now was a legitimate question of who would be liable if a club defaulted. The Spanish government wasn't about to wait for an answer. In 1990, it enacted Sports Law 10/1990, which required any club that wasn't financially viable to convert into an entity known as a sociedad anónima deportiva (SAD), the Spanish equivalent of a limited liability company. The rule applied to every club that was unable to show a positive balance in its accounts over the previous five years, starting with the 1985–1986 season. Which is to say, it applied to basically everyone.

By the time the law came into force, only four of Spain's 42 professional clubs were exempted—Real Madrid, Barcelona, Athletic Bilbao, and Osasuna. The latter three qualified as exceptions for the same fundamental reason: they are highly regional concerns. All three play in cities that have long tied their identities to their soccer teams, with Barça and Bilbao doubling as flagships for their local communities and bastions of national pride, with devoted fan bases, cavernous stadiums, and bigger memberships than some minor religions. The fan-ownership model is central to that sense of belonging. The base of support will always be there. In other words, it would have required corporate mismanagement on the scale of Enron for any of them to run into serious financial difficulties (though that was entirely possible for a Spanish soccer club).

Real Madrid Club de Futbol was a different matter. It wasn't a pillar of local pride or a symbol of cultural separatism. In fact, for many of its most devoted followers, the city in which it played its matches was entirely beside the point. For them, Real Madrid was Spain's team. Part of that was down to its unrivaled run of dominance; after all, nothing is easier than supporting a winner. "Seventy-five percent of the people who live in Madrid, including myself, aren't born there," says former Real president Ramón Calderón. "The fans don't have a link with the regional or local side, but with success. They are identified with the success."

The fact that success came on a global stage—with all those European Cup victories—led many Spaniards to view Real Madrid as a symbol of Spanishness. For them, the sight of men in white jerseys parading around with a shiny trophy was as much a bedrock of Spanish life as bullfighting, flamenco, and sitting down to dinner at 11:00 p.m.

The executives at Real Madrid had always felt this to be true. In 2001, they discovered it was quantifiably so. The results of a national poll ordered up by team executives showed not merely that Real was the country's most popular club, with 49 percent of Spanish soccer fans identifying as Madridistas, but also that there were only three cities across the entire country where Madrid wasn't the best-supported team. (It will come as no surprise that those cities were Barcelona and the Basque cities of Bilbao and San Sebastián.) The rest of Spain was Real country. Even in places with strong soccer histories and multiple top-flight clubs, people rooted deep down for Madrid. In Seville, for instance, the study revealed that Real Madrid was the number-one club, with more fans than Sevilla and Real Betis *combined*. Madridista executives celebrated the findings like yet another trophy.

Florentino Pérez understood Madrid's place in the world better than anybody. Not just because he lived only a few blocks away, but also because all those years in the stands of the Bernabéu had taught him exactly what fans expected from their team. They wanted to win, sure, but they wanted to win with honor, with a certain sense of nobility. After all, King Juan Carlos would be discussing the club's latest results at the start of official meetings.

When Pérez threw his hat in the ring for president, he was campaigning explicitly on Real's pedigree. The club had gone 29 years without winning the European Cup, and he was the man to put Real back on top. He knew all about success and conducting business in a dignified way because he felt that he embodied those very same qualities.

Then Pérez did something that definitely did not embody the Real Madrid way. He lost.

To be sure, this loss wasn't as calamitous as his last electoral setback. The final tally in the 1995 Real Madrid presidential election showed that Pérez finished less than 500 votes behind his opponent, Lorenzo Sanz, a brash self-made businessman with a taste for sports cars, Cuban cigars, and late-night card games. Far from suffering a landslide defeat,

Pérez had lost out by just 1 percent of the vote. The narrow margin only made it more painful, though. Watching his fledgling career in government unravel on election night in 1982 had stung, but Pérez could console himself that political forces beyond his control were at play. This time defeat felt like a personal rejection. The socios were his people. A significant number of them were his actual family members. And losing to someone like Lorenzo Sanz only made it more galling. In Pérez's eyes, Sanz was nothing more than a crapshooter, a boorish *nuevo rico* who lacked the requisite class to occupy the office of president of Real Madrid.

Granted, Real Madrid's grand democratic experiment isn't the platonic ideal of self-government. Presidential elections take place every four years, unless the incumbent considers it advantageous to hold them earlier, or even later. Of the 17 men who have served as president—and they have all been men—seven failed even to see out their initial four-year term, while Santiago Bernabéu, who took credit for inventing the European Cup and was the stadium's namesake, ruled like a dictator for 35 years. Like all great democracies, things have only gotten worse in the internet age. These days, the act of running for club president seems mostly to involve wild self-aggrandizement, unchecked personal ambition, and lots of mudslinging.

But that hadn't deterred Pérez, and neither had the requirement that candidates show proof that they could underwrite 15 percent of the club's budget. Even as the final votes were counted, with his defeat still sinking in, Pérez resolved to run again. He would spend the coming years making sure that the next time was different. Because in his heart, Pérez was still convinced that Real desperately needed him.

WHEN REAL MADRID'S long wait for a European Cup, now known as the Champions League, came to an end on Lorenzo Sanz's watch in 1998, there was no denying it hurt Pérez's ambitions. Real's repeat win two seasons later, when it crushed Valencia 3–0 in Paris a matter of weeks before a new presidential election, ought to have killed them off entirely.

Pérez had promised to return Real Madrid to the summit of European soccer, and now Sanz had actually pulled it off twice. To most observers, Sanz's reelection was a matter of course. The prospect of unseating an incumbent who had just delivered two Champions League titles in three years was patently ridiculous. But Pérez knew better. He was a Madridista, after all, and he understood there was one thing Real Madrid fans coveted even more than European glory: a chance to pull a fast one on Barcelona.

That's why Pérez's second campaign for Real Madrid president focused on a different pledge, one that was even more ambitious than knocking off the superclubs of Europe. This time he promised to deliver Luís Figo, the ludicrously gifted, impossibly handsome Portuguese winger, who just happened to be the star player and captain of FC Barcelona.

Pérez bet that the prospect of stealing Figo from Madrid's greatest rival was so fiendishly irresistible that the socios would have no choice but give him their votes. For one thing, Figo was Mr. Barcelona, the team's talisman, beloved by fans and teammates, a player so fiercely committed to the blaugrana that when Barça won the Copa del Rey in 1998, he dyed his hair in red and blue stripes. As if that weren't enough, there was another reason Pérez felt so convinced that the Madrid socios would do whatever it took to land Figo: they had told him so.

In the months before launching his election campaign, Pérez had canvassed Real members on a host of topics, mostly concerning the club's finances, which he believed were in much worse shape than Sanz was letting on. But he also snuck a question about personnel into his poll. Which player would the socios most like to see at Real Madrid? The leading response by far was Figo.

It was then that Pérez began hatching a plan to pull off one of the most audacious coups in modern sports history, a transfer so intricately plotted, meticulously executed, and diabolically brilliant that it amounted to the soccer equivalent of a bank heist.

Like any classic caper, it relied on some opportune timing. In the summer of 2000, Real Madrid was not the only Spanish giant holding presidential elections. Barcelona's members were also due at the polls, where they would elect a successor to Josep Lluís Núñez. (That spring he'd announced his surprise resignation after 22 years and one too many broadsides from Johan Cruyff's newspaper column.) The up-shot was that Barcelona spent the off-season immersed in presidential politicking, which was a problem, because the summer of 2000 also happened to be the precise moment when Figo's agent, José Veiga, decided it was high time his client received a raise.

Of course, soccer agents believe their players deserve a raise for correctly putting on their shin guards. On this occasion, though, Veiga had a point. Over the previous 12 months, Figo had emerged as not merely the finest player at Barcelona, but perhaps the finest player on the planet. He had scored 20 goals for club and country during the 1999–2000 season—still an absurd number for a winger in those days—and in perhaps the truest testament to his greatness, he had managed to draw unequivocal praise from Cruyff. "He can do everything: can cross, can cut inside, can shoot with his right or left," the Dutchman wrote. "Yes, he really has everything."

No one at Barcelona could dispute that Figo deserved a new contract. The issue was that no one was in a position to do anything about it. Núñez was counting down the days until his departure, while the two men vying to replace him—Joan Gaspart and Luis Bassat—were weeks away from being voted in. Three times that year Veiga traveled to Barcelona to negotiate a new contract, and three times he left without any-one's signature. By the summer, both player and agent were beginning to feel exasperated. There was a power vacuum at Camp Nou, and it offered the sliver of daylight that Florentino Pérez had been waiting for.

While the eyes of the soccer world were on the summer's European Championship in Belgium and the Netherlands, Pérez set the heist plan in motion. Pulling it off would require all his skill as a negotiator and a considerable slice of his personal fortune. The whole operation was possible only because Pérez had lost Real's presidential election five years earlier. Now, as a presidential candidate without an official role at Real Madrid, he wasn't bound by FIFA rules on contract negotiations with players on rival teams. That left him free to approach Figo and his agent with an offer that appeared too good to be true. Pérez told them he would hand over a check for 400 million pesetas—about $2.6 million—if Figo signed an agreement committing to join Real Madrid in the unlikely event that Pérez won the election. If Pérez failed to get elected, Figo was free to keep the money.

To José Veiga, who was still focused on improving Figo's contract at Barcelona, Pérez's offer looked like money for nothing, and no soccer agent worth his Prada loafers has ever turned that down. Besides, Veiga reasoned, where was the downside? Not only did Pérez have next to no shot at becoming Real president, but the merest hint of an approach from Madrid ought to have been enough to nudge Barça into finally paying his client. With Figo's blessing, Veiga signed the deal. They never even discussed it in person.

The devil, as ever, was in the fine print. The agreement drawn up by Pérez specified that if he won the election and Figo reneged on his promise to join Real, Pérez would be due a compensation fee from the player amounting to 5 billion pesetas—or $32.7 million. Neither Figo nor Veiga had given that clause much consideration, because they'd read the electoral tea leaves. For Pérez, however, it was the key, the guarantee that Figo couldn't afford to back out after the event.

That was all Pérez needed. After all, he knew Barcelona couldn't object either, thanks to another contractual loophole that was hiding in plain sight.

In Spanish soccer, every player's contract contains a *clausula de rescision*—an official price at which a player must be sold. If the specified amount is deposited at La Liga's offices, his club is powerless to stop it. These release clauses have traditionally served two purposes: most often they are set exorbitantly high so as to scare off any potential bidders from making an approach, but occasionally they are set conveniently low so that a team can get a player off the books without incurring the wrath of its own fans. Figo's buyout clause, set at 10 billion pesetas (roughly $66 million), most definitely belonged in the former category. No one had ever paid that much for a soccer player before, and in early 2000 there was no reason to think anyone would. The highest transfer fee ever paid by a Spanish club to that point was the $38.5 million that Lorenzo Sanz had plunked down the year before to sign the French striker Nicolas Anelka from Arsenal. Figo's release clause represented a 70 percent increase. It was all but unthinkable.

But when Florentino Pérez ran the numbers, it didn't seem unthinkable at all. After a few calls with his connections in the banking world, it began to make perfect sense. The banks agreed to lend Real Madrid the full 10 billion pesetas to trigger Figo's release clause on the condition that Pérez personally guarantee the amount. Pérez, who still lived in a relatively modest house in Madrid's Chamberí district, couldn't sign the documents fast enough.

By the beginning of July, two weeks out from election day at Real Madrid, everything was in place. There was just one last nagging thought in Florentino's mind. The promise to sign Figo was so outlandish that he began to worry that no one would believe him. So he threw some money at that problem too. In the final days of the race, he informed each of the club's 70,000 socios that if he was elected and failed to make good on his key campaign promise, he would pay the annual fees for every single Real member—all $8 million worth—out of his own pocket.

The news that Pérez had an agreement to sign Figo broke on July 6, catching Lorenzo Sanz somewhat off-guard. He was busy giving away his daughter at her wedding to Míchel Salgado, Real Madrid's starting right back. Sanz dismissed the story as utter garbage. "Maybe Florentino will announce that he's signed Claudia Schiffer next," he scoffed. But Pérez was one step ahead. Even the most skeptical socios had bought the membership dues gambit.

Pérez had outmaneuvered Sanz. He had also outmaneuvered Luís Figo, who tried desperately to wriggle out of his agreement with Pérez in the face of a nuclear meltdown in Barcelona. José Veiga called Pérez in tears, offering to return the 400 million pesetas he had accepted weeks earlier, while Figo appeared on the front page of the Catalan daily *Sport* wearing a Barça jersey to reassure fans he was going nowhere. He even told teammates—including Pep Guardiola, godfather to one of Figo's daughters—that the move to Madrid was entirely fictional.

But there was no going back. When the ballot boxes were emptied on July 16, Pérez had defeated Sanz by more than 3,000 votes.

Eight days later, Luís Figo was unveiled as a Real Madrid player in a presentation ceremony held, of course, in the trophy room. Barely smiling, he posed for photographs holding a white Real jersey and delivered some brief remarks. "I hope to be as happy here as I was at Barcelona," he said, before disappearing to sign his new contract, this one with a release clause set at 30 billion pesetas. On Figo's left side stood another new signing: Alfredo Di Stéfano, whom Pérez had worshiped as a child and was now hiring back to the club as honorary vice president at the age of 74. On the other side was Pérez himself, wearing his standard blue shirt and gray suit, with the smirk of a man who has just table-flipped Spanish soccer's fiercest rivalry. Hours earlier, he had deposited the 10-billion-peseta release fee at La Liga's offices. In one fell swoop, he had launched a bold new era for Real Madrid and plunged Barcelona into a new cycle of chaos. It was a Madridista's fever dream.

"It was not easy," Pérez reflected later. "Nobody had spent €60 million in 2000. But he was the captain of Barcelona! It was like ripping out their heart."

THE SIGNING OF Figo was audacious, but not as daring as what came next. Over the following five years, Pérez launched an all-out assault on soccer's established order, upending the game's economics, rewriting the rules of the transfer market, and reimagining the financial model that had underpinned club football for half a century. By the time he was done, he had turned Real Madrid into the world's most valuable sports franchise.

But before all that could happen, he needed to stop the club from going bankrupt.

Days after taking office, Pérez conducted a thorough analysis of the club's accounts. It made for grim reading. Madrid was in debt to the tune of $150 million and was losing more than $20 million a season. When Pérez and his team dug deeper into the numbers, the situation looked even worse. Wages accounted for an astonishing 86 percent of total revenue, and the biggest single source of income was ticket sales and membership fees. That was a problem, because Real Madrid had failed to sell out 18 of its 19 home games in the 1999–2000 season, and the number of socios had actually declined over the past five years. Former Real executive Carlos Martinez de Albornoz summed up the situation neatly in John Carlin's account of Pérez's early tenure. "When Florentino took over," he said, "we didn't have enough money to buy a biro."

Luckily, Pérez knew where to go to ensure the stationery closet didn't stay empty for too much longer. The banks were his friends. Pérez was already on the hook for the €18 million that he'd had to stump up to run for president, as well as the €60 million loan he'd personally underwritten to secure Figo. But his overhaul of Real Madrid had barely started—he'd just have to borrow more. To cover a loan for the signings of midfielders Claude Makélélé and Flávio Conceição, Pérez personally guaranteed another €39 million to the banks. Player sales, including Anelka's departure to Paris Saint-Germain for €36 million, paid for an additional four new signings, but the increased expenditure ballooned Real's budget. By law, Pérez was required to chip in a further €12 million to cover the shortfall. Only weeks after becoming president, Florentino Pérez's personal financial risk added up to more than €129 million. Turning around Real Madrid was no longer merely a lifetime ambition but a financial necessity.

Pérez had a plan for that too, and one a little more grandiose than taking out a loan. In his mind, fixing Real Madrid wasn't simply a matter of cutting costs and balancing the books. The club needed something bolder, something with more revenue streams and easier money. The team that had been officially declared "the Club of the 20th Century" needed to be updated for the 21st. The secret lay somewhere in soccer's commercial possibilities.

Pérez knew this because someone else had already thought of it. The same commercial transformation that he was envisioning at Real Madrid had occurred to a handful of English soccer executives nearly a decade earlier. In 1992, Manchester United, Arsenal, and Tottenham Hotspur had spearheaded a breakaway by the country's biggest clubs that led to the creation of the Premier League. In the years since, England's top clubs had become world leaders in exploiting the game's commercial opportunities. Manchester United was the benchmark. Its combination of corporate savvy, marketing might, and a constellation of stars on the pitch gave it an economic advantage that no other club in Europe could match. It was a case study in how to transform a century-old soccer club into a modern corporate empire. And conveniently enough, the blueprint it had followed was an open secret. United had floated on the London Stock Exchange in 1991, meaning that the club's accounts for the past nine years had been made publicly available. Pérez studied them like scripture. He saw that Real Madrid needed a total restructuring—its reliance on match-day income and membership fees made it a relic in the modern game. Until the 1990s, Real matches—along with everyone else's in Spain—were barely visible beyond the country's borders. The internationalization of club soccer was still in its infancy.

But already, Pérez could see what was happening. Marketing, merchandising, corporate branding—these were the new economic drivers of European football. What had been a break-even business built around ticket sales and whatever you could scrounge together from peddling scarves and sodas to a population of local supporters was turning into a gold rush for media rights and a worldwide fan base.

The Premier League had already come to that realization. Manchester United recognized that its fame and star-powered roster could make it a global marketing phenomenon, which in turn made it a serial title contender. Yet as Pérez pored over the numbers, he began to realize that United hadn't gone far enough. The English club had used its commercial advantage to stock its squad with big-time players. To Pérez, this was almost the wrong way round. The players themselves needed to be the driving force. If you invested aggressively in the game's biggest stars and their worldwide acclaim, then greater marketing riches would surely follow. And if you bought enough of them, even Manchester

United's commercial edge could be dulled. Pérez began to conceive of a virtuous circle, in which an all-star lineup would propel Madrid back to the heights of the 1950s. And Figo would be the first of his Galácticos signings.

With the help of José Ángel Sánchez, a marketing executive Pérez hired away from Sega and would later refer to as his "Galácticos in jacket and tie," he learned to identify commercial possibilities everywhere. The club studied how Disney had marketed *The Lion King*, which was a box-office smash but also continued to generate money from merchandising and spin-offs long after it left theaters. Under this new way of thinking, Sánchez and Pérez viewed players not only as assets on the pitch but also as actors in their wider commercial offering. Real Madrid Club de Futbol ceased to be just a professional sports team and became a content producer. If Pérez's job was to deliver a spectacle, then he knew that nothing in soccer was as spectacular as a superstar signing. He envisioned bringing in a new one every summer, like a Hollywood studio releasing new blockbusters. It was a high-risk strategy, but Pérez was certain it would pay off.

To make doubly sure, he indulged in some old-fashioned string-pulling.

In 2001, with a little help from his old pals at Madrid's city hall, Pérez oversaw the sale of Real's Ciudad Deportiva training ground to developers for a staggering €500 million, wiping out the club's debts at a stroke. It was an ingenious move, and one that provoked what can only be described as a total *mierda*-storm.

For years, city officials had refused to sanction development of the 15-hectare site, which once was located on the outskirts of the city but now sat at the heart of its financial district on the most expensive street in the country. The sale of the training ground, which had been valued at just €421,000 in 1998, drew fierce condemnation from the left-wing opposition and was later ruled by the European Commission to constitute an act of illegal state aid. When it emerged that ACS, Pérez's construction company, had won a clutch of the contracts to redevelop the site, the outcry grew even louder. But in 2001 all that mattered to Pérez was that Madrid's €278 million debt was a thing of the past. He could now put his Galácticos project into action.

ONE OF THE most ambitious and ultimately ill-conceived team-building strategies in corporate history kicked off in earnest in the summer of 2001. Pérez broke the world transfer record for the second time in the space of a year, shelling out $66 million to sign the French midfielder Zinedine Zidane from Juventus. In 2002, the Brazilian striker Ronaldo arrived from Inter Milan. By the time David Beckham pitched up one year later, Pérez had assembled the greatest collection of star power ever seen on a football pitch.

The most breathtaking part wasn't the succession of staggering fees, or even Pérez's desire to sign a new superstar every summer becoming official club policy. It was how the Galácticos project seemed to ignore every bit of orthodox wisdom about how to assemble a winning side. How many stars could you cram into the same lineup when there was still only one ball? Real Madrid began to look less like a soccer team and more like the Avengers.

For a while, it worked out just as Pérez planned. The Galácticos were like a soccer version of the Harlem Globetrotters. They won La Liga in his first and third seasons, either side of their crowning achievement on a cool night in the spring of 2002 at Glasgow's Hampden Park. On the same site as the club's victory in 1960, Zidane struck an impossible left-footed volley into the top corner from 20 yards out to secure Real Madrid's ninth European Cup—la Novena—in the club's centenary year. Two seasons later, Pérez celebrated another auspicious triumph when Real Madrid overtook Manchester United to become world soccer's richest team.

For Pérez, reaching that pinnacle was vindication. He had heard the detractors cluck about his reckless spending, incoherent recruitment, and brazen disregard for the rules of the transfer market. This showed he'd been right about everything. He had identified the irresistible draw of soccer's biggest stars and shown that leveraging the brands of Beckham, Ronaldo, and the rest could push Real to new heights of profitability. "Zidane cost €73 million," Pérez said, "and he was the cheapest player I signed." Indeed, Zidane started repaying his transfer fee before he even kicked a ball. Pérez had already sold the rights to his presentation ceremony to Canal Plus for 250 million pesetas.

It wasn't long before that was considered chump change. By the fourth year of Pérez's tenure, Real's income had doubled, from €138 million in 2000 to €276 million in 2004. Marketing and commercial sales now represented by far the biggest source of income, accounting for 40 percent of total revenue, a figure that delighted Pérez because it outstripped Manchester United's 27 percent proportion of marketing-related income over the same period.

The all-star roster he'd assembled didn't merely enable Real to bring in more money from its existing sponsorships; suddenly it also brought corporate partners who otherwise would never have ventured into professional sports knocking on Real Madrid's door.

In 2002, Real Madrid was hunting for a new jersey sponsor, a fact Pérez went out of his way to broadcast as far and wide as possible. Midway through the 2001–2002 season, he announced that the club's jerseys would henceforth display the "realmadrid.com" logo for the remainder of the campaign, ostensibly because he felt uncomfortable with corporate branding besmirching the pristine white jerseys during the club's 100th anniversary year. In reality, Pérez knew that it served as a beacon to interested parties that the most valuable patch of real estate in club soccer was in search of a new tenant. The news eventually made its way to a long-haired marketing executive named Rolf Beisswanger, who had recently left Hugo Boss to head up sponsorship for a new client that was sorely in need of a makeover.

In the summer of 2002, Siemens was one of the biggest multinationals in the world, a 155-year-old company with roughly €75 billion in sales and offices in nearly 200 countries. It was also virtually anonymous. For most of its existence as an engineering conglomerate focused on power turbines and transportation systems, obscurity wasn't an issue. But Siemens had recently entered the mobile phone business and realized that its staid, grandfatherly image didn't fit with its shiny new product.

To compete against brands like Nokia and Motorola, it needed some sex appeal. And Real Madrid's starry roster was just the thing to give it some oomph. "It took a lot of convincing," Beisswanger told the *Wall Street Journal*, but in 2002, Siemens's board of directors approved a deal to become Real Madrid's chief jersey sponsor. With an annual fee that rose to €17 million, it was the richest sponsorship deal in world soccer. Siemens soon regarded it as a bargain. Once its logo was emblazoned on the front of Real's jerseys, sales of the company's handsets took off. Siemens nearly tripled its market share in Latin America and added four points to its market share in Spain. The firm's internal data even showed an uptick in the one market they hadn't banked on: Catalonia.

That was before the arrival of Beckham in 2003 sent Pérez's commercial plans into hyperdrive. (When Adidas executives found out their preeminent client was joining Real, which had been outfitted by Adidas since 1998, they danced around the office.) Overnight the club found that the Beckham effect could multiply Real's fees for exhibition games tenfold. In 2005, a six-match preseason barnstorm through the United States, China, Japan, and Thailand netted $25.6 million. The shower of marketing dollars paid for upgrades to the Bernabéu, where the Galácticos now sat in a comfortable dugout warmed by overhead heaters and the adulation of the socios. Upstairs, Pérez was turning the VIP box, or Palco, into a place to see and be seen. King Juan Carlos and Kofi Annan rubbed shoulders there with Tom Cruise. There was also the occasional less salubrious grandee in attendance, like Gao Ping, a successful Chinese immigrant who years later would be indicted for his alleged role in Spain's Chinese mafia.

Regardless of its guest list, Real was the richest team in the world, it had the best players, and if the trophies didn't pile up quite as quickly as Pérez had hoped, it was clear that Real Madrid was once again soccer's gold standard. To top it all off, Barcelona still hadn't recovered from the Figo betrayal, failing to finish higher than fourth in the subsequent three seasons. In July 2004, Pérez was reelected with 91 percent of the vote.

What made the Galácticos project unique was that on top of its resounding success, it was also impossible to copy. Real Madrid was perhaps the only club that could pull it off because superstars are integral to its identity rather than late-arriving luxuries. From the days of Di Stéfano and Puskás, the entire setup of the club was designed to accommodate and appease the game's elite. Lockers in the home dressing room at the Bernabéu are arranged by jersey number, with two long benches on either side. No one chooses where they sit, no one gets special treatment. In the same way, Real long ago rejected the idea that its captain would be chosen by the coach or even by fellow players. Instead, the armband belongs to the longest-tenured player, regardless of his position or standing within the team, so as to avoid any arguments.

The Galácticos' undoing was not a problem of egos or getting the finances to add up. It was that Pérez began to focus on the finances above anything else. Commercial considerations overrode sporting ones. When Real executives looked back, they could pinpoint the moment it shifted. "We passed the limit the day we signed Beckham," conceded longtime sporting director Jorge Valdano. Beckham was by no means a bad player—you don't win 115 international caps if you're a bad player, even for a tragicomic outfit like the England national soccer team. He had undeniable qualities on the pitch. It's just that Real Madrid had no plan for using them.

Other cracks in the project began to appear, especially when the number of Galácticos began to exceed the number of available starting positions. Because the world's biggest stars are invariably attackers, Pérez ended up signing Galácticos who played in the same roles. When the English forward Michael Owen arrived in 2005, he found his spot in the starting lineup already occupied by Ronaldo. Figo was so incensed by the signing of Beckham, who typically operated in his preferred right-wing position, that he barely communicated with team officials for the first three months of the 2003–2004 season and refused to give up his job taking corners.

Then there was the problem of revamping the tactics every season to adjust to a new star. Finding the time to do that proved complicated because preseason training had morphed into yet another promotional exercise. Sponsor commitments were so numerous that players were allowed to excuse themselves from practice, and the mundane business of learning to play as a team fell by the wayside.

"It's very important that the club seeks income in publicity and so on, but there has to be a balance," Figo would say later. "We had started to break the rules a bit of what a football team should be."

Opponents with less talented players but more balanced tactics found it easier to live with the Galácticos, who suddenly looked a lot better at growing revenues than winning soccer matches. Invariably, it was the coaches who carried the can. Vicente del Bosque was on the sidelines for Pérez's first three seasons, and he paid the price for failing to deliver the Champions League in 2003. In the next three seasons, Pérez burned through five different managers. "It was a bad time to be at the club, a time when the president started to believe he knew something about football," said Carlos Queiroz, who succeeded del Bosque, but lasted just 10 months before returning to his old job as Alex Ferguson's assistant at Manchester United.

In January 2006, on a rain-soaked night in Mallorca, even Pérez could see the writing on the wall. It read Real Mallorca 2, Real Madrid 1. Two days after the team's seventh loss of the Liga season, which left Real 10 points behind Barcelona and on course for a third successive season without a trophy—the longest such run in more than half a century—Pérez announced his resignation as Real Madrid president.

He could no longer deny that the team he had constructed needed a hard reset. Figo, the first Galácticos, had left to join Inter Milan, Zidane was months away from retirement, and Ronaldo was battling injuries and a rapidly expanding waistline. Pérez didn't have the heart to tear it all down and start again. In private, he told aides he wished he'd stepped down in 2004 instead of running for reelection.

"My mistake is similar to a parent who wants to give his child only the best—you spoil them," Pérez said. "It's not the players' fault, but mine."

THAT WAS NEVER going to be the way it ended for Florentino Pérez and Real Madrid.

He had invested too much time, too much energy, and, frankly, far too much money in turning the club around just to walk away. Pérez promised to devote more attention to his day job at ACS, but within weeks of standing down he was already plotting a return to the Bernabéu. Not right away, of course, but eventually—once a few years had passed and the disaster of those last few months had been forgotten. He was certain that his image, his presidency, and his whole Galácticos project would ultimately be rehabilitated. It would just take time.

In the meantime, his successor, Ramón Calderón, spent his days trying to remind Real Madrid that it was a soccer team first and a dream factory second. "We thought that it was very important to change the mindset of the players," he says, "just being focused in training every day."

By the spring of 2009, three years after resigning as Real president, it was clear to Pérez that he couldn't stay away any longer. For several months now, he had been shaken to his core by an elemental crisis playing out across the country. This one had nothing to do with the spectacular collapse of Spain's housing bubble, which posed a serious threat to his ACS construction empire. This was much more serious.

Barcelona was back.

Pérez could feel his world order shifting, as though for the first time in history the axis of Spanish football was tilting away from Madrid and toward Catalonia. His worst fears would be confirmed a few months later when Barça ended up winning the treble of La Liga title, the Copa del Rey, and the Champions League with a demolition of Ronaldo's Manchester United. To Pérez, the season felt like one long blue-and-red victory parade.

It wasn't merely the winning that alarmed him. It was *how* Barcelona was winning. They made elite soccer look like a game of playground keep-away, piling up goals and admirers in equal measure. Pérez began to worry that, if they carried on like this, they would eclipse the achievements of his childhood Real Madrid sides. It was too much to bear thinking about.

Beyond all that, he couldn't stand the sanctimony of Barcelona's cocky purists. The veneration of Guardiola, Cruyff, and the rest killed him. The way they endlessly theorized about a simple game with a ball and a net drove him nuts. He had no time for their pseudo-intellectual nonsense about systems, shape, and "juego de posicion," whatever that meant. (Needless to say, Pérez was not an avid reader of Cruyff's column.) He always referred to the self-appointed guardians of the game at Camp Nou as *futboleros*, endlessly pontificating about the right way to play and oblivious to what he saw as the game's fundamental truth: the key to winning was having the best players.

In private, Pérez used an analogy about musicians to contrast the approach of the two clubs. If you delivered the 10 best musicians in the world to Barcelona, he would say, Guardiola would put them in a room, hand them a sheet of music, and make them start practicing until they had it mastered. Come showtime, they would be note-perfect. The difference at Real Madrid, he said, was that there would be no sheet music. He would put the musicians in a room and let them figure things out on their own. The first half-dozen performances might be painful, but given time, they would create something truly beautiful.

"It's a different kind of thing," Pérez would say. And by "different" he meant far superior.

Watching Messi emerge at Barcelona, however, was shaking the faith in Madrid. Playing second fiddle to Barcelona in the La Liga standings was one thing. But to fans accustomed to having the starriest roster in world soccer, the prospect of a supernova beginning his career in blue-and-red stripes was too much to bear.

THE MADRIDISTAS FELT it too. They needed Pérez to reset the axis. In May 2009, at a press conference at the Hotel Ritz Madrid, Florentino Pérez announced he would again run for the Real Madrid presidency. By the end of the month, every other candidate had dropped out.

Within seven days of his reelection, he broke the world transfer record for the third time that decade when he signed Kaká for $92 million. Then, three days later, he signed Cristiano Ronaldo for $131.5 million. By the time the French striker Karim Benzema and Spanish midfielder

Xabi Alonso had joined, the club's total outlay on players eclipsed a quarter of a billion euros. It was an obscene amount, especially at a time when the recession had pushed unemployment in Spain close to 20 percent. But to Pérez, all those millions were buying something invaluable for the club's supporters: hope.

"The only thing some people have to look forward to is their Real Madrid," he told the *Wall Street Journal* at the time.

Hope wasn't enough to beat Barcelona. In their first season together, the new Galácticos amassed a remarkable 96 points, but Barça won a second consecutive title with a record 99. Pérez's opposite number in Catalonia, Joan Laporta, was sitting pretty and crowing about business models and doing things *the right way*. "One model is you build a team with checks and money," the lawyer lectured. "And another model is the one we have, where we have a trajectory, where we are mature, and identified with our culture."

Florentino had a culture too. It involved using his checkbook to find the one man in world soccer who could deliver him the Barcelona antidote. The 2010 Champions League made it as obvious as a finger in the eye who that person was.

José Mourinho had cooked up the anti-Barça formula, taken some help from an Icelandic volcano, and somehow neutralized the magic—at least for an evening. Coaching Internazionale in the semifinals of the Champions League, he awaited Barcelona at the San Siro while the team took a 10-hour bus journey to Milan from Spain after the Eyjafjallajökull eruption had rendered air travel impossible. When the Catalans got there, Mourinho met them with the most confusing plan they'd ever seen.

Inter all but gave the ball away on purpose. The Barcelona pressing game was so ferocious that carrying the ball upfield came with a high risk of getting dispossessed and caught out of position, leaving Barça more room to break and build a devastating attack. In Mourinho's mind, no ball somehow meant no danger. Inter poached three second-half goals on the counter to win 3–1 at home in one of modern soccer's greatest rope-a-dopes. Mourinho's side then limited the damage to a 2–1 loss on the road with a tactic he called "parking the bus."

When he broke the spell and eliminated Barcelona on its own field, he sprinted around the pitch with his finger in the air in mad celebration. (He had not forgotten or forgiven Barça for passing him over in favor of Guardiola two years earlier.) Camp Nou was so apoplectic that it summoned the quickest revenge it could think of short of having Mourinho arrested for crimes against Catalonia. It turned on the sprinklers.

To Pérez, it was the most impressive audition imaginable.

Mourinho won the 2010 Champions League final, held by coincidence in the Bernabéu, and Pérez didn't let him leave. By offering to make him the highest-paid manager on the planet, he convinced Mourinho that Real was the only place he needed to be. He may not have encouraged the sort of all-out-attacking soccer that the Bernabéu faithful traditionally enjoyed, but stylish football could wait. The only thing Pérez cared about now was stopping Barça, and he would hire whoever it took to make that happen.

If Lionel Messi had found his Yoda in Pep Guardiola, then Ronaldo had found an Emperor to build him a Death Star.

SIX

Mes que un Clásico

EVEN FOR PEP Guardiola, it was too many Clásicos.

Too much chaos, too much "soul of Spain" tension, too much Messi versus Ronaldo, and definitely, 100 percent, too much José Freaking Mourinho. Four Clásicos in 18 days. One Clásico alone was an event large enough to bring Spain to a standstill and make anything else going on in the soccer world seem like small *patatas*. Four in a row was just ridiculous—the equivalent of a Super Bowl that lasted two and a half weeks. But by a quirk of the schedule, Real Madrid and Barcelona had been thrown together for four meetings across three competitions between April 16 and May 3, 2011. The noise was going to melt people's faces off.

Truthfully, no one should have been surprised. This is what happened when the two best teams in Europe occupied the same airspace in the same league. Come the pointy end of the season, when it was time to hand out the silverware, the superclubs found it impossible to avoid each other. They met first in La Liga, then in the Copa del Rey, and then in the two matches that mattered most: the home-and-away legs of a Champions League semifinal.

Johan Cruyff had declared that Barça needed only to win the second and fourth of those games. Do that and they'd have a trophy in hand and a spot in the most important clash of the season. But boiling it down to only a couple of victories ignored the true shape of those 18 days: an orgy of sniping, countersniping, and head games, all stirred together with seven decades of partisan history under a newly arrived global gaze. In short, it was what José Mourinho was born for. To get past Barcelona, he knew he had to get under their skin first. And by the third game in the series, he'd succeeded.

Inside the subterranean press room at the Santiago Bernabéu, down a flight of stairs that takes reporters deep below the hulking stadium, Guardiola finally snapped.

"Tomorrow at 8:45 we will play a match on the field," he seethed. "Outside of the field, he has won the entire year, the entire season, and in the future. He can have his personal Champions League outside the field. Fine. Let him enjoy it, I'll give him that. But this is a game. When it comes to sport, we will play and sometimes we will win, sometimes we will lose. We are happy with smaller victories, trying to get the world to admire us, and we are very proud of this."

Pep wasn't done. He listed all the referees he *could* have complained about, all the incidents in Clásicos that he publicly took in his stride. But now he'd had enough—he wasn't going to be drawn into Mourinho's games, he said, having clearly been drawn into Mourinho's games. If he'd had any hair left, Guardiola would've been tearing it out in front of the cameras.

"In this room, he is the fucking boss, the fucking man. In here, he knows more than anyone in the world and I can't compete with him. If Barcelona wants someone who competes with that, then they should look for another manager. But we—as a person and as an institution— don't do that."

José was getting to him.

Mourinho had been perfecting the tactic for years. He had learned ever since his own days at Barcelona that a football manager's job involved coaching football only about 30 percent of the time. The rest, as Cruyff had repeated over and over, was doing your best to control the sideshow.

When Mourinho was at Chelsea, the sideshow was driven by "the Pack"—the small cabal of local and national journalists who cover every press conference with the seriousness of a congressional hearing.

Narratives in British journalism take hold quickly because they are in fact coordinated. In a practice seen from the halls of Westminster to the cramped press room at Stamford Bridge, senior reporters huddle after a press conference to decide "the line," that one quote or nugget that will turn into tomorrow's headlines. If it often seems like the newspapers all run with the same story or angle, it's because the Pack expressly agreed on it, right down to the lead quote. And just to make sure everyone has plenty of time to get their stories together, the Pack sets itself a generous embargo.

Mourinho's brilliance was in turning the Pack into his propaganda machine. By making himself the focus of attention from the moment he arrived—"I am not one from the bottle, I am a special one," he said at his Chelsea introduction—he became a lightning rod. His players tended to appreciate it when going about their business. There could only be so many column inches about Chelsea, and he seemed to take up all of them. Mourinho had somehow weaponized his ego.

That approach was well known, even verging on parody, by the time he arrived in Spanish soccer. His finger-in-the-sky celebration with Inter on the pitch at Camp Nou lived on in his office at Real Madrid in the form of a giant cardboard cutout. For much of his first season, Mourinho played all the hits whenever he appeared in front of the media. And Guardiola was happy to keep quiet. Then one day in May, he decided he could no longer stand it.

The Barça players were sitting down to a meal in the team hotel when he launched into his tirade. The culture at the club was to ignore the outside world as much as possible. Newspapers were never brought into the training ground—some coaches even levied fines for it—and media appearances were strictly limited. But on this rare occasion, a television in the dining room happened to be showing Guardiola's press conference. For once, no one on the team asked to turn it off. Messi and his teammates watched, riveted, as their boss finally hit back at the man who had been goading them from the moment he landed in Spain. Privately, they'd all known that Guardiola could lose his temper, yet no one had ever seen him explode like this. They couldn't take their eyes off it, especially not once they understood what Pep was really doing.

He wasn't talking to Mourinho, or to the assembled media, or even to the Barcelona fans. The players realized he was talking directly to them. "That was the moment," remembers one of the players at the table. "We said, 'Okay, we will win this game, we will show that we are the best. We will show our strength.'"

"From that moment, everybody was really focused on what to do."

FOR MESSI AND Ronaldo to land in the middle of the proxy fight on Spanish unity that is the Clásico, it took some 70 years of festering bitterness between Catalonia and the central government in Madrid. The arcs are often simplified into bite-size caricature: Barcelona, the separatist guardians of Catalan identity, cultural liberalism, and afternoons at the beach versus the buttoned-up city of Madrid and the favorite team of General Francisco Franco.

The truth is more nuanced. For one, Franco, the fascist dictator who ruled the country from 1936 until his death in 1975, didn't much care about soccer. A man so unpleasant that Adolf Hitler once said he would rather have teeth pulled than meet him again, El Caudillo's hobbies skewed more toward hunting, fishing, and painting self-portraits. But during a time when Spain was effectively closed off to the world, a stylish, cosmopolitan soccer team dominating Europe through the 1950s could serve as a useful standard-bearer. As Franco's erstwhile foreign affairs minister Fernando María Castiella once put it, "Real Madrid is the best embassy we ever sent abroad."

At home, Franco was more concerned with stamping out anything he perceived to be a foreign culture. The Catalan language was banned in public spaces. FC Barcelona was made to change its name to the more Castilian-sounding Barcelona Club de Futbol, and the senyera was removed from the crest. More seriously still, the club's Swiss founder, a Mr. Gamper who loved Catalan culture so much that he changed his first name from Hans to Joan, had to flee amid the rising tide of Spanish nationalism. FC Barcelona didn't hesitate to position itself as a defender of

Catalonia. As far back as 1932, four years before the start of the Spanish Civil War, the club had rewritten its statutes to define itself as "a cultural and sporting association." Then in 1935, club president Josep Sunyol formalized the links between Catalan's dreams of self-governance and soccer under the slogan "Sport and Citizenship."

Sunyol, also a political activist, was later arrested by Francoist forces on a trip to Valencia and executed. He had not been traveling on club business, FC Barcelona's official history points out. He was a private citizen plucked off the street. "He was acting as a political figure and not attempting to sign any player," the club says.

Player signings would, however, come to play a key role in stoking Barça's hatred of Madrid. The particular move that galled Barcelona for more than half a century involved another of those dribbling wizards from Argentina. This one was named Alfredo Di Stéfano, and in Real Madrid's glorious history, his arrival in 1953 marked the BC/AD moment.

At that point, Real hadn't won a Spanish league title since 1933. It had the biggest stadium in the country, paid the highest salaries, and boasted the royal seal on its shirt, granted in the 1920s by King Alfredo XIII. But there were next to no recent trophies to speak of inside the Bernabéu. Di Stéfano changed all that. Real's first Galácticos project orbited around him. And in the 11 seasons from his arrival at the club until he left in 1964, Real finished above Barça in the league standings eight times. It also dispatched the Catalans in 15 of their 22 league meetings. The feud was so one-sided that Di Stéfano didn't even consider Barcelona to be his main foe. His principal source of concern was far more local.

"For me the rivalry at the time was with Atlético Madrid," he says in Sid Lowe's history of Real-Barça antagonism. "They were a good team and they were right here next to us. When they won, they suddenly sprang up like mushrooms and started shouting. Barcelona? They were 600 kilometers away—we couldn't even smell them."

More than Real's contempt, what still stings in Catalonia is that Barcelona once thought it had signed Di Stéfano too.

Back in 1953, the confusion arose from Di Stéfano's employment status in South America. His rights technically belonged to River Plate in Buenos Aires. Yet he was playing for Millionarios in the non-FIFA-sanctioned pirate league of Colombia. Real negotiated his transfer with one club, Barça approached the other, and both Spanish teams believed they had deals in place for La Saeta Rubia—the Blond Arrow. The Spanish government stepped in and ruled that Real had a rightful claim, because its contract was with River. FIFA also intervened and made a more diplomatic offer during a mediation process: the Spanish clubs could share Di Stéfano. He would switch back and forth every season for four years. Real first, then Barça, then back to Real, and back to Barça. That solution was completely absurd—alternating ownership barely works for ski chalets between friends, so it wasn't going to work for a soccer star between enemies. Di Stéfano, for his part, had no preference. "I always said that I didn't care if I played for Barcelona or for Madrid," he wrote later. "It was all the same to me."

Yet because the clubs had entered mediation, they were compelled to accept the world's craziest time-share. Only once the Barcelona board was replaced in its entirety did the club agree to make an era-defining error: for the sake of simplicity, it signed over Di Stéfano's rights to Real.

Just how much the Spanish state influenced the whole fiasco was debated for decades. It's now clear that it did intervene in Real's favor during various administrative processes, but it likely wasn't the highway robbery that Barcelona supporters believed it to be. Certainly, this wasn't a case of Franco himself creeping downstairs in his Real pajamas and handpicking one of the world's most exciting players for his hometown club. When the Franquista state wanted to apply pressure, its methods were usually much more ham-fisted. Like its involvement in the 1943 Copa del Generalisimo—the new name for the Copa del Rey—when Barcelona met Real in the semifinals over two home-and-away legs. Barça won the first meeting 3–0 at Les Corts, the home ground that preceded Camp Nou. But something was amiss about the second, and the score line suggested as much: 11–1 to Real Madrid.

Precisely what happened in the buildup to the return game in the Spanish capital's Chamartín stadium has been lost to history. The rumor for years was that the Barça players received a visit from a high-ranking police or military official warning them that it was in their best interest to tank the game. That version was eventually debunked. It's more likely that the referee received a few instructions before the match to grease the wheels a little for Real. What's certain is that the Barça players were met with such hostility in Madrid, from fans pelting them with stones to some form of intimidation from authorities, that they couldn't play like professionals. Even *MARCA*, in celebrating the victory on its front page, called it a game of "incomprehensible abnormality." The game that went down in Barcelona as the "Scandal of Chamartín" remains the most lopsided Clásico of all time. Given the circumstances, it doesn't get brought up a lot.

Nearly 70 years later, Ronaldo and Messi knew little about any of this. The fractious histories of fascism in Spain and Catalan separatism existed only in some distant background. To them, the modern era of the Clásico—the period when they were merely paying attention to its history without altering the course of it—dated back to 2002. That's when Messi, still eating his lunches at La Masia, followed the story of one of the Clásico's great traitors.

At the same time in Lisbon, Ronaldo was paying attention too. After all, that traitor happened to be a Portuguese legend.

THE TRANSFER OF Luís Figo from one side of the Clásico divide to the other in the summer of 2000 had stunned Barcelona, Real Madrid, and, most of all, Luís Figo himself. No one had been prepared for his get-rich-quick gamble to become a move as radical as Babe Ruth leaving the Red Sox for the Yankees or Bob Dylan going electric. But now Figo had to live with the consequences of double-crossing Catalonia. He had just made 1.5 million new enemies.

The first time he returned to Barcelona with Real, 98,000 of them let him know precisely what they thought with 90 minutes of relentless high-pitched jeering. Between injury and suspension, his second visit had to wait until November 2002. Once again, the Barça fans came prepared to greet him.

On top of the abuse that rained down from the stands came coins, lighters, empty bottles, and printed pictures of dollar bills. Under the circumstances, volunteering to take Real Madrid's corner kicks counted as an act of bravery by Figo. Every time he strolled over to the corner flag, he was separated from the Barça hordes only by a row of riot police who were powerless to stop the aerial barrage. It was during one of those trips to the edge of the pitch that the Clásico's strangest ever projectile landed near Figo to make the message as clear as possible.

Welcome back. We used to love you. You betrayed us. Now we hate you. Here's the severed head of a pig.

Smuggling the stinking thing into Camp Nou took some doing, as did launching it hard enough to reach the grass. But in the chaos of the moment, few could tell exactly what the pink blob was in the mess of bottles. In the second half, the referee had to pause the game so he could implore the Barça fans to stop. Even Barcelona players begged the hardest of the club's hard-core fans to calm down. The game eventually resumed after a 16-minute delay, only to finish 0–0. Afterward, Barcelona president Joan Gaspart did the opposite of apologizing for the behavior of the club's fans.

"I wouldn't say Figo's attitude was provocative, but if a player goes over to take a corner . . ." he said, implying that by walking over there Figo was essentially asking to be pelted with airborne porcine detritus. "In any case, none of the many objects that were thrown hit him."

No harm done then. Clásico rules were in effect.

Not that it always took bits of animal carcass to make the point. No two clubs in the world are more attuned to perceived slights than Barcelona and Real Madrid. In 2008, the final indignity of Frank Rijkaard's tenure in Catalonia—when everyone knew it was over and key players were barely showing up to practice—was having to perform a *pasillo*. With impeccable timing, Real Madrid had clinched La Liga one game before it was due to meet Barcelona at the Bernabéu. In accordance with Spanish soccer tradition, that meant that Barça would have to perform a guard of honor to congratulate the Real players as they emerged from the tunnel. It would have been less humiliating to the Barça players if they'd been forced to play in pink leather pants.

Outside the stadium, vendors hawked T-shirts that read I SAW THE PASILLO. *MARCA* turned the knife by printing a picture of the Real tunnel on the front page that morning with dashed lines and the words, "Barça, stand here."

Of all the embarrassments of that season, that one stuck with the Barcelona players and fans. Even as the club reached new heights under Guardiola over the next two seasons, the hot shame of standing on Real Madrid's pitch applauding Real Madrid players before a 4–1 defeat still burned.

Messi, still relatively new to the whole Clásico thing, had stood on the end of the line, as far away from the gloating Real fans as possible. But his emergence followed by Ronaldo's arrival the following season gave this historic battle a new dimension that elevated the Clásico to previously unseen heights.

With two squads full of box-office stars, led by the two winners of the past three Ballons d'Or, what had been a strictly Spanish concern mushroomed into a global sensation. The beauty of it was that even without any of the wider context—Franco, Di Stéfano, Catalan separatism—the game itself no longer required any explanation. Barcelona versus Real Madrid came with a catchy name, the guarantee of a hostile atmosphere, and in the Messi-Ronaldo era it acted as the one thing European sports had never been able to import from the United States: El Clásico was the All-Star Game that advertisers had been searching for a decade earlier. Now they didn't need Nike or Adidas dropping stars into a soccer cage match or flying them to North Africa to face off against Satan's team of the undead for a TV spot. The all-stars, a universal concept in sports, were all on the same field for at least two matches a year—and sometimes five. Better yet, these games came with real stakes. They weren't glorified scrimmages like the NBA's All-Star Game or the NFL Pro Bowl.

Inside La Liga's offices in Madrid, executives knew that the game was taking them to the next level. Its broadcasters claimed that the Clásico could reach 400 million viewers. Though the actual figures were probably closer to a quarter of that, Spanish soccer was being beamed to more fans in nearly 200 countries and territories than at any point in the league's history. Messi versus Ronaldo turned into the springboard for Barça versus Real, and vice versa.

"The Clásico for us was like the maximum," says Javier Tebas, a former executive of 11 Spanish clubs who was then serving as La Liga's vice president. "We had teams with the best players in the world, and we had the best coaches in the world. Mourinho, Guardiola, Messi, Cristiano. . . . We had so many circumstances come together at once. It's unlikely that we'll see the same circumstances again in any league in the world."

It was no coincidence that Real Madrid and Barcelona used that period to take over the top two spots in soccer's annual revenue standings. In 2008–2009, Real Madrid became the first club to rake in more than €400 million per year, with Barça not far behind with €366 million, according to the accounting firm Deloitte. Within three years, a period that coincided with the peak of the Messi versus Ronaldo Clásicos, both clubs had increased those figures by more than 25 percent. By the end of 2011–2012, Real Madrid and Barcelona's annual global revenues combined for more than €1 billion.

Real's international appeal was easy to understand, even to people who knew next to nothing about soccer. The silverware was shiny wherever they displayed it, and the Galácticos reflected their own fame back onto the club. In almost every era, Real Madrid could dust off photos of players in the brilliant white jerseys conquering Europe. It is the same approach taken by every self-absorbed dynasty from the Roman Empire to the New York Yankees: we have won, we will win again, let's build some monuments.

Barcelona's tack was more esoteric. The organization was, they said, "mes que un club"—more than a club. This was the phrase that Joan Laporta had commandeered for his presidential campaign, a slogan that was supposed to capture everything that came with being a soccer fan in this particular city with this particular identity. The team wanted people to know that Barça's history wasn't limited to what happened on the pitch. It was an entire culture that you lived and breathed every day. Anyone who understood the bittersweet applause when the Camp Nou clock showed 17:14—a nod to the year Barcelona fell to Philip V and became part of Spain—felt this deep in their Catalan bones.

Translating this for anyone else became the great challenge of Barça's marketing department. "It is a lot more difficult to promote the concept of 'more than a club' to an FC Barcelona football fan who is neither a Catalan nor Spanish and has absolutely no idea about the history of the club, Catalonia, or Spain," Ferran Soriano wrote. "What does 'more than a club' mean to a Chinese child?"

The whole ethos needed to be tweaked for an international audience. So Barcelona's small commercial department of around 10 people—a fraction of the dozens employed by Manchester United across offices in London, Manchester, and eventually around Asia—came up with the idea of partnering with a humanitarian cause. Unlike nearly every major club on the planet, Barça had never sullied its jersey by splashing the name of a sponsor across the front; only the small logo of its kit manufacturer appeared on the chest. Shirt sponsors had been widespread since the 1980s, and a few had even become iconic elements of jersey designs during associations that ran for years—Carlsberg beer and Liverpool, for instance, or Pirelli tires and Internazionale. But Barça had so far resisted cashing in on the stripes. Maybe a worthy cause was a way to dip a toe in the water of jersey sponsorship without offending the club's supporters. Who could argue with that?

The first partner the club considered in the mid-2000s wasn't quite the paragon of international virtue many people had in mind: it turned out to be the People's Republic of China. Barcelona entered talks to put "Beijing 08" on the shirt to promote the forthcoming 2008 Summer Olympics in exchange for €20 million a season. But when news of the negotiations leaked to the press, the whole deal collapsed. Then in 2006 a company called Bwin offered Barça even more money for the spot, according to a person familiar with the proposal, only for the club to decide that an Austrian online betting firm wasn't the right image either. (Bwin wound up on Real Madrid's jerseys from 2007 to 2013 instead.)

The perfect candidate, the worthiest of worthy causes, arrived later that year. It wasn't a problematic foreign government, nor was it a gambling company. This was the United Nations Children's Fund. Barcelona would take one of the most iconic jerseys in sports and use it to promote UNICEF.

Later, in the 2011–2012 season, UNICEF would move to the back of the shirt to be replaced by a different charitable organization, the Qatar Foundation. Only that deal came with a clause that it could eventually change to another Qatari outfit in the third year of the agreement—the slightly less charitable Qatar Airways. "What Barcelona did was spectacularly smart," Dan Jones, the head of Deloitte's Sports Business Group, told the *Wall Street Journal* at the time. "In a three-step process, each of which was difficult for people to object to, they've moved from a clean shirt to a shirt with a Middle East airline brand on it."

But in 2011, with UNICEF on the jersey and the jersey on Messi, everyone wanted to be Barcelona's friend. The club that won with unparalleled style was must-see TV. Claiming more than 300 million fans around the planet, Barça's global reach was at an all-time high.

"It was probably the easiest time to sell sponsorship, probably, of anybody's career," one former Barça executive says. "We would essentially be able to win any deal versus our competitors, with the exception, perhaps, of United."

What Manchester United did better—and earlier—than anyone else was divide up the entire world into regional markets by industry. Instead of doing global deals with, say, a soda company, it chopped up those rights into dozens of smaller local deals, sold by category and by country, all coordinated by a buzzing office in London to build the largest commercial empire in soccer. The club has been working that way since the 1990s, which is why it can now boast a global kit sponsor and a global official airline, but also a "consumer banking partner for Indonesia" and a "soft drinks partner for Nigeria."

For all of its success on the pitch, Barcelona couldn't replicate that model. The Catalan identity that made it so appealing to fans also hamstrung the club's commercial operations. Take Barça's beer sponsor. It made sense that the favorite soccer team of Catalonia would partner with the favorite brewer of Catalonia, a company called Damm, whose brewery is visible on the way into the city from the airport. Damm has been around for more than a century and distributes its red-labeled Estrella beer all over Europe, but it generates only a fraction of the turnover of the major international brewers such as Anheuser-Busch or Heineken. What would have made more sense, according to those inside the club, was a regional agreement with Damm and then a richer global deal with a larger brand. The Damm deal just proved too hard to restructure.

The same went for Barça's banking partner, La Caixa. Because it was founded right in Catalonia, the bank enjoyed a kind of most-favored-nation status with the club. But as Barça took over the world, its executives couldn't help but feel that they were leaving money on the table by throwing in their lot with Spain's third-largest lender. La Caixa was not a company that would see much point in paying a ridiculous premium to reach audiences in the United States or East Asia. Yet Barcelona, in the midst of a perfect soccer storm, was now in the business of charging ridiculous premiums—or at least trying to.

What it had was a pitch like none other. Besides selling the inherent cool of a swinging city by the beach and the defiant culture of a region, Barcelona was peddling an even more attractive commodity around the world: it was trading in purity. Here was soccer raised to a platonic ideal of what the game should be, a team of equals working in orchestral harmony around a player who could produce magic at any moment. Messi captured what anyone who'd ever kicked a ball wanted to be on the playground.

Not only that—he was putting on these shows in a jersey that literally had UNICEF on the front. The picture advertisers were buying was a boy who played and won with childlike glee, and who was doing it all for the kids. "They felt that it was pure football, it wasn't a commercial enterprise," the former Barça executive said.

"But interestingly, it allowed us to generate more commercial revenues than ever."

Still, the club felt it could have done more to capitalize on that period. Its nonticket, nonmedia rights revenues exceeded €100 million per year, according to Deloitte. Real Madrid, which had been at this game for decades, remained out in front. But Barça was finally closing the gap to become the second-richest team on the planet at the end of 2009–2010, all because it had landed on the most compelling sales pitch in the game.

It boiled down to two words: halo effect. Any brand that partnered with Barcelona was partnering with all that was good and happy about the world's most popular sport.

No one came with a wider halo than Messi. He embodied the cherubic joy of pure football skill for the sake of it. Though he was closer to the ground, fans held him on some higher plane. José Mourinho was here to remind his players that this was no angel.

"The truth is that the biggest football smart-ass is Messi," he told his team. "He covers his mouth to protect himself from lip readers when he's provoking defenders. He irritates opponents, even if he doesn't show emotions on the pitch."

Real goalkeeper Jerzy Dudek insists that what Messi whispered in the ears of center backs Pepe and Sergio Ramos would have made Maradona blush. "If I told you what he'd said, you probably wouldn't believe it came from a player who is a role model for many people in the world." Dudek insists that Messi went further than throwing out a few barbs about players' looks or relatives. "Messi was part of a provocative Barcelona team that would do things out of sight of the referee in the hope that there was a reaction which he spotted. They also knew how to fall down at the right time in the penalty area. Small details like that made a difference to Barcelona winning big games, and Mourinho wanted to open people's eyes to it."

Barcelona's greatest act of provocation, though, was beating Real repeatedly. Months before the four Clásicos in the spring, the two sides met in the league in Barcelona in November. The match was a bloodbath. Eight Real players received yellow cards, Sergio Ramos was sent off, and Barça won 5–0. Barça's Gerard Piqué walked off the field holding up five fingers, one for each goal, while Ronaldo glared with his hands on his hips. When the Real players trudged back into the home locker room, they could hear Barça chanting next door.

Mourinho's team argued and fought back tears until he slammed the door. "Be quiet and listen," he shouted. "Listen to them singing. . . . They won 5–0, but what do they get for it? Three points. Nothing else. Remember this before we play them next time."

"Tomorrow, take a day off training," he went on. "But you still have to work. Go into town. Take your wives and children out. Go to your favorite places. Let the people see you. Talk to them about losing 5–0. Nobody will say a bad word. They will support you. It will get it out of your system. Our opponent was better—tell them. But we will be ready next time."

In the weeks that followed, Mourinho made sure his players stayed angry by pinning up newspaper clippings around the Valdebebas training facility. Pictures of Piqué holding up his fingers. A headline from Xavi that compared scoring against Real to making love. Ronaldo's personal vendetta intensified in the winter of 2010 when the Ballon d'Or voters picked their entire top three from Barcelona. Messi finished first for the second year running. This Real Madrid squad had been assembled for more than one-third of a billion dollars, but Mourinho was molding them into underdogs. When the four Clásicos in 18 days materialized on Real's calendar, he wanted a siege mentality.

"They were so great, and with Madrid, we were growing, but we were still not on that level," former Real midfielder Xabi Alonso says. "We needed to be really, really . . . intense. Let's leave it that way."

Intense was putting it mildly. Mourinho was constantly in Alonso's ear: Kick whoever needed kicking. Do whatever was necessary to break up the Barça passing schemes, which were so complex that academics would later write network science papers on them. Nothing was off-limits. Cool heads were overrated.

It worked well enough to avoid embarrassment in the league game at the Bernabéu on April 16. But the 1–1 draw, in which Messi and Ronaldo each scored from the penalty spot, couldn't slow Barça's inexorable march toward the league title. With just six games left to play, Real needed a victory to keep up the pressure, and the gap was just too big to close. Piqué was happy to remind Real of this fact in the tunnel, rubbing plenty of separatist salt in their wounds.

"Eight points, eight points! Little Spaniards, we have won your Spanish league!" he yelled. "Now, *Españolitos*, we're going to win your king's cup."

The truly remarkable thing about Piqué's outburst was that many of those little Spaniards were his colleagues on the national team. He'd known some of them since childhood. He'd toiled alongside them through every age group. And nine months earlier in South Africa, he'd won the World Cup with them—for Spain. Piqué was one of seven starters in the Spanish jersey that day from FC Barcelona. It was a day of such heavy national pride that the team was visited in the locker room by the queen of Spain herself. (Carles Puyol, more Catalan than a can of Estrella, greeted her in nothing but a towel.)

None of that mattered in a Clásico. Even Barça's non-Catalan players were taken aback by the sheer magnitude of the rivalry. "You can feel it," remembers one. "You can feel it, because you work in the city, you see the passion. When you are on the side of these players, for me, it was very surprising to be honest. I had these big games [elsewhere], but thinking each day, you kind of understand that it's more than football. It's different people. There is a cultural difference. And living with these players from Catalonia, you feel how they really cared about this game."

The Copa del Rey final four days later was every bit as hostile on the pitch, even if it was played on the officially neutral Mestalla Stadium in Catalan-speaking Valencia. Mourinho persisted with his tactics, designed to spoil Barcelona's buildup play, and hoped that Ronaldo could produce something out of nothing. His decision to line up seven defensive-minded players in the league match had already invited plenty of criticism—not least from Johan Cruyff, who accused him of running scared and diagnosed him with a severe case of "Barcelonitis."

"The greatest praise for Barça came from Mourinho with his lineup," read the grenade in Cruyff's column. "To play at home with seven defenders you have to be very afraid."

As usual, Cruyff offered Mourinho some free advice: he recommended that Real practice not just 10-versus-11 situations (in case a Madrid player was sent off), but also 9-versus-11. Cruyff believed that if Pepe, the bruising Portuguese defender, tried to pull his usual shenanigans against this Barcelona team, then "the most normal thing would be that he doesn't finish the game."

Yet Mourinho's approach had something to it. By packing the middle of the pitch and hounding the ball-carrier, Real blunted the Barça attack enough to stay in the match. After the 5–0 in the fall, that counted as progress. The cup final went the entire 90 minutes of regulation without a goal. Then, in the 13th minute of extra-time, Xabi Alonso did precisely what he was supposed to do and dispossessed Messi in the center circle, sparking a move that culminated seconds later with Ronaldo hanging in the air to head a cross at goal. With a trophy on the line and Barça on the pitch, Cristiano didn't miss. After two seasons in Spain, he finally clinched his first trophy with Real with a 1-0 win.

The one he and Messi really wanted, though, was still up for grabs. The Champions League semifinals were set for April 27 and May 3, with game 1 in Madrid. Over the seven frantic days between the Copa del Rey and the first leg, the rhetoric intensified as daily talking points focused on everything from the choice of referees to Guardiola's attack on Mourinho to the length of the grass. A slightly shaggier pitch for the first match at the Bernabéu was thought to potentially put the brakes on Barça's passing. If that didn't work, there was always Pepe's studs.

As it happened, Cruyff's prediction had arrived one match early. In the most fraught match of the four-game swing, Pepe was red-carded despite making minimal contact with his high tackle on Dani Alves. Alves left the pitch on a stretcher, returned moments later, and Real finished the match with 10 men. (A Barcelona player was also ejected, but it was the unused substitute goalkeeper Diego Pinto who joined in some pushing and shoving a little too enthusiastically.) That decision made the referee the target of Mourinho's ire after Barcelona won the game 2–0.

"One day," he said, having also been sent to the stands for sarcastically applauding the ref, "I would like Josep Guardiola to win this competition properly."

Mourinho, using Pep's full name, was still sore about a Champions League clash against Barcelona during his Chelsea days and proceeded to rattle off the names of at least four different referees who had wronged him. "Por que? Por que? Por que?" went the rant. Later, Real also published a video that purported to show Barça midfielder Sergio Busquets calling Real's Brazilian defender Marcelo a monkey. The case was dismissed by European soccer's governing body "due to a lack of strong and convincing evidence."

What Real couldn't dispute was that Barcelona had effectively sealed the result with the two goals by Messi. (Every goal in all three Clásicos until that point had been scored by him or Ronaldo.) Mourinho didn't see a way for Real to turn the tie around in Barcelona in the second leg. And he was right. The fourth Clásico, a 1–1 draw, came and went to send Real home and Barça into its second Champions League final in three years. Just as it had in 2009, Barcelona brushed aside Manchester United with a performance that went down as the masterpiece of Guardiola's four-year collaboration with Messi. Leo scored the second Barcelona goal in the 3–1 victory, won Man of the Match, and collected one of the rarest prizes in football along the way: genuine admiration from Alex Ferguson.

"Nobody's given us a hiding like that, but they deserve it," the United manager said. "They play the right way, and they enjoy their football.

They do mesmerize you with their passing, and we never really did control Messi. But many people have said that."

The season's final tally showed that Ronaldo had won the Spanish Cup, while Messi had taken La Liga and the Champions League. There was just one more piece of meaningful silverware at stake, and it concerned just those two players.

How they performed in the Clásicos, the closest thing to a global dance-off, went a long way toward deciding which one of them would pick up the Ballon d'Or in the winter. Whichever way the order broke—Messi followed by Ronaldo or Ronaldo followed by Messi—new battle lines were being drawn. By 2011, the most famous sports grudge in the world was blurring into something else altogether, something simpler and further-reaching than any single club or its history. And Real Madrid versus Barcelona was becoming indistinguishable from the rivalry that piggybacked on top of it. The Clásico would always be there, but soccer fandom itself was splitting in two: you were either Team Leo or Cristiano FC.

SEVEN

Gold Rush

WHEN THE TIME came to hand out the Ballon d'Or, soccer's most prestigious individual award, there was a strict protocol in place. The votes were tallied from national team captains, coaches, and international media over several weeks leading up to the wintertime awards show. The only people aware of the results ahead of time were a small handful of organizers and the finalists themselves. Spoiling the surprise wasn't ideal, but in the hectic life of a 21st-century soccer player, arrangements had to be made for private jets, altered training schedules, and red carpet attire. Once they got the call, nominees were sworn to legally binding secrecy.

In January 2012, Leo Messi was preparing to receive that call again. With two Ballons d'Or already in his trophy cabinet, he ordered up a dinner jacket in burgundy velvet to pair with a black velour waistcoat tailored by the Italian designer Dolce & Gabbana—Domenico Dolce dressed Messi personally as often as possible. Ronaldo's gala outfit, meanwhile, remained a mystery, mostly because no one ever saw it. That year, he declined to make the trip to Zurich altogether. "Cristiano sends his regrets."

If the trophy didn't have his name on it, Ronaldo was no longer interested in sitting in the front row to applaud someone else. And even though he was entitled to a vote as the captain of Portugal, Ronaldo didn't bother to return his ballot either. (Messi, also a national team skipper, picked exclusively Barça and Argentina teammates: Xavi, Andrés Iniesta, and Sergio Agüero.) So as FIFA ran highlights of the three finalists, Messi and Xavi performed the standard awards show ritual of politely nodding and clapping from their seats, while Ronaldo was present only in a photo, wearing a Real Madrid shirt, projected on the big screen.

When the long-retired Brazilian Ronaldo opened the golden envelope, Messi was anointed the best footballer on the planet once more, with 47.88 percent of the vote. Cristiano was second. Again. This was the shape of every conversation now. FIFA's team of the year for 2011 included nine players from Real Madrid and Barcelona, but Messi and Ronaldo took up most of the oxygen. Not only did picking one or the other align you with a permanent rooting interest, it also said something about your worldview, your values, and how much you cared about style or trophies. For fans and sponsors, it was almost impossible to stay neutral.

That didn't stop at least one brand from trying.

The luxury German car company Audi first entered the fray on the side of Florentino Pérez's Galácticos. At a time when there seemed to be nothing glitzier than the white shirts of Real stuffed with superstars, sponsors were falling over each other to grab some of the magic for themselves. With what turned out to be perfect timing, Audi did that shortly before the club signed David Beckham in 2003. Real asked the automaker if it could supply transportation to ferry Beckham around all those unveiling events.

There was just one thing. Real needed not just one car, but three. Beckham required a convoy to deliver him to his medical examination and then to the official presentation in the Bernabéu. Everyone who saw footage of Beckham rolling around Madrid that day would also see him in an Audi.

"Put it this way," the president of Audi Spain said at the time. "If Audi had tried to carry off an equivalent ad campaign—one in which we received so much exposure on prime time TV and in front pages of newspapers in every country of the world—it would have been, quite simply, unpayable. In order to pay for that quality of advertising, we would have had to sell the company first."

"Never has a coup like it been seen in the history of marketing, I am convinced of it," he added. "The only comparable set of images—and I am being frivolously hypothetical here—might be if Osama Bin Laden were arrested and then driven off in an Audi."

For all the value its partnership with Real unlocked, the emergence of new stars in Catalonia during the mid-2000s highlighted a potential pitfall to Audi. No matter how well it did with Real, there was a chance of alienating half of its customer base: the anti-Madridista demographic. And Barça's marketing department was there to remind Audi just how large and rich and eager to buy German cars this particular demographic was. The company was convinced that it made perfect business sense to be on both sides of the debate.

Securing deals with Real and Barça was an expensive proposition, especially if they wanted players to appear anywhere near the product. (At Barcelona, only sponsors who ponied up more than €3 million a year received any access to the players at all.) Beyond the annual fees, Audi agreed to give every player the keys to a brand-new car, like some sort of German Oprah.

All Audi asked in return was that the players please, please, please drive the cars to practice. The company knew that paparazzi stalked the front gates at Barça's Ciutat Esportiva and at Valdebebas outside Madrid, so it dared to hope that the players might repay Audi's generosity by being seen at the wheel of their $100,000 freebies. This proved more challenging than expected. The Audis were sleek and fast and comfortable, but footballers have flashier tendencies. If it doesn't have an Italian name or gull-wing doors or a paint job that carries a public health warning, the chances of it ending up in a soccer star's six-car garage are slim. The practice arrivals should have been "an opportunity to generate media value," one Barcelona executive remembers. "But some of the players just wanted to drive Lamborghinis or Ferraris and Bentleys. It was a constant battle to get them to actually drive the Audis."

Real Madrid tried a different tactic to get its superstars to bring the right cars into practice, one pioneered by airports and fancy shopping centers years before. They used premium parking. Drive your free Audi and you could pull right up to the main building of the facility, steps from the pitches, locker room, and massage tables. Turn up behind the wheel of any other vehicle and you had to park in a different lot, farther away and surrounded by tall hedgerows for discretion. Your Lambo might have been built to be seen, but at Real's sponsor-correct training sanctum it was less welcome than a trip to the dentist. The automaker found sticking around worthwhile.

In December 2011, Audi used its access at the two clubs to launch a pre-Clásico spot with twin cars liveried in Real and Barça colors drifting around a circuit, making art with tire tracks. "Passion leaves a mark," was the tagline, absolutely not referring to the number of vicious fouls dished out whenever the two clubs met.

The double sponsorship would run for years. The squads of millionaires picking out their free cars turned into annual photo ops to show off the newest models. In 2016, *MARCA* estimated the retail value of the cars selected by each team at more than $4 million.

To the surprise of exactly no one, Real Madrid had the more expensive taste.

BESIDES A LUXURY carmaker from Germany, another business, much closer to home, was invested in both sides of Messi versus Ronaldo. This was a local Spanish concern called La Liga.

To understand the frenzy of activity that came next, it's important to understand first that, well into the 21st century, La Liga was a business backwater. Far from being the slick operation that North American sports leagues had spent 40 years becoming, with Park Avenue offices, enormous marketing departments, and even more titanic television contracts, the leadership of Spanish club soccer was mainly a compiler of schedules and employer of referees. La Liga could only look on with admiration—and deep-seated envy—at the organization that had redefined what was possible in the soccer industry, not only in achieving global popularity but also in making everyone involved unfathomably rich. The gold standard was the English Premier League.

To the small group of ambitious club executives and owners inspired by the NFL in the early 1990s, the Premier League's guiding principle was that soccer clubs could be more than ancient institutions that anchored British city neighborhoods and fielded 11 guys on a Saturday. They could also be moneymaking enterprises.

This was a radical idea. Until then, team owners saw themselves as nothing more than custodians whose sole job was to preserve the clubs for the next generation, as if they were country manors or musty libraries. To the cigar-smoking toffs and local self-made businessmen at the helm, winning was enjoyable but incidental. Besides, running clubs for profit was seen as out of step with the Victorian ideals that had created them. That was the philosophy that had accompanied the game to Spain when British merchants and returning Spanish students brought soccer to Iberia in the late 19th century. They came with heavy leather soccer balls, sportsmanlike ideals, and even Anglo-Saxon naming conventions—which is how a Basque club, for instance, wound up being called Athletic Bilbao or a team in Cantabria became Racing Santander.

What set English soccer apart in the late 1980s was that it remained stuck in one of the darkest periods since the laws of the game were first written down in the back of a London pub in 1863. Hooliganism was rampant. Deadly stadium disasters became alarmingly frequent, from the Bradford fire in 1985 to the Hillsborough tragedy in 1989, which ultimately cost the lives of 97 Liverpool fans. Soccer became the focal point of a British class battle: the conservative-leaning *Sunday Times* went so far as calling one of England's greatest exports "a slum game played by slum people in slum stadiums."

The future founders of the Premier League saw an emergency. A group of business-minded young men led by Arsenal vice chairman David Dein, Tottenham Hotspur's Irving Scholar, and Manchester United's Martin Edwards realized that they were above all in the entertainment business. Fans didn't owe them anything just because their fathers and grandfathers had supported the club. The club needed to give them something in return: safe seating, proper concession stands, bathrooms that didn't violate the Geneva Convention. Major work had to be done on infrastructure if English soccer was ever going to look like the NFL. The question was, who was going to pay for all of this? The answer was television.

At the time, what little TV revenue English soccer could generate was split equally among all 92 professional clubs spread across four divisions, from Liverpool and Manchester United at the top to Hereford and Northampton Town at the bottom. The Premier League's framers sought to end all that. Ahead of the 1992–1993 season, the top 20 clubs broke away from the other divisions and partnered with a struggling satellite outfit called Sky, backed by Rupert Murdoch. The agreement was for £192 million, more money than anyone in English soccer had ever seen. Most importantly, the Premier League clubs had now established their very own cartel. They wouldn't have to share the spoils with anyone but each other. That momentous decision laid the groundwork for Premier League clubs to steal a march on the rest of Europe with ever-spiraling television contracts that lifted the entire division. Over the next quarter-century, the price of those rights increased by nearly 2,600 percent. Teams raked in more money, spent more in the transfer market, and paid higher salaries. By 2016, eight of the 20 highest-earning soccer clubs in the world were in England. For players and investors, the Premier League was the place to be.

Spain was desperate to replicate that model. There were just two obstacles. Their names were Barcelona and Real Madrid.

FOR MORE THAN two decades, the two superclubs had the Spanish television rights market precisely where they wanted it. Unlike their counterparts in England, La Liga clubs all sold their rights individually, which was fantastic for those with already massive followings and less fantastic if you were, for instance, Rayo Vallecano, the fourth-most popular team in the city of Madrid. Real and Barça took this system to mean that it was every club for itself. The attitude wasn't born from selfishness—or at least not entirely. In 1993, a year after Premier League clubs changed the game by breaking away to sell their broadcast rights as a single entity, a Spanish competition court ruled that La Liga would not be permitted to do the same. It would take until 2007 for a European court to disagree.

In the meantime, Real and Barcelona earned more than 10 times what the clubs at the bottom brought in from broadcasting every season. A club like Granada made around €12 million from television in 2011–2012, while Real Madrid took home €140 million. Even the teams that finished at the bottom of the English Premier League were making at least €40 million a season.

For Javier Tebas, who became La Liga president in 2013, and his predecessor Fernando Roca, eliminating these imbalances became an obsession. They couldn't stand idly by while 2 of the 20 teams in the league they ran vacuumed up half of the total broadcasting revenue. Especially not when England was showing them how it could be done. "The Premier League is incredible in several senses," Roca said. "Its economic impact all around the world, everybody else is looking on enviously and playing catch-up."

More aggravating was that English soccer had pulled off this trick *without* the top two players in the world. There simply had to be a way for La Liga to make more of Messi and Ronaldo while it could still count on having both of them in Spain. Tebas argued that the solution began first and foremost with bringing together all 20 clubs to sell the league's broadcast rights collectively, even if they were 20 years behind schedule.

"We tried to do it on a voluntary basis," he says.

You can imagine how that went. The majority of clubs jumped on board with the plan right away. The big two, meanwhile, struggled to grasp why they should give up anything for the sake of less successful teams. If the likes of Deportivo, Sevilla, and Rayo couldn't attract as many eyeballs or command the same fees, then that was their issue.

Perhaps they could try being better at football. The way Real and Barça saw it, they had spent all that time building up their commercial and broadcast operations for this exact reason.

Barcelona's Ferran Soriano once recalled a meeting with a coach from Major League Soccer, the top division in the United States, who tried to convince him that Spain's model was all wrong. "I don't understand," the coach said, "why you don't see that what you should be doing is boosting teams like Sevilla FC and Villarreal CF to make the Spanish league more exciting and maximize income."

Soriano couldn't believe what he was hearing.

"I found it difficult to think about maximizing any income of any kind," he wrote later, "because all I wanted and cared for was for FC Barcelona to win all the matches, win and always win, independently of the 'tournament overall income' or suchlike concepts."

Inside La Liga's offices, the wheels were already in motion to turn those "suchlike concepts" into reality. In 2013, the league finally convinced Real and Barça to accept capping their overall share of the TV pie, though they still gobbled up more than a third of it through their contracts with media giants Telefónica and Mediapro. At least it was a start, Tebas thought. He exhausted himself arguing that, even under a collective sales approach, the two clubs would hardly see a drop-off in income, because the overall package would be that much more attractive to broadcasters and drive higher prices. La Liga's games were worth only a fraction of the Premier League's—the worldwide rights had sold for less than €800 million in 2013, compared to English soccer's 10-figure haul—yet this was the only way Tebas could envisage any growth.

"It was obvious when you've got the centralized set of broadcasting rights. . . . It's worth a lot. You can sell a whole competition—it's all very important," he says. "And we had to work a lot on the brand, La Liga. Because obviously, the competition is a lot more than just Real Madrid-Barcelona, Messi-Ronaldo."

But convincing broadcasters they also needed to air Getafe versus Eibar would take some doing. England was successfully selling Southampton versus Newcastle around the world by pushing the league's top-to-bottom intensity and competitive balance. Any given Saturday could produce a high-octane thriller between teams you might otherwise have never watched. The Premier League marketed its 20 clubs as the stars, each with its own history, foibles, and personality. Fans weren't just supporting 11 players and a crest—they were claiming a piece of England for themselves. As an added bonus, when it came to making sales in key foreign markets, the Premier League unfolded in predictable time slots, with high production values and entirely in English.

Barça and Real, under Laporta and Pérez, had consciously decided to make the opposite pitch to the world.

They chose to build their global expansion on the idea that you could tune in on any weekend and expect to watch two all-time greats smashing in a hat trick. Wasn't that what the world wanted to see anyway? No one went to a Bond film to watch MI6 drones battle Blofeld's henchmen to a 0–0 draw.

La Liga was there to serve up what the Premier League could not: no matter which team Messi or Ronaldo was playing against, fireworks were guaranteed. It didn't need to be a Clásico—a game against Elche would do. From 2010, Messi and Ronaldo were averaging more than a goal per game. In 2010–2011, they both racked up 53 goals across all competitions. The next season was even more ridiculous: Ronaldo scored 60 in 55 games, only to be outdone by Messi's 73 in 60 games. These were the kinds of numbers that no one in any serious soccer-playing nation had seen since the 1920s, when the whole concept of goalkeepers was still relatively new. Even if Messi and Ronaldo never kicked a ball again, those totals would have been historic. But they kept it up year after year. In 2014–2015, the two of them combined for 91 goals in the league alone. *Ninety-one goals.* That was more than the total scored by the entire rosters of every team in La Liga not named Real or Barça. Even when they were simply beating up on Spanish soccer's little guys, Messi and Ronaldo had become appointment viewing.

Which is precisely what Real and Barça wanted to perpetuate. They didn't need competitive balance across Spanish soccer. They needed chum to feed their sharks.

FIXING THAT MINDSET, in the end, required more firepower than La Liga had at its disposal. It took an act of government, rubber-stamped by the Spanish crown itself, to approve the law that made collective bargaining possible, the Real Decreto-ley 5/2015. Under the new rules, the ratio between the top earners of TV rights money in La Liga and the lowest could no longer exceed 3.5-to-1 (or 4.5-to-1 once those revenues surpassed €1 billion). Even then, debates over the balance of power between La Liga and the Royal Spanish Football Federation turned into a political drama that dragged in the superclubs and the players' union. Disagreements over the relative shares of broadcast income distributed to the top two tiers even led to La Liga players calling for a strike. Things became so acrimonious that the Spanish press feared the season would have to be abandoned. Work stoppages crop up once a decade or so in US sports, but never on the relentless treadmill of European soccer.

When the details were finally ironed out, La Liga was looking at a new economic future. Tebas wanted a championship with a personality beyond Real, Barça, Messi, and Ronaldo. But he knew as well as anyone who was going to build it for him.

"It was necessary," Spain's secretary of state for sport at the time, Miguel Cardenal, said. "This way, Spain wouldn't lose ground on the other great leagues. It's a historic day for Spanish football."

Everyone could tell where all that new revenue would go. The jarring realization that all owners and executives reach eventually—preferably before they've burned through a few hundred million dollars—is that football pushes nearly every marginal dollar it earns directly into the players' pockets. Most clubs can't build long-term cash reserves. As soon as their revenues increase, so does their appetite for spending on talent.

The other reality that takes some getting used to for investors arriving in football is the threat faced year after year by most clubs outside the elite: relegation. Fall far enough down the standings, even for just one season, and you risk being booted out of the league altogether. When that happens and a club faces the prospect of spending at least one season in the second tier, revenues collapse, players leave, and the club's immediate future is devoted to dragging itself out of a financial black hole. Even if it quickly returns to La Liga, its chances of staying there are not good. Of the 33 clubs that were relegated from the top tier between 2000 and 2020, 19 suffered that ignominy more than once.

This particular problem is not one that Real or Barça worries much about—neither has ever dropped out of La Liga. But running a business at the top of the standings comes with different issues. Barcelona's Soriano put it best when he laid out how different this industry is from the rest of the world. You are being evaluated constantly by a merciless public. Success is measured in the trophy cabinet, not the balance sheet. And the workforce is unlike any other. (After leaving Barcelona in 2009 to become chairman of a Catalan airline named SpanAir, Soriano would learn how few of those lessons applied beyond soccer—SpanAir was bankrupt in three years.)

"Footballers are young, very expensive, and they earn a lot of money," Soriano wrote. "All of which are aspects that make them very difficult to manage. They are the club's main asset and they need to be managed simultaneously as human beings, employees, and assets that can be bought and sold and have a market value that can either rise or fall."

No one was more concerned with that last point than Jorge Messi. He obsessed over Leo's market value (read: his salary) like it was his son's share price. The length of his contracts didn't matter to him so much as constant improvement in the terms.

This was a source of much consternation inside the Barça boardroom. Contracts were never allowed to run out entirely for any player the club hoped to hold on to. Talks around a renewal usually began 18 months out to give both parties plenty of runway. And of course, everything imaginable needed to be done to make Messi happy. But even by the crazy standards of soccer contract law, Jorge's demands were getting absurd.

Joan Laporta had bent over backward to keep the contract updates on schedule. He was the one, after all, who'd handed Messi a massive extension in 2009 tying him to the club until 2016. At the time, that decision had been seen as risky enough to earn him the disapproval of none other than Cruyff. "The extension until 2016 is something else," he wrote. "I continue to defend short contracts and not long ones, a maximum of three or four years. Even for the best, no matter what their name is." Footballers, he added, "need motivation to continue growing."

The president who replaced Laporta in 2010, a former Nike executive named Sandro Rosell, was a little less amenable. The new tension spilled into public in December 2013 when board member and Barça vice president Javier Faus objected to putting new deals on the table every six months for the player he called "this gentleman."

This was one of the rare occasions when Messi had something to say. He shot back in an interview on Catalan radio.

"Señor Faus is someone who knows nothing about football," he said, "and wants to run Barça like it's a business. Which it is not."

Only it very much is. This was the point Soriano and Laporta had tried to make when they took over in 2003 with the club $200 million in the red. That much debt makes you a business. Otherwise, it makes you a bankruptcy filing.

Six months after Faus's criticism, the Barcelona website posted a news story under the headline "Agreement with Leo Messi."

"The revised and updated contract will be signed over the next few days," it said.

It was no coincidence that Ronaldo had just signed a new deal with Real Madrid that paid him more than $50 million a year before taxes. By setting a benchmark figure, Cristiano had unwittingly helped Messi and his father know precisely what to ask for when negotiating a seventh Barcelona contract in the space of 11 years. At age 27, Messi became the highest-paid soccer player in the world.

Beyond the dizzying number of zeros, this contract came with another notable feature: Messi would split the income from his image rights with the club on a 50-50 basis. More than a decade after deciding to invest in the undersized boy from Argentina, Barcelona was about to start making money from his global celebrity.

Had he played for Barça's great rival, of course, Real Madrid would have been cashing in on him the whole time. Shared image rights were standard operating procedure under Florentino Pérez. But now both Ronaldo and Messi were in truly symbiotic relationships with their clubs. Barça and Real had a real financial stake in making them as famous as humanly possible. The extraterrestrial number of goals helped. By the mid-2010s, every soccer sponsor in the world was trying to get a piece of them.

Those who succeeded were a motley, free-spending bunch with big decisions to make. Did brands want a goal-scoring genius who could spend photo shoots doing mesmerizing tricks like they were close-up magic, but who couldn't really act? Or did they want a goal-scoring genius built like a Greek god with a million-dollar smile—who also couldn't really act?

Companies found that there was no wrong answer. Turkish Airways paired Messi with basketball legend Kobe Bryant in a 2012 spot that gained 90 million views on YouTube in its first two and a half weeks. The Swiss watchmaker TAG Heuer, meanwhile, went with Ronaldo so it could put him on its list of ambassadors alongside Leonardo DiCaprio and Cameron Diaz, following in the metronomic footsteps of Tiger Woods.

The attention was almost more than Messi's and Ronaldo's teams behind the scenes could handle. Far from the Madison Avenue suits who might have crafted their images if they'd become superstars in America, Jorge Mendes recognized in private that commercial operations weren't his strength, because he wasn't all that interested. He was an expert at moving players and coaches around soccer clubs, not at building up a public persona. Mendes gave it so little thought that he briefly put his own daughter in charge of running Ronaldo's social media accounts. The one time the agent really tried to shape the narrative around his client, the result was a strange 2015 documentary on Ronaldo's life in which Mendes appears on-screen for more than 10 percent of the movie. The rest of the film is filled with Cristiano driving luxury cars, baring his torso, and at one point singing along to Rihanna on the Portugal team plane.

Jorge Messi was even less equipped to handle his son's growing commercial empire. From a three-room office in Barcelona, he fielded requests in much the same way Mendes did, not always knowing how a specific brand might paint his son by association. That's how Messi wound up pushing Herbalife Nutrition, a wellness company based in Los Angeles and the Cayman Islands that doubles as a multilevel marketing outfit. The brand, which has denied regular allegations that it is a pyramid scheme, signed deals with Messi and FC Barcelona from 2010 to 2013 before going the Audi route and trying the other side for a while. Herbalife was pivoting to more outwardly health-conscious partners: Ronaldo and his abs. Cristiano was the ideal spokesman to keep a straight face while saying things like, "Nutrition is a weapon for me."

Not done selling self-improvement, Ronaldo then partnered with a shampoo brand in 2014. Perhaps to retain a particular section of his customer base, he would later sponsor a hair transplant clinic in Madrid.

Cristiano also modeled Emporio Armani underwear until he decided in 2013 to create his own line of tight-fitting skivvies, which he unveiled with a 70-foot installation of himself wearing nothing but bikini briefs in the center of Madrid. Leo was more focused on what went over the underpants, working on his own line of casualwear thanks to a partnership between Messi and Hilfiger—or at least their sisters, Maria Sol Messi and Ginny Hilfiger.

The extra revenue added almost 50 percent to each of their annual incomes, especially once they tapped the lucrative Persian Gulf pipeline. Messi and Ronaldo were reorienting the whole market. Companies were stumping up for individual sponsorships what they used to spend to get on the front of jerseys. Messi signed in 2013 with Ooredoo, a Qatari telecommunications firm that is majority-owned by the state and was simultaneously pushing into soccer by sponsoring Paris Saint-Germain. Ronaldo doubled down on Real Madrid's existing shirt deal with Emirates, the flagship carrier of Dubai, by also striking a personal agreement with the airline—not that Cristiano ever flew commercial anymore. Even the fraught politics of the Middle East couldn't stop them. Ronaldo might be the rare celebrity who could do a promotional photo shoot for a Saudi Arabian cell-phone provider one year and star in ads for an Israeli streaming service the next.

Nothing was too far-flung, no brand too obscure. Like Hollywood actors filming Japanese ads that they figured no one else would ever see, Messi and Ronaldo made local partnerships to rent out their faces to any brand that could afford it. Russia's Alfa-Bank borrowed Messi for the 2018 World Cup and put him on billboards around the country. (Closer to home had been Portugal's Banco Espírito Santo, Ronaldo's banking sponsor until it collapsed in 2014 and sent the country's stock market into freefall.) But as far as commercial non sequiturs went, first prize in this strange competition between Messi and Ronaldo could only go to Cristiano.

In a decade of baffling endorsements, none came from deeper in left field than his 2017 ad for Egyptian Steel, in which he spends most of the 60-second spot wandering around a steel mill in a hard hat. There's no soccer ball, no clever tagline about high performance—just Ronaldo taking in a spectacle of industry.

"Have you ever related steel to eco-friendly?" he tweeted. "I did. That's why I've partnered with the most safety-oriented steel brand #Egyptian_Steel." That and the fact that his sister was dating the company's founder.

There seemed to be no limits on how to cash in on Messi and Ronaldo. By this point, even Adidas and Nike were profiting from both of them. Nike hadn't sent Messi a pair of boots in ten years, but every Barcelona shirt with Messi's name on the back came with the Swoosh on the front. Hard to believe, then, that Nike had hemmed and hawed over renewing its Barcelona contract in 2008 until Puma came in with a rival bid and forced its hand.

The same was true for Adidas and Ronaldo. Every "Ronaldo 7" shirt sold by Real Madrid also featured the Three Stripes. Although both companies would have preferred to outfit the players from head to toe, executives knew that this was the reality of the soccer business. The manufacturers were still collecting roughly half the money from every jersey sold at retail prices that fell between $80 and $110. They had learned this lesson a long time ago with the man who laid the groundwork for both of them. "We didn't have David Beckham," recalls one Nike director. "But we sold a lot of David Beckham shirts."

Nike and Adidas were printing their competitors' names and might as well have been printing money. Between the 2011–2012 and 2015–2016 seasons, the second and third most popular soccer jerseys on the planet were Barcelona and Real Madrid. Though neither could touch the commercial juggernaut in Manchester, Real was moving 1.65 million shirts a year and Barça sold 1.28 million. No matter what board members said, whichever club did most of the winning hardly mattered to the bottom line anymore.

This was not an argument that would fly to the people who got paid to wear the jerseys. And in 2012, Messi's biggest concern was not in Barcelona's boardroom or on the pitch, but in the club's dugout. At the end of the 2011–2012 season, his universe changed in a fundamental way: Pep Guardiola left Barcelona.

Officially, Pep was tired. The four years in the Barcelona hot seat had been the most stressful of his life. The ex-player who had entered the coaching profession as the youngest manager of a major club anywhere in Europe, with flecks of gray in his hair, was now completely bald. He explained in public that he felt he could no longer motivate his players.

It had been a rough year by Barcelona's lofty standards. First, there was a defeat by Chelsea in the Champions League semifinal, which was followed by something even worse: the loss of the league title to José Mourinho's Real. In private, tension with the new personalities inside the Barça boardroom was starting to wear on Guardiola. He needed a break, maybe not from football, but certainly from the politics.

So he packed up and took his family with him for a yearlong sabbatical in New York, where he rented a plush apartment on Central Park West, sat courtside at Knicks games, and casually dropped in to give pointers to his kid's private-school soccer team. There were dinners with Garry Kasparov and university professors. He knew that his close friend and former Barcelona board member, Xavier Sala-i-Martin, taught economics uptown at Columbia, so Pep audited his class there. (He promptly made himself a hilarious nuisance by gesticulating to direct the professor's attention anytime he saw a raised hand, as if he were still in the dugout.)

Back in Barcelona, the club was working on its next evolution. Richer than at any point in its history, Barça could now supplement its core of homegrown players with pretty much anyone else who caught its eye from anywhere on the planet. And in 2012, no one was more sought after than a blond-mohawked teenager in southern Brazil who was already being talked about as a potential successor to the duo at the top of the game: Neymar da Silva Santos Jr. At his Brazilian club Santos, he'd already been granted permission to wear the number 10 jersey, which had once been owned by Pelé. Neymar dribbled like Messi, bent the ball like Ronaldo, and flopped more dramatically than either of them.

But Barcelona had competition for his attention. Real Madrid had been on the case since 2011. Chelsea, too, had pitched Neymar and his representatives on a move to London. Bizarrely, West Ham joined the running and hoped to sign him for under £30 million, before settling on Frédéric Piquionne and Victor Obinna instead. If you've never heard of those players, then it's for a good reason.

Neymar's father, a former mechanic acting as his agent, suddenly had some of the richest clubs in Europe (and West Ham) wining and dining him for his son's signature. That's when he understood that he could pretty much name his price when the moment came. The biggest question was timing. The plan was for Neymar to remain at Santos until 2014 before leading the Brazilian national team into the World Cup on home soil. He was already a powerful commercial brand at home, with Nike, Panasonic, and Volkswagen helping him amass a fortune of more than $50 million, according to Neymar Sr. Everything would come together just right with enough patience.

But the Spanish superclubs weren't keen on waiting. In May 2013, the 21-year-old Neymar announced in a statement that he had received two formal offers from teams in Europe, both in Spain, and he was choosing

Barcelona. The official fee to Santos was just €17.1 million. Neymar and his father, though, had already pocketed €40 million, dating as far back as 2011, when Barça forked over an initial sum of €10 million to the family. That kind of direct, discretionary payment—buried deep in its financial statements—was not uncommon at the club. For the Neymar transfer, it appeared on page 178 of the 2012 accounts, where it was referred to only as a "long-term purchase commitment amounting to *40,000 thousand* euros."

When Neymar was finally unveiled on the pitch at Camp Nou as one of the richest 21-year-olds in soccer, he pledged to "help Messi continue to be the best player in the world."

High-profile outsiders had been thrown into the mix before. Those whom Messi didn't like would only find out about it once it was too late. In the case of Zlatan Ibrahimović, a Swedish colossus with an ego bigger than an IKEA warehouse, Messi communicated his distaste to Guardiola via text message. As Ibrahimović put it in his autobiography, "It started well but then Messi started to talk." Specifically, Messi was complaining about tactics. He wanted Guardiola to play him exclusively through the middle, which didn't leave much room for Ibrahimović to operate. Zlatan wouldn't last long at the club after that. He left in 2011 after just 29 appearances in two seasons. His lasting legacy might have been his parting shot at Pep: "You bought a Ferrari, but you drive it like a Fiat."

Unlike Zlatan, Neymar understood early that there were two rules when you arrived at Barcelona. Rule number one: you must despise Real Madrid. Rule number two: everyone on this team is equal, except for Messi, who is more equal than everyone else put together.

What Messi needed most, as soccer's ultimate creature of habit, was players and coaches who got those rules and the way Barcelona wanted to play. The Guardiola years had worked because everyone spoke the same soccer dialect, with all of its idioms and nuance. Xavi, Andrés Iniesta, Gerard Piqué, Sergio Busquets, Víctor Valdés, and Messi—the six graduates of La Masia who started both the 2009 and 2011 Champions League finals—barely needed to speak in order to communicate. Any newcomer was required to slide in seamlessly.

In the dugout, Barça found someone who definitely spoke the language. Former Guardiola assistant Tito Vilanova took over until he was sidelined by throat cancer after only a season. Barcelona tried to placate Messi by replacing Vilanova with a fellow Rosario native, the former Newell's Old Boys player and coach Gerardo Martino, but that backfired spectacularly by the end of the 2013–2014 season. When Tata Martino played him slightly out of position, Messi sulked openly on the pitch as Barcelona crashed out of the Champions League against Atlético Madrid.

The club panicked again and sent Martino on his way. So just as it always does in times of emergency, Barça turned around and hired an ex-player. This time the new boss was the more capable Luis Enrique, who had represented the club from 1996 to 2004. On top of that change, Barcelona armed Messi with an extra weapon. The summer after Neymar, it signed the prolific Uruguayan striker Luis Suárez, who would start contributing just as soon as he had finished serving a four-month ban from all soccer activities for *biting* an opponent at the 2014 World Cup. (It was the third biting incident of his career.)

Once Suárez paid his debt to soccer society, he joined Messi and Neymar to form an attacking trident that made Barcelona look somehow more dangerous and more suffocating than they had been under Guardiola. The whole team was pointed at the front three. "To be on the pitch with them, it's not so easy," says Croatian midfielder Ivan Rakitić, whose role put him just behind the forwards on the pitch. "You have to work for them. You have to attack the space that they left for you."

Under the new approach, Messi completed his transformation from all-purpose genius into a goal machine. During the first season of the "MSN," as the three-man weave came to be known, Messi scored 58 goals in 57 appearances across all competitions as Barcelona won La Liga with the largest goal differential in club history: 110 goals scored, just 21 conceded. It made perfect sense when the club added the Copa del Rey and 2015 Champions League to its haul.

That season Barcelona also made a crucial admission to itself: keeping Leo happy was now the explicit policy of the club.

President Josep Maria Bartomeu, a longtime club apparatchik who took over from Rosell in 2014, knew better than to try things any other way. He hired a manager Messi liked and signed talent to work in his service. The club built on the ideal of interchangeable Catalan wizards sharing the ball was going to stop kidding itself. This team belonged to one man and one man alone.

"Messi is our star," Bartomeu told the *Wall Street Journal* in 2015. "He is the one star."

AT REAL MADRID, Ronaldo's status was never up for debate.

Florentino Pérez was still shopping for some of the most expensive players in Europe, but everyone who arrived at the club now had to know who was really in charge. In the summer of 2013, while Barcelona bought Messi a sidekick from Brazil, Real went looking for a Welshman.

Pérez had set his sights on Gareth Bale, a devilishly quick winger who was terrorizing Premier League defenses for Tottenham Hotspur. At 24, he was ready to make the step up to a major European club and compete for the Champions League. So Real wasted no time. Pérez made an opening bid for £55 million. But Tottenham chairman Daniel Levy, one of the toughest negotiators in the game, wasn't impressed—only because he knew Pérez was capable of going so much further. Levy had spent his whole life in soccer watching Real Madrid spend money like a drunken bullfighter. He was well aware that if the will to buy was there, the price would catch up eventually.

Once again, Levy was right. He flew to Spain twice to meet with Pérez, and each time he came home with the promise of a few extra million. There was just one thing that struck him as strange: Pérez insisted that he could go no higher than €96 million. That would have to be his final offer, not because the club didn't have the cash, but because of a self-imposed cap. Real Madrid couldn't be seen to spend more on Bale than they had on Cristiano.

The two clubs settled at €91 million—at least until Real tried to pay the fee in installments. Levy threatened to pull the plug on the whole deal, and Pérez began to sweat. In an effort to bring Levy back to the table to rescue the biggest transfer of the summer, Real shelled out €100.8 million in a single payment. The only condition was that the fee could never be acknowledged in public.

What the public did see once Bale arrived was Ronaldo demanding more than perfection. He required teammates to get on his level. For most mortals, this was clearly impossible. But Ronaldo wasn't shy about letting them know. It didn't take long for him to crush Bale's spirits, simply because Bale occasionally committed the capital offense of failing to pass to him. This manifested itself in theatrical displays of frustration and eyerolls so deep that Ronaldo probably saw the inside of his own skull. Bale, who still scored in double figures in each of his first three seasons in Madrid, found a comfortable coping mechanism. He turned himself into a nearly scratch golfer.

"This is normal to have a discussion," says Carlo Ancelotti, whose first stint managing Real Madrid lasted from 2013 to 2015. "This is positive. This kind of player has the desire to win, to do the best. It's not negative. . . . It makes the training competitive."

The third member of Real's attacking trio, the French striker Karim Benzema, fared somewhat better alongside Cristiano in the club's answer to the Barça MSN because he honored the pecking order immediately. In building the BBC—Bale, Benzema, Cristiano—Ancelotti initially thought he could use Ronaldo as a center forward. Only once he took over practices in Madrid did he realize that Ronaldo preferred to work from the left side and cut in. That was good enough for Ancelotti. The entire tactical plan would have to adapt.

"Why change the position of a player that is comfortable?" Ancelotti says. "You don't have to tell him a lot of things. Just let him go. Be creative, of course—but you have to put this kind of player on the pitch in the most comfortable way."

RONALDO AND MESSI were so comfortable that they hardly missed a game. Yet even with their two superteams slugging it out in La Liga, soccer still wanted more of all this—more marquee evenings, more heavyweight prizefights, more chances to compare greatness in single

90-minute increments. Fans wished they could see them on the same pitch more often than the two to four times a year they were being served. (Executives and sponsors didn't hate the idea of more box-office events either.) The trouble was that their appetite was bumping up against the very structure of the sport. The only guarantee was two Clásicos a year in the league—everything else was left to random draws and temporary form in cup competitions.

Consider that in a marquee playoff series in the NBA, two generational greats might face off up to seven times in the space of two weeks. LeBron James and Stephen Curry, for example, met on 22 occasions *in the playoffs alone* from 2015 to 2018. And in tennis, where the same cast of characters tours the world for 11 months of the year, the era of mega-rivalries between Roger Federer, Rafael Nadal, and Novak Djokovic had produced 148 singles meetings between any two of them by the end of 2021.

Messi and Ronaldo, meanwhile, were on the same pitch in competitive club matches barely 30 times over the course of the decade that spanned from 2008 to 2018. Which is why actors from several corners of the soccer world stumbled on the same realization all at once: there was plenty of money just sitting out there for whoever could engineer more Ronaldo versus Messi.

The avenues for doing that in Spain were complicated. La Liga's format of 38 games, with 20 teams playing each other twice, was immutable. And a competition like the Copa del Rey was difficult to expand, since the biggest teams were already complaining about overloaded schedules. Though there were ways to load the dice and increase the chances of more Real-Barcelona meetings—such as giving La Liga teams byes until the cup's round-of-32 stage—organizers and sponsors were hoping for more guarantees.

The more flexible option, discussed for years before it was finally adopted for 2019, was growing the Spanish Super Cup. What had long been a one-off game between the previous season's winners of La Liga and the Copa del Rey turned into a four-team tournament showcase that could be taken on the road. The change, when it finally came in 2019, was too late to feature both Messi and Ronaldo, but that didn't stop the Spanish soccer federation from using the rivalry while designing it. Spain found a willing partner in Saudi Arabia, which paid €120 million to bring the Super Cup to Jeddah for three seasons. At the same time, the European and world governing bodies of soccer, FIFA and UEFA, were toying with new ways to create more games between elite clubs. Over the course of years, they drew up plans for an expanded Champions League or a rejuvenated Club World Cup with more European sides. Soccer was setting the table to gorge itself on superstars.

For more than 10 years, one man had shown them that the idea might just work. Enter Charlie Stillitano, a gregarious former MLS executive with a Princeton degree and all the experience of coaching a kids' soccer team in New Jersey. Through his gift for storytelling and his encyclopedic knowledge of Italian food, he spent the early 2000s charming his way through the boardrooms of European soccer, selling them on a unique product: the United States. He convinced them that the American market was there for the taking if they just bothered to turn up for a few summer exhibitions. Full stadiums, NFL-caliber practice facilities, and merchandising opportunities were waiting for any high-profile club that would get on a plane. All that, plus a mini-vacation in the sunshine, full of shopping in Beverly Hills or lounging around pool parties in Miami Beach. Stillitano's fee to the clubs in those early days was $500,000 a game.

By 2013, Stillitano had a new business partner in this enterprise, the billionaire owner of the Miami Dolphins, Stephen Ross. Together, they had formed Relevent Sports and formalized the summer roadshow into a tournament called the International Champions Cup (ICC), because Ross was tired of calling them exhibition games. He wanted real competition with live stakes. He'd heard the idle threats that European clubs had been making for 20 years about breaking away from their domestic leagues and UEFA to form a super league, and he thought that it sounded like a pretty good idea—as long as he was running it.

ICC games could be held anywhere from East Asia to West Texas, but the US was always the primary target. They had television coverage and thirsty markets with disposable income, all desperate to experience a piece of what Americans watched every weekend from across the Atlantic. Soon teams were falling over each other to join in.

"The commercial departments went from, forgive me, knuckleheads to brilliant people," says Stillitano, Relevent's executive chairman until his departure in 2021.

A few even offered to play for free, simply to tap the commercial potential. Not Real Madrid and Barcelona, though—Relevent was still paying through the nose for them. But Ross and Stillitano knew who needed to be there to make the whole thing work. The ICC only ever wrote two players' attendance into the contracts. If Barcelona and Real Madrid were flying stateside, Messi and Ronaldo had to be on the plane.

Relevent gave them millions of reasons to play ball. Cristiano's payment merely for showing up accounted for 10 percent of Real's overall rights fee. Messi's made up an eye-watering 30 percent of Barça's.

The crown jewel was supposed to come in the summer of 2017. Stillitano had secured a Clásico on American soil. All the years of toil—of securing hotel rooms and drivers and three-star restaurant reservations to send millionaires barnstorming through the United States—were paying off for the most significant match in ICC history.

It had taken some convincing. "When they play each other, they don't want to lose to each other," Ross told *Sports Illustrated*. "That's why they don't go around playing each other usually. If you don't play often, one can't say they're definitely better than the other." But when Ross sat down with both Florentino Pérez and Josep Maria Baromeu, he made them a promise that few others in the world of sports could deliver with any credibility. If they were willing to export Real versus Barcelona, he would make this match like a Super Bowl.

As it turned out, a personal matter in Spain made Ronaldo a late scratch from the game. Stillitano gave him every chance to make it there by putting a private jet in Madrid on standby, but the timing never worked out. They had to settle for a Messi-only Clásico to delight the

65,320 fans inside Miami's Hard Rock Stadium, all of whom paid at least $200 a ticket.

OVER IN EUROPE, another investor was watching. A City of London wheeler-dealer named Robert Bonnier, who had made a dot-com fortune, lost it, and was in the process of building it back up, also thought that the gap in the soccer market was obvious. For all the talk of de facto all-star games during Clásicos and summer exhibitions, his new objective in life was to give soccer an actual all-star game. And instead of a US-style East versus West, or National League versus American League, he saw only one possible format: Team Messi versus Team Ronaldo.

"An all-star game is the last great frontier for football," says David Piper, the TV producer hired by Bonnier to make it happen.

The nearest soccer had come was in MLS, where the league handpicked its best players and threw them together to serve as preseason fodder for a major European club. This would be much, much bigger. So around 2014, Bonnier and Piper opened talks with every possible entity on the long list that would need to sign off on such a crazy project.

FIFA and UEFA, who fiercely guard their monopoly on licensing competitive matches in Europe, wouldn't hop on board easily or cheaply. Neither would the clubs. Pérez demanded €25 million for any Real player to be involved.

Anticipating some raised eyebrows from sponsors as well, Piper worked out that Messi and Friends could wear Adidas while Ronaldo and Co. trotted out in Nike kits. And to assuage concerns over neutral ground, they settled on playing the match at Wembley.

The easiest thing was piquing Messi's and Ronaldo's interest. Both camps were intrigued when they heard that the budget for the operation would exceed €100 million, leaving plenty to go directly into their pockets in the form of match fees and bonuses for the winners. Messi and Ronaldo would be finally, explicitly in the business of Messi versus Ronaldo.

Each side even asked if they could have a hand in selecting the teams.

Bonnier and Piper said sure, why not? There was no limit to how much they could tweak the format, because no one had ever tried it before. If they could make the inaugural match in 2017 work, the idea was to grow the project into a biennial event that would look more like a music festival than a friendly match, with bands, laser shows, and maybe even a boxing prize fight to cap off the weekend.

That version of the project collapsed in the end under the sheer weight of the parties involved. The web of competing interests—clubs, regulators, egos—proved too unwieldy to handle. "We were very close," Piper says ruefully.

But getting as close as they did crystallized something real that was happening on the pitch. Messi and Ronaldo were in a new phase of their careers: they were taking back control of a rivalry that they barely owned anymore. They'd each won every major club trophy available. Now it was time to ask themselves how many more times they could do it. Messi and Ronaldo were no longer building seasons—they were building legacies.

To Ronaldo, there were only two venues that mattered anymore, the Ballon d'Or and the Champions League. On the night in 2014 when Real Madrid became champion of Europe for a 10th time by beating Atlético, Cristiano knew exactly what he needed to do. Though he wasn't the game's highest-impact player—that would be his teammate Sergio Ramos, who headed home the 94th-minute goal to send the game into extra-time—Ronaldo seized his moment by scoring a late, meaningless penalty kick to make the score 4–1. After the ball hit the net, he ran to the corner flag, whipped off his shirt, and flexed every muscle in his body like the Incredible Hulk after a thousand burpees. He had no doubts about which picture would be seen around the world the next morning.

He collected his second Champions League trophy and, later that year, his third Ballon d'Or. As it turned out, Cristiano had never been more prepared for anything in his life. Six months before the final, he'd already constructed a special place for the silverware back home in Funchal: a public museum to himself.

EIGHT

The Monuments Men

FROM JUNIOR TOURNAMENTS with Andorinha to the Ballon d'Or, every trophy Cristiano Ronaldo has ever won is stored within the CR7 Museu on Madeira. So is a specially cooled, life-size statue of the man made of Swiss chocolate. There is another more or less life-size sculpture outside, this one made of bronze, where so many adoring fans have paid their respects to the bulge in his shorts that the region is now permanently discolored. (This remains an improvement on the bust that once graced Cristiano Ronaldo International Airport in Madeira, which had to be replaced because it made him look like one of the dimmer Muppets.)

Inside, down the stairs to a windowless bunker, more than 200 jerseys, balls, and pieces of silverware are carefully organized in display cases as the holy relics of Cristiano's career. The pile of medals is more than some clubs have won in a century. Pack rat that he is, Ronaldo also saved the laminated credentials he wore around his neck at major tournaments. And because Cristiano is a completist—like a collector who tracks down every Japanese pressing of the Beatles' records—he requested special permission to manufacture full-size replicas of the English, Spanish, and Champions League trophies he's won in order to display them in their hefty, shiny glory. The originals belong to the clubs (see: the trophy room at Real Madrid).

The Ballons d'Or, though, are authentic and occupy unmissable real estate by the front. Near those, Ronaldo keeps a small silver brick to mark another milestone from 2014, an award from Facebook for crossing 100 million followers. A single lap of the room is enough to understand one of his fundamental personal traits: Cristiano views success exclusively in things you can count.

"He wanted to show what he had conquered while he was still alive," says Nuno Mendes, the friend who runs the museum and rattles off Ronaldo's achievements more easily than his own phone number.

When those conquests outgrew the museum's first location in 2016, Ronaldo had to move the collection across the street to its current home. That way he could also connect the Museu to his CR7 Hotel, a brand he licensed to the Pestana group for a collection of luxury establishments decorated with his image. Others would open eventually in Lisbon and Madrid and off Times Square in New York. At the original hotel in Funchal, signed jerseys are all over the lobby, sketches of his career highlights adorn the rooms, and even the key-card envelopes read, "Prepare to Win." The wall of the men's bathroom features a four-foot picture of Ronaldo's face in aviator sunglasses. Each lens doubles as a mirror over the sinks.

Around Funchal, everyone claims some connection to Ronaldo's family, the Aveiros. They know where they live, or they went to school with a cousin, or they spotted his mother on the balcony of her fancy condo. The island's favorite son returns at least once a year, and somehow every resident of Madeira seems to know when he's back.

The same is true in Rosario, where everyone will tell you that they were good friends with the Messi-Cuccittini clan and knew from day one that little Leo was bound for greatness. It also became the case in Castelldefels, the quiet beach town 20 minutes from Barcelona's practice facility, where Messi built an enormous white house near his teammates. He set it up as a place he'd never really have to leave in a community that left him alone. When his next-door neighbors proved a little too noisy, he simply bought their house. His outings consisted of trips to the same collection of local restaurants. His neighbor was Luis Suárez. His most extravagant request was the addition of a small soccer field where he is content to kick a ball around with his sons and his gargantuan French mastiff named Hulk.

There are, to date, no plans for a Messi museum at the property. The trophies are around—and occasionally appear in Messi's Christmas messages on social media—but they are not on public display, because of an essential difference between the two men. For Ronaldo, legacy is a material thing, to be touched and photographed and polished. Lining up the silverware is the clearest way he knows to make the point overwhelming. To walk through Ronaldo's museum is to hear one argument made, over and over again: any team he played for could not possibly have survived without him. Wherever he went, success depended exclusively on Cristiano.

FOR MESSI, THAT just happened to be true—or at least things were starting to look that way. In Argentina and Barcelona, they even had a word for it. *Messidependencia*.

The worries began shortly after the two most productive seasons of Messi's career. Over the 2011–2012 and 2012–2013 Liga campaigns, he racked up an insane 96 goals. What troubled Barça watchers, even during the most exhilarating period of their footballing lives, was how much more he scored than anyone else on the team. Messi alone was responsible for 42 percent of all Barcelona goals. With Argentina, the situation was only magnified by the drop-off in quality from his club teammates to the national squad. Messi was the top scorer and most effective playmaker as the national team punched its ticket to the 2014 World Cup through two years of grueling qualifying matches. Despite flying back and forth between Barcelona and South America for only a few days at a time, he had a direct hand in 16 of his team's 35 goals and was instrumental in the buildup to at least a half-dozen more. By the time the tournament rolled around, manager Alejandro Sabella was no longer pretending that his team's fate didn't rest on Messi's narrow shoulders. "Whenever there is a player like Messi, there's a dependence," he said in 2014. "We are trying to improve, but dependence always exists. We have to try to take the pressure off him between all of us, because we are a team."

The most helpful thing the team could do was to pass Messi the ball on every possible occasion. There was no Iniesta, no Xavi to back him up when he played for the Albiceleste, as Argentina's national team is known. The magic had to come from him every time.

"It's impossible not to be *Messidependent*," his teammate Javier Mascherano said. "If you've got the best in the world and you're not depending on him, then who?"

Barcelona's response to the same problem was to build around Messi even more explicitly. What choice did it have? Who would ever argue that watching the greatest of all time pile up goals for fun was a bad thing? It hardly mattered, in the short term at least, that the team looked less and less like the Guardiola era sides of patient buildup and death by a thousand passes. Way back in 2008, Pep had urged fans to "fasten your seatbelts." Now they needed a fighter-jet harness. Barça was an all-out attacking machine with Messi completely in charge.

This was the situation that Josep Maria Bartomeu inherited when he became president of FC Barcelona in 2014, in the wake of Sandro Rosell's legal troubles surrounding the Neymar transfer. A Spanish businessman with little background in running a football club, Bartomeu had served as Rosell's vice president and before that had overseen Barça's handball and basketball departments. None of it had prepared him to run a global company that bought and sold assets worth tens of millions of dollars and bore precious little resemblance to the club he grew up supporting.

Then again, watching Barça win La Liga, the Champions League, and the Copa del Rey in the first full season of his term might have convinced Bartomeu that this gig was easy—as long as Messi stuck around.

Those who argued that Messidependencia was a fabrication of the headline writers didn't realize quite how far it went. Not only did Messi call the shots in the dressing room, albeit at low volume, but he was now taking on a much bigger role at the club, one that even Guardiola could not have imagined in the days of teaching him where to play.

In his own discreet way, Barcelona's number 10 viewed himself as the club's shadow general manager. He wasn't running the scouting department or negotiating anyone's contract (aside from his own, regularly), but Messi was no longer shy about making his feelings known in matters of personnel and recruitment. With a simple text message, or more often via his father, he would communicate to Bartomeu which players he felt should or shouldn't be wearing the blaugrana colors.

And around the summer of 2017, Messi felt strongly that an Argentine winger named Ángel Di María very much should be.

A versatile player who could fly past opponents on the flanks and run directly at defenders inside, Di María had impressed Messi ever since he was first called up to the national team in 2008. The pair linked up well during qualifying for the 2014 World Cup and found creative ways to open up space and passing channels. Di María also had the inherent quality, appreciated by Messi, of being from Rosario—even if he grew up supporting Rosario Central rather than Newell's Old Boys.

He seemed like such a natural fit that the Messis wasted no time in setting the wheels in motion. Leo piped up, and Jorge let Bartomeu know.

"Leo thinks you should sign Di María," he told Bartomeu.

Bartomeu knew from his predecessors that managing this relationship might be the most delicate task faced by a Barça president. He didn't want to dismiss Jorge Messi out of hand or tell him to leave sporting decisions to the sporting director. Yet he didn't want Di María either. He soft-pedaled as well as he could.

A player like that, he explained, didn't come cheap. Not when they were coming from Paris Saint-Germain, and certainly not when they were represented by Jorge Mendes. Barça would be looking at a fee of €60 million or €70 million, for sure, not to mention a ginormous salary. Two years earlier, Di María had moved from Manchester United to PSG for more than €50 million. Still, Jorge Messi insisted. Leo would be very disappointed if Barcelona didn't at least try.

So Bartomeu promised to try. When he came back to Jorge, he reported that he'd been rebuffed, as expected. There wasn't much else he could do about it.

"Well," Jorge Messi asked, "how much did you bid?"

As it happened, Bartomeu had low-balled PSG with an offer between €30 million and €40 million. That was as high as the club was prepared to go. Anything more would have been over market value and down-right irresponsible.

Jorge wasn't impressed. But the exchange armed him with two crucial pieces of information. The first was that Bartomeu hadn't tried hard enough—the Messis would remember that. The second was that Barcelona had at least €30 million to burn. Jorge had some thoughts on how the club might spend it.

"You should give it to Leo," he told the Barça president.

Jorge Messi's audacity in proposing such a gift one year out from a contract renewal spoke volumes about the balance of power within the club. The only thing that spoke louder was Bartomeu's decision to comply. The money turned into a hefty raise in Leo's next contract. Barcelona declined to comment on that negotiation.

Messi's ubiquitous influence inside the club was no longer a secret. Doing things the Barça way now meant doing things the Messi way—as a Barcelona staffer named Pere Gratacós had learned the hard way in early 2017. A former Barcelona B player and coach, Gratacós was in charge of the club's sporting relations with the Spanish soccer federation. During a draw for the Copa del Rey, he committed the Barça equivalent of a thought crime. "He's the best, this is true," Gratacós said, according to the Catalan daily *Sport*, "[but] Messi would not be as good without Iniesta, Neymar, and company."

It wasn't the first time Gratacós had expressed a blasphemous view in the eyes of the club. Seven years earlier, he had told *La Vanguardia*, "In Africa there are many Messis. I coached Messi for two years and later I saw these players and I can say there are many who have a similar level."

In 2010, casting doubt on Messi's immaculate, inimitable genius was not a fireable offense. By 2017, it definitely was. Within 24 hours of Gratacós's comments on Iniesta and Neymar, Barcelona issued a statement that he had been dismissed "for having publicly expressed a personal opinion that does not match that of the club."

It's not clear whether Messi noticed the comments or mentioned them to the Barça brass. Even if he had, he probably didn't need to say a word for the club to take action. Any slight, real or perceived, demanded a response. Reputation management and light censorship were now part of the day-to-day running of FC Barcelona.

One man had seen this atmospheric shift coming as far back as 2014. Though he wasn't around very long to detect it, former coach Tata Martino put the situation into words shortly after being fired in Catalonia and taking over the Argentina squad.

"Everything that happens around Lionel happens solely and exclusively for how he is feeling," Martino said. "The reality is that at Barcelona everyone ends up waiting for him to decide many things. The situation is not that different on the national team."

No one ever had to guess how Cristiano Ronaldo felt about a team set up solely and exclusively in service of his talents. He didn't merely expect this setup—it was how he wanted it. It was supposed to be all about him, because that's where the goals came from. In Ronaldo's mind, no one could survey the catalog of titles and trophies that had piled up at every club he'd ever played for and reasonably question the wisdom of building a team that way. Anyone who did would be met with the same response, his stock answer to any hint of criticism: "The numbers don't lie."

The problem was that those numbers were becoming hard to keep track of as the accolades and honors continued to roll in at Real Madrid. Fortunately, Ronaldo had a solution for that. He started keeping a record of his achievements on hand at all times. In case he suddenly needed to defend his legacy, he had empirical evidence of his greatness close by.

Carlos Bruno got the full rundown when he visited Real Madrid's training ground. The Sporting fitness coach who had chased Ronaldo out of the gym all those years ago hadn't seen his former student in nearly two decades when he arrived at the Spanish club's headquarters in 2017 for a conference on youth coaching. On the final morning of his trip, he was invited to watch Real Madrid's senior team go through a training session before lunch. At the end of practice, as the Real players hustled into the locker room and the other conference attendees hustled to the cafeteria, Bruno asked a club official if he could say a quick *bom dia* to Cristiano. The official returned a few minutes later to say Ronaldo would stop by on his way out.

After half an hour or so, the team began to trickle out of the locker room and head toward the parking lot. Cristiano Ronaldo was not among them. Thirty minutes later, another group of players filed out through the Valdebebas lobby. Still no sign of Ronaldo. Another hour passed, at which point Bruno was ready to call it a day. He approached the official at the desk to ask if perhaps Cristiano had forgotten that someone was waiting to see him. *Maybe this wasn't a convenient time?* No, he was told firmly. If Ronaldo said he would stop by on his way out, then Ronaldo would stop by on his way out. Bruno went back to his seat. He waited some more.

Finally, nearly three hours after the end of training, Ronaldo appeared, the last player to leave the locker room. He bounded over, wrapped Bruno in a bear hug, and apologized for keeping him so long. Ronaldo explained that after practice he liked to squeeze in a workout in the gym. And also a few laps in the pool. And also some hydrotherapy conditioning, a full body massage, and a quick plunge in the ice bath. Bruno began to realize he was lucky the wait was only three hours.

As they walked through the sweltering Madrid heat toward Ronaldo's car—a decent hike since, on most days, he did not make use of his free Audi—the two chatted about mutual friends, the old days at Sporting, and life back in Portugal. Ronaldo posed for a couple of photos and filmed a video for the coach's young son ("He put the video on Instagram immediately and was the king of his school," Bruno says) before Bruno prepared to say his goodbyes and hunt down some lunch. That was until he made one critical error.

"And how is everything at Real Madrid?" Bruno asked, innocently enough.

Ronaldo's eyes lit up as he withdrew a piece of folded paper from his pocket and beckoned Bruno to come look. The document in Ronaldo's hand was a printout that chronicled every major accomplishment of his 18-year career—and a good number of the minor accomplishments as well. It noted every domestic and international trophy he had won, as well as every individual award he had earned, and gave a comprehensive breakdown of his goalscoring, including every hat trick he ever scored.

"Professor, look, look!" Ronaldo said, pointing out his three Champions League titles, two La Liga championships, and two Copa del Rey triumphs in Madrid.

"And these, and these!" he continued, directing Bruno to his four Ballon d'Or trophies and four European Golden Shoe awards for the continent's top scorer.

"Not bad, eh?" he said, indicating the records for fastest player in La Liga history to reach 150 goals, 200 goals, and 300 goals.

As they pored over this archive of Ronaldo's career, Bruno noticed that both of them were starting to perspire heavily in the afternoon heat. Ronaldo plowed on, seemingly oblivious.

By the time he had finished, with a quick spin through some of the more arcane statistics—first player in Spain's top flight to hit 20 goals in the first 12 games of the season, top assist provider at the 2014 Club World Cup—Bruno realized they had spent more than 20 minutes checking off every last entry in the document.

Once Ronaldo went on his way, Carlos Bruno was left in the Real Madrid parking lot with two abiding thoughts. First, this was not normal behavior. And second, he had now definitely missed his lunch.

RONALDO FANS ALL over the world knew some version of his list by heart. Messi fans knew it too—they just decided it wasn't important. With both men certain of their places in the pantheon, the debate about which name was holier had long moved out of their hands.

"For me, this fight doesn't exist," Ronaldo told a Chinese newspaper in 2017. "You can't compare players. Cristiano is Cristiano and Messi is Messi. The two are great players, individually and on a collective level."

Although there had once been a frostiness between Messi and Ronaldo—"They barely say hello to one another," Ruud Gullit remarked after hosting the 2013 Ballon d'Or—it seemed Messi and Ronaldo were ready to move on from their rivalry. But the rivalry was not ready to move on from them. Because the whole time they had been fighting to prove which of them was the world's greatest player, millions of complete strangers around the planet had been fighting *about* which of them was the world's greatest player. The Messi-Ronaldo Debate had become an entity unto itself, the biggest, dumbest, most pervasive argument in sports. And both sides were far too entrenched in their position to give up now.

It was probably inevitable that the happy accident that landed two all-time greats in the same sport *at the same time* would degenerate into a howling, hyperpartisan argument on social media. The two constituencies involved—soccer fans and the extremely online—are not exactly known for their sense of moderation. For anyone even vaguely plugged into soccer during the 2010s, the Debate was inescapable—even if staying out of it was part of their job description. In October 2013, FIFA president Sepp Blatter dived headlong into the dispute during a spectacularly ill-advised interview at Oxford University. "I like both of them, but I prefer Messi," Blatter said, adding that the Argentinian was a "good boy that every father, every mother would like to have at home." Ronaldo, on the other hand, represented "the other side of football" and "has more expenses for the hairdresser," Blatter quipped, before comparing the Real Madrid forward to a military commander and illustrating his point by marching back and forth across the stage.

Even for Blatter, a man who had mastered the art of putting his own foot in his mouth, it was a bizarre gaffe, like the host of the Oscars announcing their favorite before opening the winners' envelope. Within days, he was forced to apologize for his inappropriate comments following an angry phone call from Florentino Pérez at Real Madrid, where Blatter was an honorary socio.

"I'm ordering you to Madrid immediately to explain to our socios and to the press why you said Messi and not Ronaldo our player," Blatter recalls Pérez fuming. "I told him, 'Calm down a bit. It's my opinion and I have a right to express it.'"

Blatter's remarks were positively deferential, however, compared with the discourse online, where the Messi-Ronaldo argument has, like everything else during that time, metastasized into a cesspool of rabid tribalism. In the darkest wastelands of the internet—obscure subreddits, men's fitness forums, the YouTube comments for any half-popular soccer video—it has become a forever war, fought on a battlefield of rage-tweets, vitriolic screeds, and dubiously sourced statistics wielded like a blunt weapon.

Of course, arguments about the greatest players have been around since the game started out as a series of semi-organized riots between rival villages. And soccer has seen its share of polarizing athletes before. Diego Maradona was a scoundrel and a self-confessed cheat who once used a fake plastic penis to evade drug testers. Suffice to say he wasn't everyone's cup of yerba maté. But his antics never produced anything as ferocious or interminable as the Messi-Ronaldo Debate.

Part of it is down to timing. Their rise coincided with the emergence of another world-changing duo: Facebook and Twitter. The arrival of social media fundamentally changed what it meant to be a soccer fan. For the first time in history, two all-time greats were hitting their peaks at a time when we could watch their every move, every stepover and then another stepover, as it happened. You didn't even have to sit through entire matches. Their rivalry played out online in real time.

This visibility helped propel them both to a level of global superstardom unmatched by any other athletes in history. They accessed a level of recognition normally reserved for US presidents and popes. Their magnetism can be measured in dizzying numbers. Messi has more than twice as many Instagram followers as LeBron James. Ronaldo's tally is 50 million higher than Kim Kardashian's. He has more Twitter followers than Twitter itself.

More importantly, their followings far outstrip those of the clubs they play for. For many of their fans, the sense of attachment they feel to Messi or Ronaldo is far deeper than any affection they might have for Barcelona or Real Madrid. Consider that pictures on Ronaldo's Instagram showing him brushing his teeth, working out in the pool, or drinking coffee in his underpants draw twice as many likes as those of him playing the sport that made him famous in the first place. An image of Ronaldo celebrating his seventh career league title in 2020 attracted

10 million fewer likes than a picture a day earlier of him posing shirtless next to his Bugatti.

At times, the fact that they play soccer seems entirely beside the point. Ronaldo and Messi have become lifestyle brands whose appeal transcends sports itself, inspiring a level of individualistic devotion that has less in common with pro athletes and more the kind of obsessive fandom and cult of personality associated with pop stars, Hollywood actors, and celebrity couples.

"People are constantly comparing us," Ronaldo said. "They even compare our children, how they grow, what they do at school, who is faster, smarter."

If social media ushered in an age in which soccer is in greater thrall to the individual than ever before, it's undeniable that Messi and Ronaldo cultivated it to some extent too. Watch how Ronaldo's free-kick routine has changed over the years, for instance. In his early days at Manchester United, he simply ran up, blasted the ball toward the goal, and ripped off his jersey to celebrate. But by the time he was at Real Madrid, things had changed. Ronaldo was the star now, and he wanted everyone to know it. When the whistle blew, he no longer ran straight toward the ball. He waited. Deep breath, eyes fixed on the ball, letting the anticipation build and build. He had transformed a simple set piece into a small piece of theater, or a 30-second commercial in the middle of a match. The same goes for penalty shoot-outs: Ronaldo usually insists on shooting fifth because that position offers a greater chance for glory, despite statistics showing that earlier penalties have a higher correlation with success. Messi, meanwhile, was such a superstar in his own locker room that after winning any trophy with Barcelona, he'd find himself standing with the silverware while his teammates queued up to pose for photographs with him.

The gravitational pull between the two explains why something that could have been one of the harmless "who's better?" debates found across all sports has turned into something nastier. Siding with Messi or Ronaldo has become not merely a statement of preference for one footballer over another, but something closer to an article of religious faith. For more than 15 years, people have found new ways to squabble over the same simple question, even as the central tenets have barely changed: Messi needs to prove himself at another club, Ronaldo only scores penalties, Messi is a fraud, Ronaldo is a bad teammate, Messi is a choker, Ronaldo is a fraud, and on and on. The Messi-Ronaldo Debate has endured so long that it has even given rise to a debate about the debate. *Why can't we appreciate two of the greatest players of all time without arguing over who is better?* Yeah, right.

In another, saner world, the fact that two superstars who had spent the majority of their careers playing in the same position could be so stylistically distinct would be a cause for celebration, a reminder of soccer's essential variety. In the early 21st century, however, it only made people even madder. Because their games were diametric opposites, admitting the greatness of the other required some small admission that our entire understanding of how the game is supposed to be played must be wrong.

Their longevity has also contributed to the acrimony of the Debate. The sheer weight and tyranny of numbers—the records and statistics that Messi and Ronaldo have put up or torn down over the years—provides an endless supply of data to be skewed, distorted, and weaponized by the competing factions in an effort to definitively prove their man's superiority. Obscure numbers like most goals against top-eight clubs or the highest Champions League tally against English teams (not including the group stage) are used to elevate one while denigrating the other.

That they have been around for so long also makes it feel like the only way to situate Messi's and Ronaldo's greatness is in relation to each other. Which makes for an oddly joyless way of experiencing soccer. When one of them does something remarkable, the response often focuses directly on the other one and whatever remarkable feat he has or hasn't accomplished to match it. Even Ballon d'Or voters, who not only weighed up the year's performances but were instructed to consider the players' histories as well, found they were really only left with two possible choices, year after year.

"It became almost Pavlovian," says Pascal Ferré, the editor of *France*

Football magazine, which runs the award. "When it comes time to vote, people see it as time to vote for one or the other."

Messi and Ronaldo can say they don't feel the weight of it—and most of the time they don't. But on a few rare occasions, the pressure of expectation has nearly broken them. Not by coincidence, it's when their entire countries are watching.

LIONEL MESSI NEVER pictured his international career ending in a noisy hallway in New Jersey. But there he was inside the Meadowlands, bereft again in an Argentina shirt, choking on another defeat like it was last month's milk. The 2016 Copa America had been a failure, like every Copa America he'd ever played in before that. "I was thinking about it in the locker room, and that's it," Messi explained, while Chile celebrated victory. "It's over with the national team. As I just said, it's now four finals. Unfortunately, I tried, and this was what I wanted most."

Messi was now 29. The Copa America had come and gone four times since he became a national-team regular, and Messi's Argentina still hadn't won it. Organizers even threw him a bonus one. Though the tournament varied between two and four cycles, the 2016 edition was held only one summer after the previous edition. The official reason was to celebrate South American football's 100th anniversary with a Copa America Centenario. The real motivation was the opportunity to generate more money from television, marketing, and ticket sales for South American soccer's governing body, Conmebol. That's why this championship of South America was held in North America. And in keeping with the soccer world's unceasing efforts to engineer more high-profile matches, this was another way to grant Messi a major stage.

It merely fixed the spotlight on his greatest frustration. Messi had now played in three Copa finals and lost all of them in a manner that was either utterly heartbreaking or completely embarrassing, or both. In 2007, Argentina was stomped 3–0 by a forgettable Brazil team. Then, in 2015, a 0–0 bloodbath against Chile saw the two sides combine for 50 fouls in 120 minutes before Chile won in a penalty shoot-out. In 2016, Chile figured the tackle-first-ask-questions-later approach might work again in a stadium built for the NFL. The bet paid off. Another 0–0 led to another penalty shoot-out and another Chilean victory, as Messi blazed his spot kick over the bar. Crushed by disappointment, he struggled to make any sense of it.

The feeling was all too familiar. Throughout his career, a strange dynamic took over any time Messi pulled on the Albiceleste stripes of Argentina. In most other places, a world-beating talent appearing out of the sky-blue would have been worshiped like a monarch. Brazil dubbed Pelé simply "O Rei," the King. Ukraine took its top scorer, Andriy Shevchenko, and made him manager of the national team before his 40th birthday. And George Weah, the first African player to win the Ballon d'Or, was so venerated back in Liberia that he was later elected president.

But Argentina was a country that had known all-time greatness before. Fans had a more discerning palate. They weighed up Messi and Maradona like they were fine glasses of Malbec—comparisons were inevitable.

On the pitch, there was little to set them apart. Away from it, however, two things stood out in the minds of fans. (Surprisingly, neither of them was Maradona's party animal lifestyle.) For one, Messi was the boy who left. He hadn't lived in Argentina full-time since he was 12 years old, nor had he ever played professionally for a club at home. And then there was the inevitable conversation-ender, the fatal flaw in Messi's career that in the eyes of certain supporters amounted to a cardinal sin.

Maradona had won the World Cup. Messi hadn't.

The closest he came was in 2014, at the World Cup in Brazil, where he was expected to carry Argentina through the tournament with the captain's armband, exactly as he had in qualifying. Except Messi was visibly exhausted, physically and mentally. He didn't score at all in the knockout rounds and faded in the final as Argentina lost 1–0 to Germany in extra-time, though he was still voted the tournament's most valuable player. Sepp Blatter, who presented him with the award, later called this decision "incorrect."

Sabella, the Argentina manager, could see how badly Messi wanted to put the team on his back that day in Rio. He knew that he would try whatever it took on the pitch for his country—in practice drills, Messi was not only the most dangerous attacker, he was also the smartest defender. But the realization stared Sabella in the face, just as it had for his predecessor and the men who followed him. Coach after coach was left finding new ways of saying the same thing.

The problem wasn't with Messi—it couldn't be. The problem was that Argentina couldn't get on Messi's level.

"He put the group first, before the individual, and he personally sacrificed himself for the benefit of the team," Sabella said in 2014.

"The reality of the Argentine squad clouds Leo's brilliance," Jorge Sampaoli would say four years later. "Leo is limited because the team doesn't gel ideally as it should."

It didn't help the new Maradona that the actual Maradona was piling on from the peanut gallery. Before the 2016 Copa, El Diego came right out and said that he believed Messi lacked the leadership skills to carry Argentina to glory of any kind. "He is a great person," Maradona said, "but he has no personality." He wasn't the first to think that.

Maradona then turned the knife when he addressed the other tournament going on that summer, the European Championship in France. "Cristiano, without a doubt, is the star," he declared. "He's one of those players who can single-handedly put his team in the final. He is football culture. Anyone who likes football, likes Cristiano."

So when Messi announced in New Jersey that he was retiring from international soccer, he said it was "for the sake of everybody."

"I think a lot of people want it," he added. "They are obviously not satisfied—and we are not satisfied either—by reaching the final and not winning it. . . . I am the one who failed. So that's it."

Of course, that wasn't it. Within a few months, Messi would be back in the fold. But in July 2016, for the first time in his career, he was admitting total defeat. The environment was wrong, the tactics were wrong, and the attitude was wrong. Once again, being surrounded by something other than the structure he was used to in Barcelona had left him trying to plug too many gaps at once. It simply couldn't work.

Messi was willing to concede international football to everybody else.

NEWS OF ARGENTINA'S failure made its way to Marcoussis, in a southern suburb of Paris, where Cristiano Ronaldo was in his version of paradise. In a facility borrowed from the French national rugby team, he was surrounded by more weights and machines than he'd ever seen in one place. Making things even better, he was playing for his favorite team in the world: Portugal.

He only wished in that moment that Portugal looked a little less like Messi's Argentina. The European Championship couldn't have begun further from the way he'd hoped. Portugal's opening match was against Iceland, whose population of 330,000 made it the smallest nation ever to qualify for a major tournament. It only took 11 of them, defending for their lives, to hold Ronaldo to a 1–1 draw and seemingly disgust him with the whole enterprise. "It was unbelievable," he said. "We tried hard to win the game, and Iceland didn't try anything. This, in my opinion, shows a small mentality and they are not going to do anything in the competition."

Iceland, which went on to knock out England, could only laugh. And the Cristiano haters kept on chuckling when he missed a penalty in the next group-stage game against Austria. Portugal found itself staring down the barrel of elimination.

But if this was the summer of Messi's leadership credentials coming under fire, then Ronaldo began treating his time in France like he was General Patton blasting his way out of Normandy. Every match—every team meal—represented yet another opportunity for ostentatious displays of command. (Unlike Patton, however, Cristiano did not go around slapping people.) That's why, on the night after the Austria game, Ronaldo called a players' meeting in the team hotel. He kept his message brief.

"Boys, we are alive."

Portugal had only two points from two games, but the Euro organizers had accidentally done the team a favor years before the tournament by expanding the field. Now that the event had grown from 16 countries to 24, a couple of third-place finishers from the group stage would still advance. And if Portugal had to be one of those teams, there was no shame in it, because the important thing was getting through. Cristiano wasn't ready to go home yet.

With Portugal needing at least a point against Hungary, he scored twice in a 3–3 draw. Then, in the round of 16, he teed up the winner in the 27th minute of extra-time by opening up Croatia's defense and forcing a save from the goalkeeper, only for Ricardo Quaresma to put away the rebound. Ronaldo celebrated as if the goal were his own.

He didn't score in the quarterfinal against Poland either, as a 1–1 draw sent the match to a penalty shoot-out. That's when Ronaldo made his presence felt again. He took it upon himself to organize the roster, insisting that a nervous João Moutinho step up for a spot kick. "You hit them well!" he shouted on the pitch. "If you miss, screw it. Be strong. . . . It's in God's hands now."

And where God couldn't help, Ronaldo would do the rest.

After Portugal drilled all five penalties against Poland, Cristiano gave his team a decisive lead in the semifinal victory over Wales. Four weeks after its disastrous start to the Euros—and nine days after Messi had quit international soccer altogether—Ronaldo was back in a major-tournament final with Portugal. This was where he was born to be. All he had to do now was beat the heavily favored host nation at the Stade de France in front of 80,000 fans.

Twelve years earlier, in his only other major international final, Ronaldo and Portugal *were* the heavily favored host nation. But that night in Lisbon had turned to disaster as the team somehow choked against lowly Greece and lost 1–0. This time, Ronaldo told himself, things would be different. After all, he would be leading out the team. Far from the brash 19-year-old he was in 2004, Cristiano was now something akin to Achilles, an inspiration on the field of battle, a man inseparable from his grand role. (The difference was that Ronaldo was always camera-ready too: he kept a bucket of ice by his locker at the Bernabéu, not to treat postmatch swelling in his knee, but to reduce postmatch puffiness in his face.)

Except in the biggest match of his life, Ronaldo's time on the pitch lasted all of 23 minutes.

After France's Dimitri Payet crashed into him during the opening exchanges, Ronaldo found that he could barely run anymore. A searing pain shot through his left knee anytime he pushed off. He tried to play on, gritting his teeth as he hobbled, but the knee wouldn't let him. With less than a quarter of the game gone, Ronaldo slumped to the turf in tears.

He gathered himself long enough to beg the physios to strap his knee and let him keep going, even though a scan would later show a sprained medial collateral ligament. That only bought him a few more instants on the field. One excruciating sprint later, Ronaldo signaled to the bench that he couldn't go on. He ripped off his captain's armband and knew his final was over. He was stretchered off to a standing ovation from the Stade de France.

For 15 minutes in the nearly empty dressing room, Ronaldo was disconsolate. He wept while his teammates outside kept the French forwards at bay. The doctor poked and prodded at his knee. The first piece of good news was that he didn't believe Ronaldo required surgery. Then, as the doc tidied up the strapping, the handful of other people in the locker room noticed a sudden shift in Cristiano's mood, as if he suddenly remembered that there was a final going on out there.

Ronaldo needed to be with his teammates. And his teammates, shell-shocked after watching him leave the game, needed to hear from him. He pulled on a mint-green tracksuit top and a fresh pair of sneakers and prepared to give the halftime talk.

"Listen, people," he told them at the break, with the game still scoreless. "I'm sure we will win, so stay together and fight for it."

By the second half, Ronaldo was back on his feet and pacing the touchline like Fernando Santos's taller, more muscular shadow. What the entire stadium could see was Cristiano shouting instructions, waving his arms, and telling Portuguese players what to do. To anyone not in the dugout, it looked like Ronaldo was doing his best to steal the show— along with Santos's job as manager. As it turned out, this was one time Cristiano wasn't being a diva. He was simply repeating every word out of his coach's mouth at fantastic volume. Santos had lost his voice.

What little direction Santos managed to get out was clearly working.

France squandered chance after chance, while Portugal bent without breaking. There was no question it was ugly. But none of Portugal's tournament had been about earning style points. The team hadn't won a single match in regulation until the semifinal. This was a side built around three things: hard work, discipline, and getting the ball to Cristiano. When Cristiano was no longer an option, Portugal had no choice but to double down on the other two and hope to catch a break.

In the 109th minute of the night, deep into extra-time, they caught that break.

It came in the form of a 28-year-old, Guinea-Bissau-born substitute named Eder, with all of three international goals to his name. From 20 yards out, he shook off one defender and fired through the legs of another into the bottom corner of the goal to set Ronaldo crying for what seemed like the 10th time of the evening.

"We lost our main man, the man who could score a goal at any moment," Portugal defender Pepe recalled. "But we were warriors on the pitch. We said that we'd win it for him."

Eleven minutes later, Portugal had the first major trophy of its soccer-playing history. And Cristiano Ronaldo was a European champion. After attempting to play through the pain, he was now partying through the pain—on the pitch, in the locker room, and all the way back to Marcoussis. Inevitably, he was at the center of the celebrations and his teammates didn't mind. On the contrary, Eder said, "he still gave us all his strength and bravery." Though Ronaldo hadn't even been in the game for most of the final, the squad knew that he'd put it there. Ronaldo had grown so vital to Portugal that he could somehow be its most important player without kicking a ball.

So it was only fitting inside the Portuguese locker room at the Stade de France that Ronaldo—the captain, talisman, and sometimes coaching megaphone—gave the definitive victory speech. "To all the players, to all the staff, to everyone involved in this conquest," he said with his shirt off. "Nobody believed in Portugal, but the truth is, we made it. . . . I am very happy.

"This is one of the happiest days of my life."

PART 3

Twilight of the Gods

NINE

Messinaldo, Inc.

CRISTIANO RONALDO WAS furious.

Without any warning one evening late in 2016, he summoned his team of friends, advisers, and hangers-on to an emergency meeting at La Finca, the exclusive gated community outside Madrid where he and Jorge Mendes both kept sprawling homes. They gathered first at Ronaldo's and then migrated to Mendes's living room, where everyone but Cristiano took a seat. He was too agitated to keep still.

Ronaldo's name had just come up, over and over, in a trove of documents unearthed by a Portuguese hacker named Rui Pinto and published by the German magazine *Der Spiegel*. The project was known as Football Leaks. Based on more than 18 million documents concerning dozens of players and clubs, it painted Ronaldo's finances as a vast web of offshore holdings and letterbox companies allegedly designed to hide income from Spain's inland revenue service. He'd been caught cold and felt there was plenty of blame to go around.

"I told you!" he shouted, pointing at each of the people sitting around the room. "I don't want any problems. And now, you bring me problems."

The group included Ronaldo's entire inner circle, from Mendes to the financial adviser Mendes had hired, to Ricardo Regufe, the former Nike rep who managed the company's relationship with CR7 and wound up working for him instead. They'd all known Cristiano for most of his career as he racked up unimaginable wealth and made them rich in the process. None of them was able to assuage Ronaldo.

The rant went on and on, according to a person who was there. He was fed up with his team, he was fed up with the prying, and he was fed up with Spain. In one of its more stunning headlines, Football Leaks had previously revealed that Ronaldo's contract with a Saudi cell-phone provider paid him €1.1 million for a single day's worth of photo shoots. But now the intricate workings of his whole financial empire were laid bare for everyone to see. The files contained so many inside details that much of it was news to Ronaldo, whose personal reputation was being shredded in real time.

"I pay you to avoid problems," he told his advisers. "And when problems come, it's my name out there, not yours!"

For as long as Cristiano had been a professional, his life was organized by GestiFute, the company Jorge Mendes founded as a fledgling agent in 1996. It negotiated his contracts, managed his money, and found him endorsement deals. In 2015, 13 years into his career, GestiFute documents showed Ronaldo's personal wealth to be somewhere around €227 million, according to *Der Spiegel*, though that was probably just a best estimate. Mendes's agency oversees such a complex structure, those close to him say, that Cristiano has no clue how much he's actually worth.

Whatever the amount, the bulk of that money was kept nowhere near him. Almost all of the income he earned away from the field circled the globe between Bermuda, Hong Kong, Panama, Switzerland, and the British Virgin Islands—a virtual Champions League of banking secrecy.

Where Cristiano's name didn't appear directly in the hacked documents, there were always nearby proxies. The Ronaldo files were littered with the names of offshore companies, like the Brockton Foundation. Set up in Panama in February 2003, before Ronaldo's move to Manchester United, Brockton controlled all of his marketing rights and funneled every dollar he earned from sponsorship through those offshore entities. The advantage of having Brockton in Panama was that it could not be compelled to reveal in which other jurisdictions the money was banked and where taxes might be owed. In 2004, those responsibilities slid over to a company called Tollinn Associates, located in the British Virgin Islands—another tax haven—and eventually they landed with something called Multisports & Image Management, based in Ireland. The country's 12.5 percent corporate tax rate, the lowest in the European Union, made it a favorite of firms much larger than Cristiano Ronaldo, Inc., such as Apple and Google.

Offshore banking, in itself, is not illegal. It only becomes a problem when it's used to dance around tax jurisdictions—which happens to be the number-one purpose of offshore banking. Those revelations around Ronaldo's accounting practices were enough to arouse the interest of Spanish investigators, who began poking into his finances in late 2015. Ronaldo denied any wrongdoing and insisted that he always paid his taxes on time and in full.

Ronaldo (along with nearly every other foreign star in Spain) had, in fact, enjoyed extremely privileged standing with the taxman during his early years in the country, thanks to something known as the "Beckham Law." This legislation, passed in 2005 by José María Aznar, the former prime minister of Spain and a Bernabéu Palco regular, was intended to make the country more enticing to foreign talent of all stripes, from sports to music to science.

But few benefited from it more than Florentino Pérez's Galácticos, who viewed the loophole as an open goal. Players arriving in Spain were granted a special status that capped their tax on Spanish income at around 25 percent—as if they were Spanish citizens who had lived outside the country for more than a decade. Anyone else in their tax bracket was coughing up roughly 50 percent. That provision ended in 2010 for athletes earning more than €600,000 a year, though anyone who'd arrived before then was grandfathered into a grace period for years to come.

The combination of legal changes and massive leaks was all the encouragement the tax authorities needed to start diving into footballers' books. And in Ronaldo's case, it didn't take long to spot the streams of cash that seemed to flow everywhere but in Spain. By 2017, those would lead to Spanish authorities circling some $16.7 million that they believed Ronaldo withheld from the state between 2011 and 2014. He was charged with four counts of tax fraud—including three of "aggravated" tax fraud—carrying a possible jail term of around seven years. The case dragged on until 2019, when Ronaldo finally pleaded guilty, accepting a two-year suspended jail sentence plus a fine. Appearing in person in a Madrid courtroom, he wore a black turtleneck, black blazer, and white sneakers to sign away the problem by paying the Spanish state $21.6 million.

The money stung, but the reasons behind the whole cock-up were even more troublesome. What the whole episode had made clear was that the management of his own fortune was a black box to him. Ronaldo's singular focus on becoming the best soccer player in the world hadn't prepared him to also become one of the richest athletes on the planet. And around that time Nike was about to make him even richer, handing him only the third lifetime sponsorship deal in the company's history, after Michael Jordan and LeBron James. When it came to handling that money, however, all Ronaldo understood was whatever he knew from Mendes, the man he'd implicitly assumed knew best. Yet standing in his agent's living room in 2016, the realization hit Ronaldo: Just who was doing what with all of that cash? Whenever he wanted to add another sports car to the garage or hop on the private jet, the payments always cleared, but he had no sense, really, where any of it came from, how it was being invested, or even how much of it there was. Most of all, Cristiano Ronaldo could now see there was an entire world of liabilities out there that could resurface at any time—and his autograph was on all of them.

"You tell me to sign, I sign," he yelled at Mendes. "What the fuck do I know about the British Virgin Islands?"

THE FINANCIAL DISCLOSURES were not the most damaging headline to emerge from Football Leaks. That would be the eventual revelation that a woman named Kathryn Mayorga had accused Ronaldo of rape in 2009.

The previously unknown allegation was first published by *Der Spiegel* in 2017, based on what the magazine had obtained from Pinto, the hacker. It detailed how Ronaldo, spending his 2009 summer break in Las Vegas, had met Mayorga in the VIP area of the Rain nightclub at the Palms Casino Resort before inviting her up to his penthouse suite. Once they were there, Ronaldo forced himself on her while she repeatedly told him to stop, according to Football Leaks and a civil complaint filed in Clark County District Court.

"When Cristiano Ronaldo completed the sexual assault of the plaintiff," the complaint read, "he allowed her to leave the bedroom stating he was sorry, he was usually a gentleman."

Mayorga, a part-time model who was then 34, reported the alleged sexual assault immediately to Las Vegas police without naming Ronaldo—she referred to him only as a "well-known celebrity." She didn't specify where the incident occurred either. But, her lawyers said later, the police let her down. Instead of guiding her through the next steps of the complaint, the officers Mayorga spoke to warned her that whoever the well-known celebrity was would likely accuse her of lying and trying to extort him.

Ronaldo soon proved them partially right. In a rare public statement, released by his legal team, he said, "Rape is an abominable crime that goes against everything that I am and believe in. Keen as I may be to clear my name, I refuse to feed the media spectacle created by people seeking to promote themselves at my expense."

Not knowing where the assault had occurred, police didn't spend long on the case. They also said that video evidence showing Mayorga's interactions with Ronaldo that evening had been lost. But because Mayorga reported it immediately and underwent a medical examination that noted several lesions, there was no statute of limitations, according to local law, and the case could be reopened down the road.

That it would ever come up again seemed unlikely after she accepted $375,000 from Ronaldo's lawyers in exchange for her signature on a non-disclosure agreement. But by 2017 the Me Too movement had emboldened women everywhere who'd suffered sexual assault to speak out and shed new light on the rampant, insidious use of NDAs by powerful men to silence their accusers. In breaking her silence, Mayorga hoped to tell her side of the story and explain what a devastating effect that night in Las Vegas had on her life. In the aftermath, she suffered "post-traumatic stress disorder and major depression," her lawyers said, which "rendered her incompetent to participate in negotiations of a non-disclosure agreement."

The Football Leaks documents purported to show exchanges between Ronaldo and his legal team in which he answered a questionnaire about his encounter with Mayorga. In it, he recognized that he had proceeded violently and against her will. Ronaldo's international team of lawyers, private investigators, and crisis managers, led by the celebrity attorney David Chesnoff, said that the documents obtained by Football Leaks were fabricated.

On social media, every new development in the case was met with legions of fans who were suddenly experts on Nevada state law—people who were quick to dismiss the real trauma suffered by a woman they'd never met. The allegations were covered widely, all over the world, and yet remained strangely dissociated from the mainstream discussion of Ronaldo on the field. He countered them with repeated denials and confidence that, if he waited long enough, the issue would fade away in European soccer's onto-the-next-thing environment. The story struggled to regain much traction when investigators reopened the case and issued a warrant for a DNA sample from Ronaldo, only to find that they had no way to compel him to provide one from across the Atlantic.

In July 2019, Clark County announced that it was declining to prosecute the case. "Based upon a review of the information provided at this time," the district attorney's office said, "the allegations of sexual assault against Cristiano Ronaldo cannot be proven beyond a reasonable doubt."

Mayorga did, however, press ahead with a civil suit in federal court, where the burden of proof is simply "a preponderance of the evidence" rather than the criminal standard of "beyond a reasonable doubt." In mid-2022, the civil matter was dismissed by a US district court judge.

LIONEL MESSI'S LEGAL troubles were strictly of a fiscal nature.

With his financial life organized by his father and a cabal of hand-picked advisers from Spain to South America, he happily ignored anything that didn't happen within the white lines of a football pitch. He had his goals, his house, his dog, his children, and his partner Antonela, whom he'd known since childhood. For Messi, happiness stemmed from simplicity. It's possible that he never once laid eyes on a tax return.

Those filings, however, became a major problem for him in 2013, when Messi and his father Jorge were also caught in Spain's sweep through footballers' taxes and accused of defrauding the state of €4.1 million between 2007 and 2009. Like Ronaldo, the specific concern was around sponsorship payments that were kept offshore and away from the prying eyes of the Spanish tax authority. (Messi hadn't profited from the Beckham Law because he'd been a Spanish citizen since the days when Barcelona was trying to ward off interest from other clubs.)

The matter wound up going to trial. Messi appeared in court in Gava, his local district outside of Barcelona, in June 2016, days before he was due to leave for the Copa America Centenario. The strategy there was always to plead ignorance. Leo couldn't possibly know about his tax situation, he argued, because it was Jorge's job. And Jorge couldn't know because taxes were the lawyers' and accountants' jobs. The banking structure for all of Messi's nonsalary payments—set up since his earliest endorsements and involving alleged shell companies in Uruguay and Belize—had been explained to Jorge, who nodded along. But now, in court, he insisted that he hadn't fully understood it.

"It's all Chinese to me," he told the judge.

As for Leo, he was kept on a strictly need-to-know basis regarding his own finances: "I didn't think it was necessary to inform him of everything," Jorge said.

Messi stuck to that line of defense too, even under fierce questioning from prosecutors.

"So you signed all contracts with your eyes shut?" they asked.

"I signed them because I trust my father, and it never entered my head that he would try to cheat me," Leo said.

The court didn't buy it. The following month it slapped Leo with a 21-month suspended prison sentence and a 2.1-million-euro fine. Jorge also received a 21-month suspended jail sentence (reduced to 15 after appeal) and a fine of €1.6 million. Neither was ever likely to see the inside of a prison cell, since Spain tends not to jail people convicted of tax fraud when sentenced to less than two years. All Leo wanted to do was pay the penalty and get out of there.

Messi's and Ronaldo's issues with tax authorities were not unique. Around that time, the Spanish state was cracking down on all high earners in sports. News that yet another soccer person was being investigated came with alarming regularity. José Mourinho, another Mendes client, was also charged with and convicted of tax fraud, as were several of Messi's teammates at Barcelona. Even outside Spain, authorities knew that footballers' accounts could prove to be happy hunting grounds. In Brazil, Neymar ran afoul of the state and, in March 2016, was ordered to pay a fine of $52 million.

Barça knew little about what happened to players' salaries once it paid them, and even less about their outside income. But when it came to supporting its one superstar, the club was smart enough to defend Messi unconditionally. So after the ruling, it didn't think twice about publishing a statement about the Spanish Tax Office right next to the latest photos from training on Barcelona's official website.

"The club, in agreement with the government prosecution service, considers that the player, who has corrected his position with the Spanish Tax Office, is in no way criminally responsible," Barça wrote.

That didn't do much to improve Messi's mood. Feeling like the court had gone out of its way to make an example of him, he was so disgusted that for the first time in his life he gave serious thought to leaving Barcelona. The problem was that the list of clubs a player like Messi could move to was shorter than Messi himself.

Anywhere else in Spain was out, since there was really only one other club on his level, and Messi couldn't possibly entertain a move to Ronaldo's Real Madrid—even though Florentino Pérez had dreamed about it since forever. Germany was out too, given Messi's distaste for cold weather. That left just a handful of major leagues for him to find a team fantastically wealthy enough to afford his salary. And none, at that point, was richer than the English Premier League.

Chelsea had weighed up a move for Messi in 2013, when Adidas was rumored to have offered at least half of the transfer fee to pry its poster boy out of Barcelona's Nike shirt and into an Adidas-sponsored blue jersey. The trouble was that Messi despised the London club, dating back to his early clashes with it in the Champions League. "There are players here who hate Chelsea more than Real Madrid," he told the *News of the World* in 2006. "I never thought I would hear myself say that."

But another English team had recently and suddenly made itself very attractive. Not only did nouveau riche Manchester City have plenty of cash, but in the summer of 2016 it had hired the man who knew Messi's game like no one else on the planet—Pep Guardiola. So Messi made the call. What would be required to leave Camp Nou, reconnect with Pep, and take another shot at winning the Champions League? City was prepared to listen.

"He felt persecuted in Spain," says a person with direct knowledge of the conversation. "He didn't think he was getting fairly treated."

For most of Messi's life, the idea of approaching a club like Manchester City would have seemed entirely preposterous. That's because for most of Manchester City's life, it wasn't a club that attracted world-class playmakers from South America—blue-collar Englishmen with names like Colin and Mike were more its speed. But City now had a few things going for it that Messi had never considered before his expensive spin through a Spanish courtroom. The club boasted a clear plan, boundless ambition, and a manager who knew precisely how to build around a brilliant number 10.

Though Messi was sincere about leaving, the deal never materalized. There simply wasn't a way for City to find a way around the release fee that Barcelona had set for him, which now exceeded half a billion dollars. Messi would have to remain a Spanish taxpayer.

As for City, well, the club figured it could live without him.

THAT MANCHESTER CITY, a club playing in England's second tier as recently as 2002, could realistically consider Messi's price tag—and then decide it didn't need him after all—says a lot about the other force that was reshaping soccer in the 2010s: massive investment from oil-rich Gulf states.

Few had seen it coming during the sport's first financial boom in the 1990s. Usually owned and operated by local wealthy businessmen, clubs were transformed by the explosion of television rights payments driven by the English Premier League. More than a century into the sport's existence, investors were seeing it in a new light: club ownership might actually be a moneymaking business. Cash poured in from around the world as globally minded money men sought to trade in soccer's universal popularity.

But after the initial wave of foreign ownership in the 2000s—led by people such as Chelsea's Russian oligarch Roman Abramovich and the billionaire Glazer family at Manchester United—a new set of investors arrived seeking something else entirely. They didn't care about profits, because to sovereign wealth funds from the Gulf, the soccer economy was a drop in a barrel of oil. These unfathomably rich investors were looking to buy a platform.

The United Arab Emirates arrived first. A country that was only founded in 1971 as an association of kingdoms in the desert, the UAE spent its first three decades of existence tending to its domestic growth. A nation previously known for pearl-diving was now going to build around energy and real estate. Qatar, also established in 1971 and flush with natural gas, followed close behind. These young countries laid out their projects in documents they each called "Vision 2030," which served as roadmaps to development, sustainability, and, above all, global influence.

"Qatar is at a crossroads," the Qatari government wrote in 2008. "The country's abundant wealth creates previously undreamt of opportunities and formidable challenges."

Top of the list of challenges was crafting an image. Not only were these countries relatively small, but they were seen as suspicious of the West, dependent on oil, and unburdened by adherence to human rights. The sports world, never known to turn down a dollar, became the ideal partner. The UAE and Qatar each developed strategies that played out on three fronts: sponsorship, event hosting, and eventually full ownership of institutions.

Sponsorship was the easy part. These Gulf states could throw money around and create name recognition without having to develop any infrastructure. Getting into the hosting game was a little more complicated, but that happened quickly too. Early on, Dubai and Abu Dhabi focused on golf weekends and tennis tournaments, horse racing and Formula One. Stars came from all over—and luxury brands came from Switzerland—to promote their products in one of the most affluent markets on the planet. And what were those markets acquiring beyond watches, shoes, and handbags? A veneer of worldliness and sophistication.

But there was nothing quite like piggybacking on the reach of soccer. In 2008, a group led by the brother of the ruler of Abu Dhabi acquired a distressed asset called Manchester City in one of the most audacious image-building exercises sports has ever seen. With enough money, they were going to build a winner. And by hiring the brightest people, they were going to make that winner too big to fail. For millions of people, this slick, smart glory machine would be the first point of contact with Abu Dhabi. The strategy was made explicit from the get-go.

"If you're developing your nation and you're looking to be on a global stage," former City chief executive Garry Cook told the buyers from the Gulf, "we are your proxy brand for the nation."

It was during the 2008 takeover that City made its very first overture to Messi—although as flirtations go, it was less locking eyes across a crowded dance floor and more spilling coffee all over someone on the bus. City's bid of €50 million on transfer deadline day that summer was entirely an accident caused by a misunderstanding in City's London office. Barcelona barely acknowledged receipt of the fax.

Manchester City's spending would soon become considerably sharper. In its efforts to work from a clean slate and make every aspect of the club "best in class," City realized it needed a new football culture. The trauma of being Manchester United's kid brother for decades had saddled it with an inferiority complex. So it looked around Europe and simply chose who it wanted to be. In the early days, when City's biggest competition for a Champions League place was Aston Villa, it raided the club for its best players. Then, as its stature grew, it set its sights a little higher. City aimed to import some of Arsenal's easy-on-the-eye style by literally importing Arsenal players. But by 2012, with Premier League and Champions League contention in the cards, there was only one club anyone else in Europe wanted to emulate. If City was going to be "best in class," as its executives always said, it had to be like Barcelona.

Manchester City systematically hired executives away from Catalonia to revamp itself from top to bottom in an environment where money was no object. Ferran Soriano, who had brought Barça's finances back from the brink in the 2000s, became chief executive. Txiki Begiristain, a former member of Cruyff's Dream Team and onetime sporting director, joined City in a general manager role. And in 2016, the Barcelona conversion culminated with the arrival of Guardiola, whose team would go on to break the Premier League's records for points and goals scored in a season. In the space of a decade, Abu Dhabi's money and Barcelona's smarts had built an era-defining team in England. City, which hadn't won a top-tier championship since 1968—before the UAE was a country—claimed five Premier League titles in nine years.

"They have petrol *and* ideas," Arsenal manager Arsène Wenger said, paraphrasing a former French finance minister. "So that makes it even more efficient."

Man City wasn't the only state-funded club turning its league upside down. Across the English Channel, Qatar was doing the same with Paris Saint-Germain. In 2011, one year after its stunning coup to secure the hosting rights to the 2022 World Cup, the country acquired the only major club in the French capital. Neither would have happened without the blessing of one of Qatar's favorite business allies: the French government.

PSG had, until that point, been something of an underachiever for a club of its size. Founded in 1970, it had won only two French league championships and one European title, the now-defunct Cup Winners' Cup. The takeover was orchestrated by Qatar Sports Investments, an arm of the country's sovereign wealth fund. From the start, the new owners made it clear that their sole sporting objective was to win the Champions League. "Dream bigger," they said in the club's new motto.

Signing 37-year-olds wasn't necessarily the quickest way to do that. But when PSG picked up an aging David Beckham in 2013, the purpose was much more about renting some of his stardust. Though he made fewer than a dozen appearances, he instantly broadened the club's exposure. The player who gave the club both brand value and goals was Zlatan Ibrahimović, who came to embody the early Qatari years in Paris. But even he couldn't carry the club past a Champions League quarterfinal. By 2017, the club understood that to truly dream bigger it needed to spend bigger too.

Following an embarrassment against Barcelona in Europe, which saw PSG throw away a 4–0 first-leg lead by losing the second leg 6–1, the emir of Qatar himself took action. He signed off on two of the biggest transfers in soccer history. In August 2017, PSG sent Barcelona a single wire transfer of €222 million to break up Messi's MSN and sign Neymar. The Brazilian was ready to step out of Leo's shadow, and Paris told him it had a stage waiting just for him. Later that month, PSG also struck a deal that would make the French striker Kylian Mbappé the most expensive teenager of all time for a fee that reached €180 million.

It was the kind of money that none of Europe's old guard had ever spent in accumulating soccer's generational wealth. But Qatar and Abu

Dhabi were condensing decades of European extravagance into a few summers. PSG had its poster boys. Manchester City had its imported culture. And the Gulf-backed clubs were out to remake soccer's world order.

Messi and Ronaldo would fit into those plans eventually. Other ties between the two players and the Gulf, however, had been firmly in place for years. In the eyes of the richest consumers of sports on the planet, their image—and occasionally their presence—was yet another luxury brand to be collected.

That's how Lionel Messi, the working-class kid from Rosario, Argentina, wound up among the close personal friends of one Turki Al-Sheikh, a royal adviser and chief political enforcer of Saudi Arabia's Crown Prince Mohammed bin Salman.

It's safe to say that Sheikh is one of the planet's more flamboyant soccer fans. Entirely on a whim, he once bought a soccer team in Egypt and renamed it Pyramids FC, until he got bored and sold it after a year. He then moved into the second division of Spanish soccer, where he acquired the club from Almeria on the south coast and proceeded to plow in more than €50 million of his personal wealth over his first two years of ownership. Part of that investment was spent on buying a dozen Audis that the club raffled off to drive season-ticket sales. The campaign drew so much attention that even Messi wanted to know more about it—despite having his own Audi hookup back in Barcelona.

More than dabbling in ownership, Sheikh was an example of an uber-rich soccer fan with the money and contacts to collect visits from soccer superstars the way other supporters collected sticker books. He routinely flew world-class managers to Saudi for private coaching seminars, from José Mourinho to Zinedine Zidane, to the mastermind of Argentina's 1978 World Cup triumph, César Luis Menotti. In his role as chairman of the Saudi Entertainment Authority, Sheikh in 2018 organized international exhibition matches between Brazil and Argentina in Jeddah, then again in 2019 in the Saudi capital. Messi scored the Riyadh game's only goal.

What seemed to excite Sheikh most about his friendship with Messi, however, were the personalized greetings from Leo. The two men are on a first-name basis, though Sheikh speaks no Spanish and Messi has only limited English. Yet any time Sheikh receives a video, like on his birthday, he shares it immediately with his millions of Instagram followers. "Turki . . . Feliz cumple."

In case there was any doubt, Sheikh was not on Team Cristiano. No matter—Ronaldo cultivated his own coterie of powerful admirers in the Gulf, namely, the government of the United Arab Emirates. In 2020, the country issued Ronaldo with what it called a UAE Gold Card. And while it sounds like a fancy credit card, it might actually have been more valuable: the piece of plastic was in fact a 10-year visa for the country, reserved for "specialized talents" that granted Ronaldo residency privileges and the right to own local businesses.

That visa comes in handy for Ronaldo's annual trip to the Dubai Globe Soccer Awards, another glitzy awards show with no history and invented from whole cloth by a marketing agency. The award gave itself some legitimacy by partnering with the European Club Association, which acts as a lobby to protect the interests of clubs rather than leagues, and with the European Football Agents Association. Precisely who is pulling the strings of the operation is unclear, but the Dubai Globe Soccer Awards clearly have some healthy admiration for Jorge Mendes and his number-one client. Since their inception in 2010, Ronaldo has won player of the year on six occasions (compared to one for Messi) and Mendes was named agent of the year in 9 of the first 10 editions. In 2020, Ronaldo and Mendes were also dubbed player and agent of the century, respectively, 80 years ahead of schedule. The early announcement didn't bother anyone—Dubai had anointed them and soccer's greats were playing along. All the awards served to do was underscore precisely who was now calling the shots in the global game.

Florentino Pérez had never paid much attention to Manchester City or Paris Saint-Germain.

He was the president of Real Madrid, after all, officially recognized as the best football club of the 20th century. Manchester City wasn't even the best club of the 20th century *from Manchester*. And Paris Saint-Germain had only been around for 30 percent of it.

But as Pérez sat at his desk in the fall of 2017, reflecting on the state of his club and his presidency, his thoughts were consumed by the two state-owned clubs, or *clubes estado*, and the threat they posed to the empire he had spent nearly 20 years and €1.5 billion building up.

Outwardly, it looked like business as usual for Real Madrid. In June, the club had celebrated another Champions League triumph—its second title in a row and third in four years—behind two goals from Ronaldo. But Pérez knew that underneath, the entire edifice was shaking. The massive and barely regulated influx of petro-wealth had warped the entire business of professional soccer. In a few days, he would address the socios at Real's annual general meeting. They needed to hear some home truths.

"We invented a model where it was shown that having the best players increases income," Pérez's address began. "[But] it is getting more and more difficult to compete on a level playing field."

Pérez was still incensed that PSG had scuppered a move to make Mbappé his next Galácticos. That July, he'd been convinced that Madrid had a €180 million deal with AS Monaco to sign the French teenager, whose bedroom walls were once plastered with pictures of Ronaldo in action for Real. Pérez knew that Mbappé was desperate to play along-side his idol at the Bernabéu. And Monaco liked the idea of not selling its best player to a domestic rival in Paris. The agreement was so close that *MARCA* had published the full details of Mbappé's six-year contract, which was due to pay him €7 million per season after tax. That is, until Wilfried Mbappé, the player's father, informed Real that PSG was offering €14 million, double the amount they had agreed on. Months later, Pérez was still fuming.

PSG's move summed up everything that was wrong with the state-backed clubs. It wasn't the absurd spending on player transfers that irked Pérez, a man who had broken the world transfer record five times. It was the way they were driving up salaries, handing out superstar wages to merely serviceable players. Maintaining a roster of all-stars was hard enough when it was only Real Madrid and Barcelona shopping at the top end of the market. Now it was becoming next to impossible. Real and Barça didn't merely have the largest annual wage bills in soccer: they were spending almost €100 million more per season on payroll than anyone else.

Pérez had felt the shift personally. Over the past year, he had signed off on new contracts and pay rises for a dozen first-team players, including his entire forward line of Ronaldo, Gareth Bale, and Karim Benzema; key midfielders Toni Kroos, Luka Modrić, Lucas Vázquez, and Isco; and both starting fullbacks. In the space of 12 months, the club's wage bill had jumped by 32 percent—and it still wasn't over. Despite agreeing to a new deal with Ronaldo the previous fall, Jorge Mendes was already bugging Pérez about another new contract and another pay rise. In light of the tax business, Mendes wanted Ronaldo, who took home €24 million net, to have parity with Messi and Neymar, both of whom earned more than €35 million net.

Ronaldo, for his part, was doing plenty to help his case. At the age of 33, he was now a half step slower than in his prime, but his mind was quicker than ever, allowing him to change matches with moments of brilliance—like his gravity-defying, mind-bending, back-breaking bicycle kick against Juventus in the 2017–2018 Champions League quarterfinals.

On that April night in Turin, Ronaldo sized up a cross from Dani Carvajal and decided his best chance to score from it was to launch himself into the air upside down. For this feat of improvised gymnastics, every part of his body needed to work in careful coordination—all from a starting position with his back to goal. Launching off his right foot, he twisted in midair to bring both legs to shoulder height, spreading his arms to stabilize his upper body. Nearly every defender around him had come to a complete standstill, because *mamma mia!*—Cristiano was actually trying this. His left leg swung first, then his right, in perfect instinctive harmony to meet the ball's trajectory some seven and a half feet off the ground. Ronaldo connected.

Juventus goalkeeper Gianluigi Buffon could only watch the shot fly past him to his left and shake his head in disbelief. Real manager Zine-dine Zidane, a man who knew a thing or two about stunning Champions League goals, brought his hand to his head and gasped in awe at what he'd just witnessed. Even the Juventus fans, still unaware that Ronaldo would one day play for them, felt compelled to salute this goal by their opponent with a standing ovation.

"Cristiano made up the second goal," Juve defender Andrea Barzagli said afterward. "It's a PlayStation goal."

"Are You Not Entertained!?!?!" tweeted LeBron James. "That's just not even fair. Nasty!!"

Former Real defender Álvaro Arbeloa said that this went far beyond mere entertainment. With one giant leap, Cristiano had done something extraterrestrial. "Ronaldo can now leave Earth and play with Martians," he wrote. "He has done everything here."

Back on Planet Real Madrid, Pérez was unswayed in his determination to keep costs under control. He held firm, even as the calls from Mendes grew more frequent and more fractious. The situation was quickly becoming untenable. Even when PSG and Manchester City weren't mentioned explicitly in contract negotiations, they were always lurking in the background. The state-owned clubs weren't just pricing him out of players on the open market, they were starting to price him out of players already on the team. The virtuous circle he had conceived all those years earlier was in danger of coming apart.

"If we do not renew the contracts of Modrić, Kroos, etc., they will go somewhere else," Pérez told the socios, each of whom knew exactly which "somewhere else" he was talking about. "And without those players who win the Champions League, we will lose sponsors."

Real Madrid had already lost its place as the world's richest club to Manchester United in 2017, the first time in 11 years that its revenues weren't the highest in soccer. Man United had also taken away ownership of the world transfer record at that time by signing French midfielder Paul Pogba for €105 million the previous summer, ending an unbroken 16-year period during which the record had resided at the Bernabéu. And Pérez's grand ambitions for redeveloping the club's stadium had also veered off course following the collapse of a €400 million naming-rights deal with Abu Dhabi's International Petroleum Investment Company, whose chief executive happened to be Khaldoon Al-Mubarak, also the chairman of Manchester City.

(One thing Florentino Pérez was not in danger of losing anytime soon was the Real Madrid presidency. Through a series of incremental changes to the club's bylaws, he had steadily raised the barriers to entry for would-be candidates, who now needed to have been socios for at least 20 years and be able to personally guarantee more than €75 million to a Spanish bank, among other requirements. It's entirely possible that the only person on the planet who could fulfill each of the requirements is Florentino Pérez himself. Consequently, he has not faced a single challenger in any election since 2009.)

As Pérez looked ahead to the rest of the season and beyond, it became clear that something had to change. He had reshaped European soccer once before—it was time to do it again. For months now, a radical idea had been crystallizing in his mind, one that, if he could pull it off, would keep Real Madrid at the top of the soccer food chain where it belonged.

There would be pushback, of course. Pérez knew that the traditionalists would howl about commercialization and the soul of the game. He didn't care. Drastic times called for drastic measures. And if Pérez could just get the public to buy in, he knew this was the sort of bold reordering of the status quo that would herald a golden new era for Real Madrid Club de Futbol.

It was time to build a theme park.

ROLLER COASTERS AND bumper cars weren't exactly the off-season acquisitions the Bernabéu faithful had been hoping for. By early October, Barcelona was already five points clear in the Liga standings, and no new Galácticos had arrived since James Rodríguez in 2014.

But in Pérez's mind, a theme park and a Galácticos were no different. It was all part of the same overarching philosophy, the next logical step in his plan to transform Real Madrid from a mere soccer club into a global superbrand. He had put Real on top of the world by drawing marketing inspiration from Disney's *The Lion King*. Now Pérez was planning to keep the club there by building his own Space Mountain.

He had been toying with the idea of an amusement park for years. The club held internal discussions on the subject as far back as 2004, and more recently it had agreed to license the Real Madrid name to a luxury resort in the United Arab Emirates featuring a theme park, a club museum, and a marina in the shape of the Real crest—only to see the project fall apart owing to a lack of funding. The difference now was that this sort of bold innovation was no longer simply a wishful fantasy—it was a financial necessity. The only way for Real Madrid to keep pace with Manchester City and Paris Saint-Germain was by identifying new revenue streams.

Pérez was so bullish on the idea that he had even begun sketching out designs for individual rides, which would be named after legendary players from the club's history. Having seen the Ferrari World amusement park in Abu Dhabi, he had visions of dizzying descents and stunning loops that would evoke the ball's flight through the air from iconic goals, like Zinedine Zidane's volley in the 2002 Champions League final. He knew nothing about mechanical engineering, of course, and even less about the business of operating an amusement park. But to Florentino Pérez, those were minor issues. He knew people. And as it happened, he knew just the people to ask for advice on how to make his new project a success.

Pérez invited a group of former Disney executives, led by longtime CEO Michael Eisner, to join him in the boardroom of the Bernabéu to hear his pitch for RealMadridLand. "In our world, we are as big as Disney," he said proudly, according to one of the executives in the meeting. "Real Madrid must do things like this because we are the number-one club, and the only way we will remain there is by always being the first big innovator."

As Pérez proceeded to lay out his vision, the execs in attendance quickly understood that this was a bigger innovation than they had initially realized. Pérez's plan was not simply to build a Real Madrid theme park, but to construct a new headquarters for the club—a sprawl-

ing multipurpose training and entertainment complex that would house
an amusement park and a practice facility running from the under-7s
through to the first team. He even had designs for a special new attraction that would hold 90,000 people and never provide the same experience twice.

Pérez was going to build Real a new stadium and leave the Bernabéu
behind.

By the time Pérez finished speaking, Eisner and his advisers were
floored by the scale of this proposal. Building a theme park was a risky
undertaking at the best of times. Building a theme park, a training
ground, *and* a state-of-the-art stadium simultaneously seemed border-
line reckless. Sensing their concern, Pérez motioned toward the collection of silverware on display in the boardroom. Replicas of each of the
club's 12 Champions League trophies were arranged in two lines, either
side of a small silver circle sitting on a glass plinth that bore an inscrip-
tion officially recognizing Real Madrid as FIFA's best club of the 20th
century. "Everyone else is fighting for these trophies," Pérez said, waving toward the European Cups. Then he pointed at the smaller award
in the middle. "Real Madrid is fighting for this. We want the next one
of these."

Eisner's team was impressed by Pérez's confidence and clarity of
vision. They were less impressed by some of the fundamentals of his
proposal. They spent almost three months studying the plans before
reporting back to Pérez with a laundry list of worries, among them the
fact that the city of Madrid already had a Warner theme park that risked
eating into his potential audience. Lacking a plan to attract customers
for visits longer than one or two days, it was highly unlikely that the
theme park could break even, much less turn a profit.

Beyond the basics of theme park economics, they gently questioned
the wisdom of situating a public theme park at the headquarters of a
professional soccer team. Specifically, they saw a pitfall in Pérez's idea
that the theme park would lead directly to the training ground, allowing
visitors to take in a first-team practice session like it was Disney's Animal Kingdom. The American executives explained that it would give

members of the public unfettered access to the team's activities in training, potentially disclosing key information.

"If you have an upcoming match against Barça, you might not want people watching practice, because there could just as easily be a Barcelona fan recording the whole thing and figuring out your tactics," one of the executives said.

Pérez considered this point carefully, and then dismissed it. "People see all that stuff anyway," he said.

What ultimately doomed Real Madrid's theme park was something much more elemental than spies from Catalonia: money. Pérez had secured almost €1.4 billion in funding and had provisional agreements with the local government to occupy a 130-acre site near Madrid's airport that included part of the team's existing Valdebebas complex. Eisner's team felt both were far short of what was needed to pull off such a project. Though aerial shots of the site showed it was big enough to house a stadium, training ground, and theme park, that wasn't all that came with a project of this magnitude. Once you began accounting for the hotels and conference centers, you needed a plot of land closer to 250 acres. They also estimated the total cost of the project at roughly €2.5 billion, or 75 percent more than had been budgeted.

It was a price tag that even Florentino Pérez wasn't willing to meet. In the weeks that followed, the theme park project was quietly shelved while Real marched to the 2018 Champions League title. But the forces that had made a football club building a theme park seem like a reasonable idea weren't going anywhere.

His quest to unlock new money for soccer went on.

TEN

Mergers and Acquisitions

LIKE REAL MADRID, Barcelona also had a money problem: it was sitting on too much of it.

The €222 million that dropped into its accounts from Paris Saint-Germain for Neymar was a windfall like no soccer club had seen before. Barcelona president Josep Maria Bartomeu hadn't wanted to lose the Brazilian, but he knew that the sudden injection of cash presented him with a once-in-a-lifetime opportunity. With sound strategic planning and financial prudence, the club could bankroll a wholesale regeneration of Barcelona's squad, surround Messi with fresh, young talent, and set up Barcelona for a run of success that would stretch well into the next decade.

He also knew that no one bought jerseys with "strategic planning" or "financial prudence" on the back.

In the eyes of the socis, Bartomeu was the man who lost Neymar. And in soccer, there is only one surefire way for a club president to appease angry supporters. Bartomeu needed a marquee signing to parade in front of them, like a shiny trophy. In his quest to find one, Barça would burn cash like a teenager with a trust fund and a sneaker habit.

Over the 18 months that followed Neymar's exit, Barcelona embarked on a spending spree that ranks as perhaps the wildest and most reckless ever seen in professional soccer, a sport where wild and reckless spending is the only kind of spending. By the time it was over, Barça had blown more than $700 million in transfer fees, frittered away tens of millions more in wages, and effectively mortgaged the club's future for a collection of players who would never deliver the short-term gains they were signed for.

But the splurge wasn't solely an act of self-preservation. As much as Bartomeu felt the heat from the club's fans and from Real Madrid, the biggest reason he felt compelled to splash out was the smallest member of the Barcelona team. The mere presence of Messi was a mandate to go for broke every season.

When you have one of the greatest players of all time operating at the peak of his powers, there is simply no other way. There is no such thing as a rebuild or transition season, no buying players with one eye on the future. Winning right now was all that mattered. The hierarchy at Barcelona felt obliged to spend every last cent to surround Messi with the best team that money could buy while he was still in the prime of his career. Anything less would be taken as a crime against soccer. The awkward thing was that Messi's prime was now well into its second decade and showed no sign of coming to an end anytime soon.

Even as he entered his thirties, an age when most soccer players begin worrying about creaky knees, thinning hair, and unexpected feelings of mortality, Messi wasn't slowing down. In fact, in his 14th professional season, nearly a decade since he was first recognized as the world's best player, all indications suggested that he was getting even better.

The loss of Neymar and the arrival of a new coach, Ernesto Valverde, for the 2017–2018 season saw Messi move into a slightly deeper position in the middle of the field, behind Luis Suárez. Playing more centrally only made him more crucial to Barcelona's attack: he still scored all the goals, but now he created most of them too. Messi would finish the season with 47 goals and 21 assists, topping the Liga charts for most goals, assists, shots, chances created, successful dribbles, goals from outside the box, goals from inside the box, and goals from free kicks. His numbers at age 30 weren't merely good for most players—they were good for Lionel Messi.

He showed no hint of physical decline either. In fact, he was in the best shape of his life thanks to some tweaks to his eating habits. Messi, who once subsisted mainly on a diet of pizza, Pepsi, popcorn, and prime beef, began consulting a nutritionist after the 2014 World Cup. He lost nearly seven pounds after cutting out sugar, pasta, wheat, and white rice and became less susceptible to the nagging injuries that had blighted the early part of his career. From the 2009–2010 season on, no outfield player in La Liga had spent more minutes on the pitch.

All of which only added to the anxiety Bartomeu felt about the €222 million burning a hole in his pocket. Messi's remarkable longevity and sustained excellence meant there was no blueprint for Barcelona executives to follow. And there wasn't time to grow another generation of midfield wizards, the way Barça had done for Cruyff's team and later for the players inherited by Guardiola. In those days, the money wasn't available to spend anyway, so the club's transfer practices rarely became the focus. (One secret of the Guardiola years was that his signings from outside the Camp Nou system were often his most disappointing players.)

But now, a decade into his reign, Messi had completely changed the calculus for constructing a championship team.

Alex Ferguson once remarked that great squads come and go in four-year cycles, a period that reflects the length of a typical player's peak. As with everything else uttered by the former Manchester United manager, this instantly became part of the game's accepted wisdom. Yet Ferguson had never reckoned with a player like Messi, a one-man championship window that had now stayed wide open for nearly 15 years. Messi was there for the Guardiola cycle. He won a Champions League during the MSN cycle. Now he appeared ready to embark on a brand-new cycle, in which he pretty much did everything himself.

The way Bartomeu saw it, he was left with no choice. He said all the right things publicly, of course, promising to invest the Neymar fee "with prudence, rigor, and serenity." But privately, Barcelona's directors let it be known they were after immediate upgrades to bolster the third act of Messi's career. Three weeks before the 2017 summer transfer window closed, the scuttlebutt among agents, intermediaries, and rival executives was that Barcelona was looking to make a splash.

In soccer, spreading that kind of info around is less than ideal. Barcelona's brass would soon discover that there's nothing more costly in this business than wading into the transfer market when everyone knows you're ready to spend—the equivalent of strolling into a used-car dealership and handing the salesman your checkbook.

The directors at Borussia Dortmund saw them coming all the way from Germany.

In late August, Bartomeu traveled to a meeting with Dortmund executives to discuss a deal for a young French forward named Ousmane Dembélé. (Because this is European soccer, the negotiations between the German club and the Spanish champions took place in Monte Carlo.) Before the meeting, Barcelona had settled on a firm plan to land Dembélé, who had joined Dortmund a year earlier for just €15 million. Barça would agree to pay up to €80 million for the Frenchman, as reported by the *New York Times*. Anything more than that and they would walk away. Before they entered the meeting room, Bartomeu and his chief negotiator exchanged hugs, as if they were in the tunnel at Camp Nou.

Once inside, they received a nasty surprise. The Dortmund executives said they had a plane to catch. They had no time for small talk and no interest in negotiating. Dembélé would not be sold for any less than €162 million, they announced, a price that would make him the second-most expensive player in history at that time. Barcelona's resolve proved to be flimsier than a Spanish flan. In short order, Bartomeu agreed to pay almost the full amount, settling on a fee of €105 million up front, with another €42 million in bonuses. He simply didn't dare to return home empty-handed.

Just a few months later, Barcelona plunked down €160 million to sign the Brazilian playmaker Phillipe Coutinho from Liverpool. Again, Barça's executives seemed completely lost at the negotiating table, allowing Liverpool to haggle the fee up from an initial offer of just €81 million.

It took less than six months for Barcelona to burn through the entire Neymar windfall. It took only slightly longer to realize they had completely blown it. Less than half a year after Coutinho's arrival, the club was actively trying to sell him. And the only reason they weren't putting Dembélé back on the market was that he was constantly inactive. In the four and a half years after he joined Barcelona, the French forward made just 58 starts and missed 102 games because of injury or illness.

The Neymar money was gone, but the Neymar-shaped hole in Barcelona's lineup remained. So Barcelona did what any inveterate gambler does when they've been wiped out by a couple of bad hands. They borrowed some money and got back in the game. In July 2019, Barça took out a loan backed by future income to pay the €120 million release clause demanded by Atlético Madrid for the veteran French forward Antoine Griezmann. He also flopped.

The combined €427 million spent on Dembélé, Coutinho, and Griezmann accounted for only a portion of the hundreds of millions Barcelona squandered. But in many ways, overpaying on transfer fees was the least of its problems.

More troubling was what it said about the club's entire approach to the business of recruitment. Every team has its share of misfires in the transfer market. What was remarkable about Barcelona's string of busts is that everything about the players' profiles suggested they were bad bets to begin with. Coutinho was billed as a replacement for Andrés Iniesta, yet he was hopelessly miscast in Barcelona's pass-happy midfield, where he lacked both the skill to combine with Messi in tight spaces and the room to make the driving runs that were prized at Liverpool. Griezmann, who had thrived as the primary threat in a counterattacking side at Atlético Madrid, looked lost in a team that dominated possession and asked him to be the secondary threat behind Messi. Unsurprisingly for a club that burned through five sporting directors in the space of six years under Bartomeu, there was no sense of a coherent plan, no vision for how new signings would function. It wasn't bad luck, it was bad process.

That Barcelona's executives could burn through the biggest windfall in soccer history without making any significant improvements to the playing squad seems almost inconceivable—until you consider that the people running the football club did not conceive of their jobs as running a football club. When Bartomeu was elected president in 2014, his primary goal was not to lead Barcelona to glory on the pitch, but to make it the first club in history to break €1 billion in annual revenue. He opened offices in New York, Hong Kong, and Shanghai and crisscrossed the globe wooing blue-chip companies, all to leverage Barcelona's status as a global brand. The whole point of focusing on business off the pitch was to insulate Barcelona from results on the pitch. The upshot, as Barcelona tried to mimic the empire-building of Manchester United, was that wins and losses ceased to be the primary consideration at every level of the club. In that context, it's hardly surprising that the strategy for life after Neymar was bungled. It was practically inevitable. In fact, one specialist in spotting structural weakness saw the whole debacle coming a few years out. "Money is secondary," Johan Cruyff had said in 2015. "Before anything else, there should be principles, values. Barça has lost them."

Worst of all was the impact of this ill-conceived spree on the club's wage bill. The influx of so many big-money signings to a squad already stocked with pricey veterans pushed Barça's outlay on salaries to the limit. When Messi signed a new contract in November of 2017, making him the highest-paid player on the planet with a buyout clause of $835 million, it pushed it over the edge. Barça was now spending €487 million on wages each year, not merely the most in world soccer, but nearly €100 million more than anyone else. Salaries accounted for 70 percent of annual turnover, up from just 42 percent in 2012–2013, and the maximum allowed under UEFA rules.

"The spending spree was phenomenal," former Barcelona presidential candidate Victor Font would say later, "with most decisions being wrong decisions."

FLORENTINO PÉREZ KNEW all about phenomenal spending sprees and wrong decisions. It was called the Galácticos project. And as he considered what to do about his own aging superstar, it was the lessons of the early 2000s that weighed on his mind.

The longevity conundrum was by no means unique to Messi and Barcelona. Real Madrid had been grappling with the same awkward question for several years now. Ronaldo turned 33 in February 2018 and was still a phenomenal scorer, a talismanic presence, and, in his own mind at least, the handsomest man on the planet. But how much longer could it go on? And how much would Pérez spend to find out?

The contrast with Barcelona and Messi was that Real's strategy to squeeze the most out of Ronaldo's peak years was actually working. In May 2018, the club defeated Liverpool to win the Champions League, becoming the first team in the competition's modern history to lift the European Cup three seasons in a row. That unprecedented run, expensive as it may have been, was possible only because the three most important people at the club were all perfectly aligned in their objectives: Ronaldo, Florentino Pérez, and manager Zinedine Zidane knew that winning more Champions Leagues was the only way to burnish all of their legacies at once. While Messi was busy falling out with a string of Barcelona managers, Pérez in 2016 had tapped Zidane, the former Galácticos, to keep the Ronaldo show running, because only a former Galácticos could understand Ronaldo. Handling a talent like his required a combination of coddling, tactical deference, and knowing when to stay out of his way. Most importantly, Zidane's career list of sparkling achievements made him someone Ronaldo would listen to.

"You need the experience of having been a high-level player, because the psychology of players has changed so much," says former France manager Raymond Domenech, who coached Zidane to a World Cup final. "With their outsize egos, you need someone who is still able to put the lid back on."

Together, Zidane and Ronaldo agreed that the smartest approach was to rest Cristiano against certain weaker opponents and then turn him loose, all guns blazing, on the biggest European nights. In three consecutive seasons, Ronaldo was the Champions League's top scorer, averaging more than a goal per game. That was all the evidence Cristiano needed.

"The truth is—and don't ask me why," Ronaldo said at the time, "but the players feel more empathy for Zizou."

For his part, Pérez was still blowing money hand over fist. But Madrid's spending went mostly toward wages and trying to keep its starry lineup together. Unlike Barça, Pérez had quietly ceased spending huge sums on acquiring big-name stars. There had been no new Galácticos after Ronaldo's 30th birthday. When Real Madrid published its financial results in September 2017, it showed a cash balance of €178 million.

This was no coincidence. Ever since his first spell as Real Madrid president ended in a humiliating press conference announcing his own resignation, Pérez had vowed that he would not repeat the mistakes that doomed the Galácticos. He had allowed that project to run past its expiration date because he didn't have the stomach to tear it down and start again, to bid farewell to superstars who had brought so much excitement and *ilusión* to the Bernabéu. This time had to be different. He would not allow another project to slowly atrophy under his watch and on his payroll.

So Pérez came up with a novel solution to the longevity problem. In the summer of 2018, weeks after Ronaldo lifted his fourth Champions League trophy, and months after negotiations over a new contract had reached an impasse, Pérez arranged a meeting with Jorge Mendes. He wanted to deliver the news personally.

After 450 goals in 438 games, Cristiano Ronaldo was free to leave Real Madrid.

RONALDO'S SUBSEQUENT MOVE to Juventus wasn't so much a transfer as a merger.

On one side, Cristiano Ronaldo, Inc.: a multinational corporation with a global brand, high profitability, and one key man. On the other, Juventus FC, a 121-year-old company run by scions of the Fiat Chrysler empire and publicly traded on the stock exchange. Based in Turin, the club nicknamed "La Vecchia Signora" (The Old Lady) was by far the most successful in the country's long soccer history, the Yankees of the Italian game, right down to wearing stripes at home. Juve had racked up more than 30 championships and grown so powerful that it could essentially bend the league to its will, if not always legally. In 2006, the club was briefly booted out of the top tier following a sprawling bribery and match-fixing scandal popularly known as "Calciopoli." But the embarrassment of playing in the second division was only temporary. By the time Juventus turned its attention to Ronaldo in July 2018, the club had been firmly back on top for years. And under this new alliance of heavyweights, it was relocating Cristiano's operations as an athlete-slash–global pitchman to Turin on a four-year contract.

Rumored since early in the month, the news broke on July 10 and became the biggest story in sports. Never mind that a World Cup semifinal was being played in Saint Petersburg later that night. "He's called Cristiano Ronaldo and he's now officially a Bianconero!" the club said, immediately dwarfing France versus Belgium.

By July 18, Juve's share price had spiked 32 percent and increased its market capitalization to nearly €900 million. Ronaldo hadn't kicked a ball yet, but the tea leaves were encouraging: the enormous bet on Ronaldo might just work.

Juventus desperately needed it to, because it wasn't exactly sitting at the penny slots here. This was the biggest gamble in club history. Never before had it pushed so many chips onto just one player. The transfer fee to Real Madrid alone was €117 million, and Ronaldo's salary was €31 million a season, after tax. But Juve's real bill amounted to much more.

Between his gross pay and the amortization of the transfer fee over the life of the contract, the true cost of having Ronaldo in Italy would show up on the club's books at €86 million per year.

This being a corporate merger, Juve's due diligence looked a little different from the usual work it does in the lead-up to a signing. For one, you don't *scout* Cristiano Ronaldo. There's no need to sift through his game film like he's some prospect to know if he might eventually deliver for you. He's Cristiano—just look at the trophy list.

Still, the club was aware that it wasn't buying 2003 Ronaldo or 2009 Ronaldo, or even the 2016 vintage. Though he worked as hard as ever on maintaining his physique, Ronaldo was 34 years old. He'd be 38 by the time the contract was up. (Jorge Mendes had broached the possibility of a return to Manchester United that summer, only to be told that the English club was strictly focusing on younger talent.)

What Ronaldo might or might not achieve on the pitch, however, was only part of the equation. For the first time in its history, Juve made the call to sign him with input from its sporting and commercial teams. When both sides gave the green light, it took Juventus chairman Andrea Agnelli, the great-grandson of Fiat's founder, hopping on a jet to Greece to meet Ronaldo on vacation and push the deal over the line.

Juventus was investing in goals, maybe some titles, and above all, a slice of the global attention lavished on Cristiano every day of his life. At the moment he signed, Ronaldo counted 332 million followers across the main social media networks, more than six times as many as his new club. To Juventus, the exposure alone was worth paying for—CR7 was, in effect, a human retweet button.

On Instagram, Juventus went from 9.1 million followers in March to 16.1 million in September. And on Twitter, it added 5 percent to its follower total in the space of two months. Just as remarkable was what happened to Real Madrid's Twitter base: in the weeks after dealing away Ronaldo, it actually *lost* some 300,000 followers.

That was only the beginning. Juventus signed him counting on Ronaldo-driven uplift across all of its revenue streams, to put it in corporate-speak. During the secret negotiations—and long before the deal became public—the club discreetly bumped up the price of season tickets by 30 percent and sold all 29,300 of them. It also anticipated that its jersey sponsorship deals with Adidas and Jeep (part of the Agnelli-led Fiat Chrysler family) would finally achieve liftoff and help close the gap with soccer marketing's Big Three of Man United, Barça, and Real. While those clubs pulled in €156 million, €140 million, and €95 million a year, respectively, on the kit front, Italy's most successful club was languishing at €40 million.

A large part of that gap came down to the simple fact that Italian soccer had spent 20 years in decline. Despite being the world's most prestigious league in the 1980s and 1990s, Serie A had stagnated badly since then. In 2018, it was bringing in €1.4 billion a year from broadcasters, less than half of the Premier League's haul. Stars were flocking to England and Spain, where television money flowed more freely to clubs, which turned around and invested that cash in top talent, elite managers, and gleaming new arenas. Serie A, meanwhile, was operating with an inferior TV product and ancient stadiums, many of which hadn't seen a facelift since Italy hosted the 1990 World Cup. Juventus was one of the few to build a new venue from scratch, opening what became known as the Allianz Stadium in 2011.

The summer of 2018 was a time for optimism at the club. Juventus expected a bump in every facet of the business thanks to Ronaldo. Juve could shake down existing sponsors for more money by association with Cristiano. And it could comb the globe for new sponsors while cashing in on a share of his image rights, particularly in Asia. Surely, Serie A would see a bump in revenue too, as the world tuned in to watch Juventus the way it used to follow Real Madrid. And if Cristiano did what he was supposed to on the pitch, then there would be even more prize money flowing in from the Champions League. All told, Ronaldo would more than pay for himself inside the four years of his contract, as long as everything went to plan.

Ronaldo didn't take long to make an impression. The previous time he stepped into a new locker room, at Real, he was the most expensive player in the world and a recent Ballon d'Or winner, but he remained another mortal. No one was putting him among the greatest of all time just yet. At Juventus, he arrived as a fully formed history-maker. Ronaldo became the team's highest-paid, most successful player the moment he walked through the door.

He'd been around for so long that some of his new teammates had idolized him as preteens. Now he was still going strong. Ronaldo was the living legend, the elder statesman, and the jacked older guy who hung around the weight room correcting people's dead-lift technique.

"As a person, I'm competitive . . . this guy's *competitive*," says the American midfielder Wes McKennie, who grew up watching Ronaldo from Little Elm, Texas, and soon found himself under his wing. "I'm like, 'Well, if he's going to the gym, I've got to go to the gym now.'"

Football had spent nearly 20 years getting smarter and more detailed about performance since Ronaldo was sneaking into the Sporting Lisbon weight room. Players ate healthier, recovered better, and lasted longer at the top level than at any point in the game's history. Studies found that the average age of players participating in the Champions League increased from 24.9 in 1992 to 26.5 in 2017. Yet by soccer's new standards of physical excellence, no one took better care of themselves than Ronaldo.

After every match, Juventus gave players the option to get a massage right in the locker room. Cristiano never missed it. When they flew back from far-flung road games and stopped by the training center to pick up their cars, often after 2:00 a.m., Ronaldo stripped down to his jockey shorts for an ice bath.

His teammates thought he was a psychopath. They also wanted to be just like him.

"His drive, his mindset, his consistency, his dedication to his body is on a different level," McKennie says. "Just seeing him do his thing pushes you to be better."

What the rest of the Juventus squad watched up close was Ronaldo making a radical transformation to his game in his mid-thirties. Ronaldo 1.0 had been the tricky winger at Sporting Lisbon and Manchester United. The 2.0 upgrade turned him into the all-purpose, unstoppable attacking threat at Real Madrid. His next system update refashioned him into a pure goalscorer.

Most attackers' careers see them evolve backward on the field as they age and their legs let them down. They go from the pointy end of the attack to more creative roles that involve less running, closer to midfield. Ronaldo, defying all logic, went the other way. If he recognized privately that he couldn't move like he used to, in public he saw nothing but upside. The version of Ronaldo that left Madrid and arrived in Turin practically lived in the shadow of the goal frame.

"He's nearer to the box every time, and he's making better decisions," his former coach at Sporting, Leonel Pontes, said of the new Cristiano. "Before, he had more opportunities, but he made them for himself."

There would be none of that now. He all but stopped dribbling the way he used to and concentrated on his finishing, all those individual sessions with René Meulensteen at United still anchored in his memory. And as he shed the more running-intensive aspects of his game, his body allowed him to hone new weapons. Somehow, the six-foot-two Ronaldo (not enormous by soccer standards) turned himself into one of the greatest attacking headers of the ball who has ever lived. His combination of technical proficiency and a 30-inch vertical leap made him one of the rare athletes who could score off a corner kick and dunk a basketball if he wanted to. The gem in the collection was Ronaldo's goal against Sampdoria in December 2019, when he hung in the air and met the ball with his forehead some eight feet, five inches, off the ground. Even opposition manager Claudio Ranieri thought he'd just witnessed something out of Madison Square Garden. "Ronaldo scored in NBA style," he said. "He was up there for an hour and a half."

The question for Juventus was precisely how to deploy Cristiano's new array of weapons. Any attack built *with* Ronaldo needed to be built *for* Ronaldo. This was a problem that perplexed three different Juventus managers over three seasons, and none of them arrived at a clear solution. All they agreed on was that Ronaldo's playing time in domestic matches had to come down a little, much the way it had in his final two seasons in Spain. The man who had said as far back as the 2014 World Cup that he couldn't remember the last time he played without knee pain didn't need to appear in all 38 league matches anymore. The idea was to save his legs for the moments that mattered most in the Champions League.

If only it had worked. In Ronaldo's first two seasons in Italy, Juventus was knocked out of Europe in the quarterfinals and the round of

16, a source of existential angst to him. After lifting the trophy in three consecutive years, Ronaldo suddenly found himself with a lot of free evenings in late May.

MESSI WAS GETTING a little closer to the final, but his exits were some-how more traumatic. In 2018, two years after orchestrating Barcelona's *remontada* against PSG, he found himself on the other end of a stunning comeback in the quarterfinals against Roma. That result was stuck in his mind a year later when Barça flew to Liverpool with a 3–0 lead. Anything but the most crushing defeat would have put the club back in a Champions League final. Messi did his best to make the point in his pregame speech at Anfield.

"We can't waste this opportunity, okay?" he told his teammates, wearing the captain's armband. "We have to start strong. Remember, Rome was our fault. Nobody else's."

Barcelona did not start strong. In a game played at breakneck speed from the opening whistle, Messi's unhurried approach seemed at odds with the match unfolding around him. At his best, which is to say most of the time, this low-energy style could be devastating. Messi would pace the field like a predator stalking his prey, conserving energy until the moment to strike arrived. When it didn't work, though, all that strolling around only added to the sense that entire matches could pass him by. Which is exactly what happened at Anfield.

Over the course of 90 wild minutes in which Messi barely saw the ball, the 3–0 advantage turned into a 4–0 deficit. At the final whistle, Messi could only stare off into space. Back in the dressing room, he seethed in silence. "Leo was really screwed up after," Barça's Sergi Roberto said.

For the first time in six years—and only the fourth time since 2007—neither he nor Cristiano would appear in the final. Messi and Ronaldo were taking on a new role in their Champions League careers: at-home spectators.

"We are the only ones responsible for that match," Messi said days later. "We knew that the same thing as last year couldn't happen, but it did. I think the match we played was pitiful."

The humiliations were brutal, and yet Messi wasn't surprised. He knew that the quality around him had dropped. He could see it every day at training. Where was the next crop of Masia kids? Where were the boys who knew how to play Barcelona soccer? He thought back to the last time things felt good and the answer was obvious. The MSN team had been strong enough to blow away La Liga and dominate Europe. He needed to get the band back together.

In a WhatsApp group they'd kept since those days, Messi and Suárez invited Neymar back to Barça. How the club might orchestrate the return of the world's most expensive player wasn't Messi's problem. All he knew was that he needed someone of that quality and flair in the Barcelona attack.

As it happened, the timing couldn't have been better. Neymar, who was tearing up the weaker French league but failing to make a major impact in the Champions League, was more than receptive to the idea. In his first two seasons in Paris, he'd been injured right when the Champions League knockout stages began, and the club hadn't progressed past the quarterfinals. Then, in 2018–2019, the wheels truly started to come off when he slapped a spectator after losing the French Cup final and publicly criticized the team's young players. "The kids, they're a little lost," he told reporters. "They don't listen. The veterans give them advice and they talk back."

Neymar decided he wanted nothing else to do with them. Opening up the WhatsApp group chat, he told Messi he was in.

So just as he did in his failed attempt to reconnect with Ángel Di María, Messi let it be known to the Barça brass that he wanted his compadre back. Bartomeu, knowing better than to disagree, initiated the talks. But the reality of the situation, according to those inside the negotiations, was that Barça wasn't really buying and PSG wasn't really selling. Every official statement from Paris always included the phrase "at the right price," except Barcelona could never afford the number on the sticker. That July the club had already needed to borrow €35 million just to pay the €120 million for Griezmann.

The whole thing was an elaborate dance, choreographed for the benefit of Messi and Neymar. The players needed to believe that their clubs were doing their best.

Things progressed far enough that Neymar skipped the start of pre-season camp and Barcelona's sporting director, Eric Abidal, traveled to Paris thinking he had a chance to make a deal. Yet even by the figures thrown around in the French and Spanish sports press, the two sides remained tens of millions of euros apart. PSG was never going to re-coup enough of its €220 million to let Neymar go.

The 2019–2020 season only got uglier from there. Barcelona's Messi-dependencia continued even as Messi grew visibly miserable. Barça relinquished the Liga title to Real Madrid, which was proving it no longer needed Ronaldo to win. And in Europe, years of hubris and mis-management all came crashing down on a single night. In a Champions League quarterfinal against Bayern Munich—the most important game of its season—Barcelona lost 8–2. The club hadn't lost any match by six goals since 1951. Two Spanish newspapers, one Catalan and one Madrileño, ran the same gigantic headline: "Humillación Histórica." No translation necessary.

More telling than those headlines was the snapshot that leaked from the Barcelona locker room at halftime, when the score was already 4–1. Goalkeeper Marc-André ter Stegen leaned against a door frame, en-tirely shell-shocked. And by himself, Messi sat forlornly on the end of a bench, looking every bit the silent 12-year-old who'd arrived in Barce-lona two decades earlier.

The shame merely confirmed what Messi already knew: Barça was a shell of its former self. The crest was the same, and so were a few of the names, but the edifice had collapsed around him. Messi's mind was made up. When he looked at the club's leadership, he saw no one who he believed could put things back as they were.

MESSI HAD WARNED Bartomeu all season that he was ready to quit the club, but Bartomeu never quite believed it. He put off the conversation until the summer. Bartomeu thought he had played this game with Leo and Jorge before. *Leo is unhappy, etc., etc.* Experience told him that this was nothing a new contract with some fresh incentives couldn't fix.

Except Messi didn't want to hear any of it—especially not from Bartomeu. As far as Leo was concerned, Barça's problems started with the president himself, from the hollowed-out youth system to the misguided focus on marketing. "The truth is that there has been no project or anything for a long time," Messi would say later. "They juggle and plug holes as they go."

It seemed crazy to say, but Messi no longer wanted any part of it. What he was after was another Champions League trophy, not a reconstruction. Never before in his career had he gone five years without winning Europe's biggest prize, and the way Barça was playing, he could easily go another 5, or 10, or 20. The situation was unacceptable. In typical fashion, Messi poured his heart out as quietly as possible. He spent days ensconced in his home, mulling over his options with his father and his partner. He fired off text messages to friends and board members and whispered in the ears of confidants.

And when things got truly, irreversibly serious, Messi sent a fax.

This was the moment when everyone in soccer learned that official business in Spain is conducted through something called a *burofax*. It is the equivalent of a notarized letter, tantamount to a legal document. (And despite the name, it does not necessarily need to be delivered via technology from the 1980s.) The message he sent on August 24 was short. Now that the season was over, Messi wanted to exercise his contractual option to leave Barcelona.

"Hereby, and in accordance with the provisions of clause 3.1 of the contract dated November 25, 2017," it read, "I express my wish to terminate my employment contract as a professional footballer with effect from August 30, 2020."

The contract Messi was trying to break happened to be one of the most absurd documents in the whole world of sports. Signed in November 2017—and leaked by *El Mundo*—it did two things at once. On one hand, it quickly paid Messi the highest salary of any athlete anywhere. On the other, it slowly bled Barcelona dry. Over the course of four years, the agreement with its best-ever player put the club on the hook for some €555,237,619. For the same price, Barça could have bought six F-35 fighter jets from the US Air Force.

The breakdown was laid out in 30 pages of bewildering numbers that consisted of agreements for employment and for his image rights. His signing bonus alone, paid in two installments, was worth €98 million. Performance incentives were doled out a couple million at a time for achievements that ranged from appearing in 60 percent of Barça's matches to reaching the Champions League round of 16. A league title came with a €2.4 million bump. And for his loyalty, the club threw in a bonus of €66 million.

Secretly, a few inside Barcelona breathed a sigh of relief when the burofax arrived. No matter how good Messi was on the pitch, the club was being held hostage by a salary that accounted for nearly one-third of its entire wage bill. Every new dime into Barça seemed to go straight to its number 10. Bartomeu, of course, could never come out and say it. His official position was that Barcelona would fight to hold on to its star.

The news rocked the soccer world so violently that, for once, it wasn't quite sure how to react. Was this for real? Was Messi going to wear another team's jersey? Or was it just a ploy to extract more concessions from a board of directors that he hated? Was there even another club that could afford him?

Carles Puyol, the former Barcelona captain and self-appointed defender of the club's values, knew which side of the fence he fell on. "Respect and admiration, Leo," he tweeted. "All my support, friend." Asked about his son's future by a scrum of reporters, Jorge Messi was more evasive. He answered only that the situation was "difficult. Difficult."

Those who genuinely wished to keep Messi at Barcelona were rescued by an unlikely source: a global pandemic. Because soccer took a hiatus in the spring of 2020 as Covid-19 ripped through Europe, La Liga's calendar had stretched into July. Messi was convinced that his exit option was valid at the end of the season, no matter when that happened to fall. Instead, it came with an expiration date that had already passed.

Had the season ended on its regular date in May, he would have had all of June to weigh his future and punch out. The club would have been powerless to stop him. But as he and his lawyers noted in the burofax, a global pandemic amounted to force majeure and rendered the deadline invalid. Barcelona's attorneys insisted that the deadline very much still applied. So Messi was stuck unless some other club was prepared to stump up the money to pay his release clause. In 2020, that number had reached €700 million. The shocking part is not how much money it was—roughly the GDP of Samoa—but that a couple of clubs gave it serious thought. Front of the line again was Manchester City, according to a person familiar with City's thinking. The Abu Dhabi–backed club scrambled around trying to find a way to make the numbers work and bring Messi to the Premier League. But after days of searching, it couldn't figure out how to blow close to a billion dollars at once and not violate every breakeven rule in the book.

So if Messi was going to leave, he'd have to get the release clause scrapped. That meant going to court and arguing—fairly—that exceptional circumstances had rendered the expiration date on his option meaningless, making him a free agent. But Messi didn't have the stomach for a legal fight.

"I would never go to court against Barça because it is the club that I love, which gave me everything since I arrived," he said later. "It is the club of my life, I have made my life here. Barça gave me everything and I gave it everything. I know that it never crossed my mind to take Barça to court."

That left him no choice but to climb down. Messi was staying home.

ELEVEN

Super League Supernova

BY THE TIME Lionel Messi accepted that he wasn't leaving, the rest of the world had plenty of practice staying home as well.

In early 2020, a highly contagious new virus began to spread like wildfire around the world and, well, you know. The global Covid-19 pandemic brought life to a grinding standstill, infected tens of millions, and would cost the lives of millions around the world. In all facets of life, Covid-19 sparked a general reassessment as people, families, and businesses took stock now that human contact was forcibly limited. Professional sports, a trillion-dollar business built on live human contact, was no different. What was even the point of putting on live entertainment if no one could be there in person?

During the early days of the plague year, while sports shut down across Asia, matches continued in full stadiums all over Europe, turning into silent superspreader events. In northern Italy in February, a large chunk of the city of Bergamo crowded into cars and trains for Atalanta's Champions League match against Valencia in Milan. After Atalanta won, they returned and partied in the streets and bars of Bergamo deep into the night.

Within weeks, the city was the European epicenter of the virus. Yet soccer held out as long as it could into March 2020. Even in the week after the United States shut down its major sports, starting with the NBA, the Champions League pressed ahead with games. In the French capital, Paris Saint-Germain beat Borussia Dortmund and thousands of fans cheered them on from outside the Parc des Princes. In England, a full-stadium game between Liverpool and Atlético Madrid contributed to a massive spike in cases across Merseyside.

But soon soccer—a sport that plays through driving snow, extreme heat, and occasional outbreaks of hooliganism in the name of a television product—recognized that the show needed to stop completely.

It wasn't long after March 2020 that club owners started putting numbers on the damage. On top of the global health crisis came an economic crisis. With matchdays canceled, there were no more ticket sales, concessions, or visits to the souvenir shop. The relentless visibility of teams and sponsors stalled practically overnight. Except salaries to the playing squad kept coming due. Even when games resumed gingerly in May and June, under strict health protocols, they unfolded without anyone in the stands. They were playing soccer to fulfill contract requirements, not because a weird product delivered in virtual silence was a brilliant moneymaking idea. Whether or not they played, clubs braced for massive losses. In this world of spiraling player salaries, where Ronaldo and Messi had shown the way for more than a decade, there would have to be immediate belt-tightening.

Some tried, with mixed results, to convince their squads to accept pay cuts. Barcelona, where the absence of its normally huge ticket sales and visits to the club museum made the crisis particularly acute, was one of the few places where senior playing staff took temporary reductions in salary to be repaid at a later date. Elsewhere, players insisted there had to be another way, though few offered concrete solutions. Dozens of clubs put their nonsoccer staff on furlough—cleaners, security guards, and cafeteria workers. Arsenal, owned by a real estate magnate who married a Walmart heiress, cut some of that staff altogether and fired the man who wore the club mascot's eight-foot dinosaur suit.

The situation devolved so quickly that, by May, Premier League clubs expected to pay a rebate to broadcasters for lost airtime in the spring. Manchester United estimated the bill at £20 million.

In Spain, La Liga president Javier Tebas leapt into action. Cost controls and payroll limits had already been part of his platform for years—

he'd seen too many clubs spend their way into near-bankruptcy as they tried to follow the example of the big boys. He summoned club directors right away to come up with whatever measures were necessary to find help for his struggling teams.

"The most important aspect of this is that we protect our future," Tebas said in April 2020. "What we're working towards here is to save the future of football."

That future looked less rosy by the month. Within a year, most of it spent almost entirely behind closed doors, Tebas assessed the total damage to Spanish soccer to be €2 billion. The only real solution, he knew, was finding a way to reinject some cash into the game.

Florentino Pérez, for perhaps the first time in recorded history, happened to agree with Tebas. The clubs did need money, fast. Even though Real had scraped together a €313,000 profit in 2020, he could see that the rockiest times lay ahead. In the space of 18 months, he had sold the world's most marketable athlete and kicked off a massive renovation of the Bernabéu shortly before the pandemic struck.

Unlike Tebas, however, Pérez wasn't all that interested in drumming up cash for the other 19 Liga clubs. Real Madrid's focus was, as ever, on Real Madrid exceptionalism. "We all know we'll have to travel a long path full of obstacles, facing up to this adversity," Pérez told his club's general assembly. "But we're a unique club, one that never gives in, the one that's won 23 European Cups—13 in football and 10 in basketball."

Being that unique club meant leading the way on new ideas, before anyone else had a chance to think of them.

"Football must adapt to these new times," Pérez went on. "Real Madrid will be at the forefront as it always has been," he said. "Reforming football cannot wait, and we have to get down to it as soon as possible. The biggest clubs in Europe have millions of fans spread across the world. We have the responsibility to fight for this change."

Pérez had a very specific idea in mind—and it didn't involve adding more basketball trophies. The superclubs of Europe that had been on the receiving end of some discreet phone calls from him knew exactly what he was referring to. So did a Madrid-based American financier named John Hahn and a fund called Key Capital Partners, which had a long-running relationship with Pérez's construction firm. The message was always the same. This pandemic was a crisis, Pérez told them, but it was also the ideal moment to light the fuse on a soccer revolution he'd been fantasizing about for years—at least since his whole theme park scheme fell apart.

This time he was proposing a European Super League.

CONTRARY TO WHAT he might have you believe, the concept of a Super League did not spring forth from the immaculate mind of Florentino Pérez. The concept had in fact been bouncing around European soccer for decades.

As far back as 1987, another powerful club chairman, the media magnate and future Italian prime minister Silvio Berlusconi, declared that the European Cup was ancient and obsolete. He wanted his AC Milan to play a larger round-robin league instead of a knockout tournament, featuring more games for television and greater guarantees that heavyweights would meet heavyweights. Five years of debate and compromise turned Berlusconi's idea into the modern Champions League, which launched in 1992 featuring both a group stage and knockout rounds.

But it wasn't long before Ajax, Barcelona, Bayern Munich, and Manchester United agreed that the new Champions League format wasn't radical enough. Backed by an Italian media company, they explored ways to start a 36-team Super League that would look a lot like the National Football League—which made perfect sense, since the founders of the Premier League had also been inspired by the glamour, pizazz, and turnover of the NFL, whose 32 team owners were all in business with each other. The European clubs were looking to create their own cartel.

For soccer investors looking across the Atlantic, the concept of a closed shop involving only elite clubs seemed attractive enough—as long as you were one of those elite clubs. You had more command over the schedule, could charge more money for broadcast and commercial rights, and could legitimately promise nothing but barn burners featuring the most famous teams on the planet. More importantly, a closed shop solved the problem that ate away at every investor who'd arrived in European soccer during its 20th-century wave of foreign acquisitions. It boiled down to two words: guaranteed income.

No one who bought a soccer team hoping to run it as a legitimate, profitable business was ever completely able to digest the risk that performance on the pitch could create eight-figure swings on the balance sheet. Missing out on the Champions League, for instance, might easily blow a $50 million hole in the following year's finances. (This became a particular problem in the English Premier League, where six rich clubs found themselves competing for just four Champions League berths every season.) And relegation, remote as the possibility was for most rich clubs, created something much worse than a $50 million hole—it meant financial oblivion.

In a way, it's the problem the International Champions Cup was trying to solve. With a packed schedule of exhibition matches, the summers in North America were a proto-Super League. All that was missing were live stakes. That's why Relevent Sports, the company behind the ICC, launched legal action in 2019 against US Soccer and FIFA for the right to organize official games—it had hoped to begin with a La Liga match featuring Barcelona in Miami before pulling the plug.

But while none of the Super League concepts of the 1980s, 1990s, or 2000s ever got off the ground, the concept evolved into something much more useful—and more powerful. For the wealthiest teams, the threat of the Super League became a permanent bargaining chip.

Whenever they needed to extract concessions from anyone around them—whether it was the 14 clubs outside the so-called Big Six in England or the powers that ran the game at FIFA and UEFA—they wielded the Super League plan as a weapon. Why, they asked, should FIFA or UEFA have monopolies on organizing major competitions? Didn't they need the clubs more than the clubs needed them? The clubs, after all, were the ones delivering the superstars. And in a few places—namely, wherever Ronaldo or Messi happened to be playing—the superstars had come to define those clubs.

Simmering in the background of all this was a larger battle for control of the global soccer calendar. In the same spirit as those trying to engineer more Messi versus Ronaldo confrontations on the pitch, FIFA and UEFA were locked in a bitter feud to add more events and marquee games and to grab an ever-larger share of the public's attention. While UEFA sought to expand the Champions League, FIFA was toying with the idea of a lavish Club World Cup, which would have brought together 24 of the top clubs on the planet for a self-contained tournament backed by whichever tycoon, billionaire, or petro-state made the highest bid.

What these projects all had in common was a need for Europe's bluebloods to buy in. In 2021, the bluebloods simply decided they were better off organizing this thing themselves.

The plan they concocted was for the European Super League to feature 15 permanent members plus a rotating cast of five qualifiers. But in the weeks leading up to the announcement, the group hit a snag. It failed to convince the likes of Paris Saint-Germain, Bayern Munich, and Borussia Dortmund to hop on board, at which point the group decided that 12 was enough to push the button. Surely others would follow once they saw how lucrative and popular the Super League could be. The organizers had already secured a $4 billion line of credit from JPMorgan.

The 12 clubs in question were the good and great of European soccer history: AC Milan, Arsenal, Atlético Madrid, Chelsea, Barcelona, Internazionale, Juventus, Liverpool, Manchester City, Manchester United, Real Madrid, and Tottenham Hotspur—all Champions League winners or commercial powerhouses, or both. Their owners were a collection of American billionaires, Spanish business aristocrats, a Chinese retail tycoon, a British currency trader, an Emirati royal, and one Russian oligarch. This motley group had come together with the sole conviction that European soccer's existing system was broken and if they didn't look after their own business interests, no one else would. Each club had been promised an "infrastructure loan" of around $350 million as a welcome bonus.

"This is going to be spectacularly difficult," an adviser told them in the final days before the Super League's unveiling in April 2021. "Are you sure you want to do this now?"

Riled up by Pérez, Andrea Agnelli from Juventus, and Joan Laporta—who had just won an election to replace Bartomeu for a new term at Barcelona—the clubs didn't flinch. At least not until they screwed up the timing. On a spring Sunday afternoon, word that something was brewing leaked to the *Times of London*. Within a few hours, it was clear that the Super League plan had moved from idle threat to this-is-happening-right-now.

What came next was one of the swiftest, most chaotic reactions soccer has ever seen. In short, all hell broke loose.

Fans went up in arms, openly denouncing their own clubs and vowing to cancel season tickets. Uninvited clubs freaked out, worried that a Super League would irreparably cut into the revenues of domestic leagues and damage any team left out in the cold. UEFA, in a joint statement with the English, Italian, and Spanish leagues, condemned the ESL as a "cynical project . . . that is founded on the self-interest of a few clubs at a time."

The Super League organizers, meanwhile, were practically invisible. They waited until nearly midnight that Sunday to publish an initial press release that confirmed everyone's worst fears. Yes, the 12 clubs would be permanent members of this thing, all committed for a term of 23 years. And yes, they would start as early as 2022 if possible. They were formally rejecting the Champions League in favor of a larger round-robin format that would culminate in an eight-team playoff at the end of every season. This was a momentous shift in soccer history all because, the organizers said, "The formation of the Super League comes at a time when the global pandemic has accelerated the instability in the existing European football economic model."

That much was true. The problem was that the 12 rebel clubs were addressing that instability only for themselves. No one bought the Super League's arguments for trickle-down economics in soccer—there was simply no way that Real Madrid and Barcelona earning more money in the ESL could help the likes of Deportivo.

The Super League organizers had always been prepared to weather some flak. The executives were experienced enough to know that soccer outrage tends to burn hot and flame out quickly. If they could hold on through that first barrage, including the assault from UEFA, then the Super League might survive. "They knew what they were walking into," one insider says.

What caught them off guard wasn't so much the level of opprobrium as the source. On Monday, the rage in England grew so fierce that even UK prime minister Boris Johnson bumbled into the conversation. He accused the rebel clubs of throwing themselves a private party, defiling Britain's cultural heritage, and he vowed to "drop a legislative bomb to stop it." In Madrid, organizers hadn't been prepared for an actual sovereign government to step in. Frustration with the United Kingdom was palpable. As one key actor behind the Super League put it, "Boris Johnson is not normal."

Yet for 24 hours following their initial announcement, the organizers didn't say anything else on the record. When they did, they conveyed their message via the most unexpected vector: after midnight, on low-budget television, and exclusively in Spanish.

The man they chose to deliver it was Florentino Pérez. He appeared that Monday night on a television show called *El Chiringuito de Jugones*, which translates loosely as "The Players' Beach Bar." The show has all the gravitas of sports talk radio crossed with *Wheel of Fortune*. This being a Spanish football program, it spends most of its airtime, five nights a week, from midnight to 2:45 a.m., shouting about the only two topics that matter: Barcelona and Real Madrid. There are flashing lights, goofy sound effects, and many, many outrageous opinions. The outrageous opinions are, in fact, the whole point of the show. And Pérez played along with his own hot take to justify his seismic breakaway.

"No one has interest in the Champions League until the quarterfinals," he said. "What generates the most interest? Let the greats play. We're doing our best for the sport. The Champions League has lost its attraction. We have created the Super League to save football."

Pérez would be even more forthright later.

"There are games that nobody watches," he said. "The truth is, I struggle to watch them. In Spain, in England, in Italy. Somebody has to give us another format, to earn more money. Without earning more money, this will all die."

By Tuesday, the Super League was on life support. The blowback from officials turned into fan protests on the streets. In West London, with Chelsea due to play a home game that evening, supporters rallied outside Stamford Bridge to condemn the naked greed of their own club. Four hundred miles away in Manchester, executives at City had also taken notice of the firestorm and began to get cold feet. The club had been the last one to join the group, and now it was thinking about being the first one out.

The project had no chance of succeeding without a perfectly united front and perfectly aligned incentives. In the space of 48 hours, it became clear that the Super League had neither. Almost simultaneously, Man City and Chelsea initiated formal proceedings to back out. And it was no coincidence that the two clubs least committed to the whole enterprise were also those that needed money the least. The mega-wealthy owners of Chelsea and City were in the soccer business in large part as an exercise in image management, not to generate a profit. "I have many much less risky ways of making money than this," Roman Abramovich told the BBC after acquiring Chelsea in 2003. Turning their own fans against them was the last thing they wanted to do.

One by one, the other Premier League clubs arrived at the same conclusion. They were the Super League members least desperate for cash since the Premier League had proven the most pandemic-proof, at least compared to those in Spain and Italy. If Real and Barcelona felt that only the Super League could rescue them, the English clubs realized that they didn't really need it. Truth be told, the Premier League already *was* a kind of Super League: broadcasters paid astronomical sums for its television rights, any one of six clubs could realistically dream of winning the title, and the quality of the product was higher than anywhere else in the world.

That Tuesday night the Super League was all but dead. On Wednesday morning, the apologies began from the English club owners. "I'm sorry, and I alone am responsible for the unnecessary negativity brought forward over the past couple of days," Liverpool's John W. Henry said, in something resembling a hostage video. "I hope you'll understand that even when we make mistakes, we're trying to work in your club's best interests."

Even JPMorgan expressed its contrition for simply lending money to the Super League, conduct far less heinous than many of the actions that the bank had paid out massive settlements to resolve in the previous decade.

"We clearly misjudged how this deal would be viewed by the wider football community and how it might impact them in the future," a spokesman for the bank said. "We will learn from this."

The players, meanwhile, made no bones about calling out their employers. "We don't like it and we don't want it to happen," read the note posted by the entire Liverpool squad. On the WhatsApp thread of Premier League captains, a group of men who normally spend their weekends kicking the stuffing out of each other, they all agreed that what some of their employers were doing was plain wrong. They'd never had much cause to think about owners, or club turnover, or Florentino Pérez, but this was going too far.

"We could not comprehend how these people could do this to our game," Burnley captain Ben Mee wrote. "Footballers play for the fans, not people in boardrooms. . . . Pérez sounds like someone who is a little bit desperate to earn his money for a club in a lot of debt."

Yet while fans and players made themselves heard for the good of the game in a battle for soccer's soul, one pair of voices went missing. Through the thick of the Super League uproar, the two most important figures of their generation remained silent.

Or at least nearly silent. Messi and Ronaldo remained active on social media with important and current messages for their combined half-billion followers. On April 19, the day after Super League Announcement Day, Cristiano wanted everyone to know that he'd had a good day at practice, so he shared a photo of himself flexing in his under-wear—10.4 million likes on Instagram. The next day Messi broke his silence too—to advertise a pair of Adidas cleats with a photo of himself lacing them up. The caption wasn't quite the powerful message the soccer world was hoping for from one of the greatest of all time in this moment of existential uncertainty.

"New boots," Messi wrote in Spanish. "[Fire emoji]"

THE SUPER LEAGUE was in tatters, but three clubs refused to give up the ghost.

In May, Barcelona, Real Madrid, and Juventus issued a joint state-ment insisting they were still committed to the breakaway league, de-crying UEFA's "monopoly over European football," and accusing the organization of applying illegal and "intolerable" pressure on the three clubs to back down.

It was no coincidence that these were the same three clubs that had spent a fortune to own a piece of the Messi-Ronaldo era and were now badly overdrawn. Juve lost €210 million in 2020–2021, the third-highest figure in Europe—Barça's losses of €481 million topped the charts. For more than a decade, the three clubs had been engaged in an arms race, splashing outlandish sums on players they could scarcely afford in a bid to remain atop a global soccer market being reshaped by a rapid influx of billions of dollars of sovereign-wealth petro-cash. Even as their reve-nues kept climbing, helping to cover the shortfalls and overpays, there was a growing sense that some of the world's most storied clubs were on the edge of a financial abyss. One wrong move—an unlucky injury, a sudden run of mediocre form, one bad season—could bring the entire debt-laden structure crashing down.

Which is exactly what happened. The pandemic slashed their reve-nues, squelched the value of their players, and left a giant gaping crater in the middle of their balance sheets. The Super League was supposed to be their "Get Out of Jail Free" card. Now the escape plan had gone up in smoke too.

No one had invested more hope in the Super League than Florentino

Pérez. But at least he knew he would survive the reckoning. He had rewritten Real Madrid's presidential bylaws to be certain of it. Juventus chairman Andrea Agnelli was insulated from the fallout too, mostly by virtue of his last name. At Barcelona, however, Joan Laporta was left holding the bag. He had been elected as president on a promise to reverse the mismanagement of the Bartomeu years and clean up the financial mess left behind. Post–Super League, his quick fix was gone.

To make matters worse, the full extent of the financial ruin was becoming clearer with each passing week. The club's debts stood at €1.2 billion. Even before the pandemic, Barcelona's business model had looked unsustainable. Now it looked like a raging tire fire. An audit by Deloitte found that when Laporta took over in March 2020, what had been a nearly $5 billion business, and one of the richest, most celebrated clubs in the world's most popular sport, was technically bankrupt.

As usual, when confronted with a major threat to the club's way of doing business, the first consideration of Barcelona's president was attending to the happiness of his most important employee. Messi's contract was due to expire in June 2021 and Laporta promised fans that he would renew his deal at Camp Nou. The club would figure out how to pay for it later.

"The most important thing," Laporta told the *Wall Street Journal* in 2021, "is that Messi feels loved."

For most of the past year, that was definitely not how Messi felt. He had reluctantly agreed to stay at Barça in the summer of 2020, only to see the club reward his loyalty by offloading his best friend on the team. Luis Suárez was not only Messi's favorite strike partner on the pitch but also his next-door neighbor in Castelldefels. Their families spent Sunday lunches and vacations together. Their sons were teammates on the Barça under-8s.

So when Barcelona informed Suárez that he was surplus to requirements and promptly sold him to Atlético Madrid, a direct title rival in Spain, Messi felt utterly betrayed. And at this point he was no longer shy about letting the Barça brass know exactly what he thought of them.

"You deserved a sendoff to match you," Messi wrote to Suárez in a rare Instagram statement. "One of the most important players in the club's history. Not to be kicked out like they did. But the truth is that at this point, I'm not surprised."

He was even less ecstatic when Barcelona was eliminated from the Champions League in a round-of-16 defeat by Paris Saint-Germain in March 2021. Barça's loss, by a score of 5–2 over two legs, came just 24 hours after Cristiano Ronaldo's Juventus crashed out against FC Porto. The twin defeats, meant that for the first time in 16 years, the tournament's quarterfinals would take place without either one of them.

All of that should have had Messi running for the hills. Except somehow Laporta's charm offensive was having its desired effect. Messi took Laporta's reelection in the spring of 2021 as a positive development, and his mood suddenly brightened. The 59-year-old lawyer was running the club when Messi broke into the team, appointed Pep Guardiola as manager, and oversaw the club's first treble in 2009. He knew what the good days looked like. Plus, Laporta had a clear understanding of the club's hierarchy. One of his first presidential acts upon his return to office was to take Messi out to lunch.

They agreed that when Messi's contract expired on July 1, when he'd become the most valuable free agent in soccer history, there was no need to panic. One year on from the burofax, he would stay at the only professional club he had ever known.

There was just one problem. The only professional club he had ever known could no longer afford to keep him.

Under La Liga rules, the club's spending on salaries was capped at 70 percent of its income. Back in the days when Barcelona was raking in €1 billion every season, those regulations hardly registered. Barça's annual wage bill had ballooned to more than €600 million before the pandemic. But now that Barcelona was losing half a billion euros a season, wage limits sounded a lot more menacing. Unless the club could cut its spending on salaries by €285 million before the start of 2021–2022, it would be unable to register its own players. To put that in context, consider that the NFL salary cap for 2021 amounted to roughly €154 million. Barcelona had to clear almost two full NFL rosters' worth of salary just to meet the limits.

Messi offered to do his bit and take a 50 percent pay cut to help reduce costs. But that barely made a dent. Quickly offloading some of its transfer busts would have helped, but in this climate the likes of Ousmane Dembélé and Phillipe Coutinho were toxic assets, too overpaid and overpriced to be moved. As the summer transfer window dragged on, with no major player sales to offset the losses, it became clear the numbers no longer added up. With Messi's new contract, Barcelona's wage bill amounted to 110 percent of revenue. Even without it, the wage bill was at 95 percent. There was no way to make it work without an exemption from La Liga. And La Liga was in no mood to give Barcelona special treatment.

Barely three months removed from the Super League debacle, La Liga president Javier Tebas was still smarting. Even under normal circumstances, this was not a man inclined to help Barcelona find any breathing room. Tebas had been the driving force behind the rules on sustainability that Barcelona was now directly violating. This situation was the precise scenario his laws were designed to prevent.

"The rules have to be complied with, we are not going to change them," Tebas said. "We are not going to make an ad-hoc rule for Messi."

Besides, Tebas had already offered Laporta an out that didn't require bending the rules. One month earlier, he'd met with the Barcelona president to outline a new plan to inject cash across La Liga that might have bailed out Barcelona. The proposal was for the league to consolidate its business interests into a joint venture among its 42 constituent clubs and sell a 10 percent stake to the private-equity group CVC Capital Partners in exchange for €2.7 billion. That money would then be divided among all La Liga teams and keep the immediate danger of widespread bankruptcies at bay.

Crucially, Tebas explained, the influx of cash would allow Barcelona to register Messi's contract. It seemed like the perfect solution at the perfect moment.

Not for the last time, Tebas would find that La Liga's interests didn't always align with those of its biggest clubs. Barcelona and Real Madrid both rejected the proposal, arguing that it would mortgage their TV rights for the next 50 years. Days after the league's executive committee approved the deal in a unanimous vote, Florentino Pérez announced that he was suing La Liga, Tebas, CVC Capital, and the fund's director.

At that point, Tebas wasn't offering any other lifeboats. This was Barcelona's problem now, and La Liga would wash its hands of it. Whether he liked it or not, Messi had to leave.

On August 5, a little after 7:30 p.m., Barcelona announced the departure of Lionel Messi, the greatest player ever to wear its colors, via a 102-word statement uploaded to its website. Ronaldo's exit from Real had overshadowed a World Cup semifinal. Messi's exit from Barça was turning into a Thursday evening news dump.

"Despite FC Barcelona and Lionel Messi having reached an agreement and the clear intention of both parties to sign a new contract today, this cannot happen because of financial and structural obstacles (Spanish La Liga regulations)," the statement read. "As a result of this situation, Messi shall not be staying on at FC Barcelona. Both parties deeply regret that the wishes of the player and the club will ultimately not be fulfilled."

Messi was as stunned as anyone. Even three days later, sobbing through a farewell press conference, he didn't seem ready to leave. Speaking before a room full of current and former teammates, Messi mumbled through a whole *paella* of emotions, from disbelief to melancholy to bitterness.

"I don't know what to say here. . . . I'm not ready for this," he said in the Argentine accent that even 20 years in Catalonia couldn't fully dislodge. "And honestly, last year, with all the nonsense with the burofax and everything, I was convinced I knew what I wanted to say, but this year, this year is not the same."

As he blew his nose, the abiding impression was that neither he nor Jorge Messi, nor their legal advisers, fully understood how it had come to this: the best player in Barcelona history was leaving the club that had signed him as a boy, not because he wanted to go, and not because the club wanted to lose him, but because La Liga's financial controls had crashed into Barcelona's financial incompetence, leaving everyone involved with no other choice. Messi no longer knew who to trust. He couldn't even say for sure whether Laporta had done all he could to keep him at the club. (Jorge Messi suggested as much when asked whether anyone was to blame: "Ask the club.")

"What I am clear about is that I did everything I could," Leo said, his tally of 672 goals in 778 Barcelona matches now consigned to history. "Laporta said we couldn't do it because of the league. I can tell you that I did all that I could to stay, because I wanted to stay."

It was too late for any of that now.

"I've had a lot of difficult moments, tough moments, a lot of defeats," he went on. "But at the end of the day, I'm not going back to train. I'm not going back to the pitch. I'm not going back. This is the end with this club."

By then, Jorge Messi was already on the phone to Paris Saint-Germain.

TWELVE

The Last Dance

I T WAS 10:00 P.M. in the heart of Champagne country when the soccer world's focus snapped to the substitutes' bench at the Stade de Reims football club. On a warm night in August, some 20,000 people had packed into the stadium to bear witness to this precise event, the moment when a Paris Saint-Germain assistant coach informed the official on the touchline that number 30 was coming into the game.

Never before in a century of French soccer had a substitution been more hotly anticipated. And somehow, the Stade Auguste-Delaune two hours from Paris was the place to see it. More than 200 journalists had applied for accreditation. Reims sold 4,000 tickets for the match so quickly that it had to halt sales to jack up the price—all for an ordinary league match where few beyond Reims or Paris truly cared about the outcome.

After 63 minutes, the match stopped and the visitors made their switch. There he was, under a shower of home-and-away applause: Barcelona's greatest-ever player jogging onto the field in a PSG jersey.

The sight of Lionel Messi in the wrong shirt would never cease to be confounding to anyone who had paid the slightest attention to soccer over the previous 15 years—not least because his transfer to Paris happened so fast. Joan Laporta had met with Jorge Messi on a Thursday and within hours Messi Sr. was in talks with PSG president Nasser Al-Khelaifi, the Qatari former tennis player who had risen to the head of Qatar Sports Investments, an arm of the country's sovereign wealth fund. By Friday, Khelaifi was calling the various departments around PSG and summoning them back from their vacations—it was mid-August in France, when the entire country goes to the beach. This deal was happening now.

The entire Qatari project at Paris Saint-Germain had been building to this moment for 10 years—or more when you consider the arc of relations between France and the very tiny, very rich emirate. Qatar started pouring money into the French economy in the mid 2000s by taking stakes in major French companies, investing in dozens of flashy real estate properties, from the Champs-Élysées to the Hôtel Martinez on the Croisette in Cannes, and becoming one of the country's largest military defense clients. Long before it spent tens of millions of euros to put Messi in Parisian colors, the Qatari state shelled out more than €15 billion on French fighter jets and Airbus airliners.

So after more than a decade of Qatar acquiring luxury properties and sophisticated weaponry, it seemed only fitting that Qatar's flagship soccer team should acquire its own luxury weapon.

There was much more to it than what Messi, now in his mid-thirties, could offer on the field. Since the takeover in 2011, PSG was run unlike any other club in the world. All at once, it was a group of sports teams, a lifestyle brand, an influencer collective, a fashion collaborator, an e-sports franchise, a content factory, and a celebrity destination. How many other sports teams had manufactured designer skateboards, limited-edition sneakers in partnership with the Rolling Stones, and a high-end fly-fishing tackle box targeted specifically at the Japanese market? Who else hosted runway shows and gallery openings? The strategy from the beginning was explicitly to put the Paris Saint-Germain logo on as many A-listers as possible and then to put those A-listers in the Parc des Princes VIP box. They rolled out the red carpet, now they needed to parade people across it. The club wanted Mick Jagger and Rihanna rubbing elbows with longtime PSG supporters like former French president Nicolas Sarkozy. The inspiration was the see-and-be-seen courtside seats at Madison Square Garden during New York Knicks games. Not by coincidence, PSG made sure to invite Spike Lee.

"We try to surprise people, to go where no one else has gone," says one PSG insider. "There is always football, but it's not the most important part."

With an eye forever turned toward fashion, influence, and social media, Paris Saint-Germain had become Hypebeast FC, brought to you by Nike's Air Jordan. This was the only soccer club in the world with the Jumpman right there on the shirt—all part of the plan to make everything exude hip and be immediately Instagrammable. PSG even hired a fashion photographer, rather than a sports shooter, to follow the players around for 80 days a year and make them look like pouty models and clotheshorses. The creative minds inside the club saw no reason why PSG couldn't be as iconic as those other French exports, Chanel, Dior, and Louis Vuitton.

Why? "Because Paris," says Fabien Allègre, the club's brand director. "Without being arrogant, all that's best in the world—in terms of architecture, design, food—is all done here."

From his earliest days at the club, Allègre's instruction from Khelaifi was to turn the PSG shirt into Europe's answer to the New York Yankee cap—a symbol of the city that didn't need to connect to the sport. It didn't matter if the people buying them cared about soccer or baseball. Here was a logo that could show up in rap videos, on catwalks, and around every departure lounge between Kennedy Airport and Charles de Gaulle.

The whole aesthetic had taken years to assemble and curate. Now it was time to point that noisy, colorful, eccentric hype machine at Messi.

As executives scrambled back to Paris the weekend before he was unveiled, they immediately set about crafting a new image for him and ringing sponsors to tell them the two-part news. One: Leo is coming. Two: the price of sponsorship is going up, by the way.

In one instance, PSG happened to be in talks with two companies bidding to be the club's cryptocurrency sponsor. The regular price for what the club calls a "category partner" was between €3 million and €6 million a season. Once it factored in the Messi tax, the price nearly doubled—and only one of those companies stuck around to pay it.

Khelaifi himself jumped on the phone with the club's most important partners to explain how much new value they were about to enjoy. Though PSG was signing Messi on a free transfer, it desperately needed to find ways to cover his gargantuan salary. (To the state of Qatar, $100 million was the equivalent of digging out change from between the couch cushions, but the club still had to pay him from soccer-related revenue streams to stay within European soccer's rules on breaking even.)

And all the while, PSG was trying to keep the deal a secret. Because once the news got out, this would make bold-faced headlines in every country on Earth.

"You've had Neymar," Messi's entourage warned the PSG brass. "But you'll see. This is something else."

After the papers were signed, everything about the experience became disorienting to Messi. Thousands made the trek to Le Bourget's private aircraft terminal on the outskirts of Paris just to catch a glimpse of him after his plane touched down. The last time so many people descended on Le Bourget to watch a plane land was in 1927, when Charles Lindbergh completed the first solo crossing of the Atlantic.

Messi's journey from Spain was considerably shorter, but he still felt a world away.

As he stepped off, he managed to give the crowds a wave in a new T-shirt that read ICI C'EST PARIS. This is Paris. The club whisked him around from the training ground to the stadium to his new home at the Royal Monceau hotel, a stone's throw from the Arc de Triomphe. Everywhere he went, he was trailed by a PSG video crew. The club produced 200 clips of him in the first week alone—Messi, they knew, was tremendous content. PSG's communications team put him up for 11 sit-down interviews on his first day, more than he'd probably agreed to in the previous decade.

The club did notice that even though Messi was speaking, he wasn't exactly saying much. Previous stars in Paris, like Beckham and Ibrahimović, had given fans a little more to go on. Putting it kindly, the club's communications department found Messi a bit shy, kind of a straight-edge. "He's the opposite of a Zlatan," says Allègre. As it turned out, people on social media didn't seem to care. In the space of four days, PSG added some 13 million followers across all platforms. People couldn't get enough Messi.

Orders for jerseys went through the roof, and PSG and Nike could hardly keep up. Because the club places shirt orders 18 to 24 months beforehand, they never know which players may or may not be on the roster to wear them two seasons down the road. At the club's megastore on the Champs-Élysées, customers queued for hours to buy Messi shirts only to be told they couldn't leave with more than two. Less than six months later, PSG had sold more merchandise than in the entire year preceding Messi's arrival.

The club did whatever it could to capitalize as widely as possible as quickly as possible, despite the pandemic. PSG understood, as few others did, that 34-year-old Messi had somehow been undermarketed his entire career, far below what might have been organized for him as a star in US sports. Pere Guardiola, Pep's brother and agent, had watched it unfold at Barcelona. As an acquaintance of the Catalan basketball player Pau Gasol, he knew how much bigger an athlete could be once they moved stateside and got their brand right.

"How to approach the media, how to approach commercially, how to act in front of the camera. . . . In Europe, these things, we're worse," he says. "This is changing, but in football, it was like, 'Hey, my business is on the field.'"

So PSG got to work. While Messi struggled with the French language and Parisian traffic, the club even made him look different. Off the back of Messi's signature, it added Christian Dior as a partner. Leo would trade his jean shorts for cashmere coats and tailored trousers. It all felt deeply unusual, considering where he'd just spent 20 years.

When Messi arrived at Barcelona as a preteen, he was taught about "mes que un club"—how a soccer team could represent a set of political ideals and a community. He'd never had cause to think about Catalan identity until he wore the senyera over his heart and felt the wrath of 90,000 Madridistas in the Bernabéu. He understood that when you played for Barcelona, you played for a city and its history.

PSG had always been up front about its lack of history. It knew that everyone else had about a century's head start, so it would have to manufacture something else—a lifestyle brand, an image, a buzz. The boy who once embodied all the childlike glee and purity of football—at least on the pitch—now played for a team where what happened in the games was almost incidental, a single pillar of a larger marketing strategy. In Paris in 2021, Messi learned the new meaning of "more than a club." The commercial-driven thinking that had so frustrated him when it took over Barcelona (all to cash in on him) was now the very essence of modern PSG. Messi had chosen to join a club that stood for little else.

All he could do was try to concentrate on the one task he felt he was being paid an absurd amount to do: winning the Champions League with PSG in the spring. The downside was that it meant playing for PSG in "Ligue 1, sponsored by Uber Eats," the rest of the year.

When people challenged Messi's all-time greatness by saying he hadn't won trophies in another country, the French league—scored by UEFA as the fifth best in Europe—was not what they had in mind. The drop-off from PSG to the other 19 teams was steep. Sure, Spanish soccer had plenty of minnows too, but any one of three clubs could hope to compete for the title each season. Before Messi arrived, PSG had won seven of the previous nine championships and six of the previous seven French cups. This was not a team that needed a Messi to improve. Where he could truly add value was limited to perhaps seven Champions League knockout matches a season.

"People say we've got a shitty league, that lots of things are wrong with it," Brest manager Michel Der Zakarian said after Messi landed in Ligue 1. "But if we can get a player like that here, it's extraordinary. It's going to be delicious."

Der Zakarian went as far as saying that the prospect even aroused him, in a sexual way.

That's how Reims-PSG became the hottest ticket in France once the club confirmed that it would be the site of Messi's debut in late August. And no one was more excited to be in the Stade Auguste-Delaune that night than the 11 guys across the pitch in Reims jerseys.

As soon as the final whistle brought his first PSG match to an end, Messi found himself surrounded by five opponents all hoping to trade jerseys with him, like the conclusion of a charity match. Reims goalkeeper Predrag Rajković was the boldest: he plucked his two-year-old son out of the stands and handed him to Messi for a picture. Messi obliged and the photo of the highest-paid athlete on the planet hugging a toddler he'd never met went instantly viral. Reims defender Andrew Gravillon, meanwhile, was one of several players to ask Messi for his shirt, hoping to grab it for his little brother. Messi told him he'd already promised it elsewhere. This would soon become a weekly ritual at stadiums all over France.

"We've been watching him on TV since we were kids," Gravillon said. "I tried anyway. Next time."

WHILE MESSI ADAPTED to his new surroundings in France, Ronaldo was trying to abandon his in Italy.

He had spent three years at Juventus, padding his numbers, filling his trophy case, and stretching the official list of Cristiano achievements. There were Serie A titles in his first two seasons, as well as a Coppa Italia and an Italian Super Cup. And there were goals, of course. Even in his autumn years, he still scored nearly every game—101 in 134 matches to be exact. But the statistics couldn't disguise the fact that his move to Italy had been a disappointment. He fell out with coaches who he felt weren't using his talent properly. His teammates, almost starstruck in his presence, expected such magic from him that they somehow played worse. Juve lacked any discernible style beyond "Get the ball to Cris," which worked some of the time but couldn't lift the team to the heights that the whole project was designed to reach. There was only one trophy Ronaldo really cared about, and it wasn't the Italian Super Cup.

In mid-July 2021, days before he was due to report for preseason training, Ronaldo instructed Jorge Mendes to reach out to potential suitors. He wanted a new challenge and a better shot at a sixth Champions League winner's medal, which really meant he wanted a new set of teammates.

The issue was that Messi soon made the small group of clubs that might consider signing Cristiano even smaller by moving to PSG and bolting the door behind him. Mendes sounded out the usual suspects—Real Madrid, Chelsea, Manchester City, Manchester United—but none seemed totally sold on a 36-year-old player whose powers were undeniably diminished and whose salary demands definitely weren't.

For Mendes, that represented only a minor inconvenience. He was a solutions man. He began working on a transfer anyway.

By the final week of the summer window, his efforts looked set to pay off. Mendes was in talks with Manchester City, which Cristiano saw as an ideal choice. If the sole objective was to win another Champions League, then he felt the world-beating setup at City, combined with the coaching of Pep Guardiola and one of the most expensively assembled squads on the planet, gave him the clearest chance. He could plug into the system as a classic center forward, with the sole job of finishing off the team's intricate attacking play. It was just the role Ronaldo 3.0 was looking for.

City was coming round to the idea too. One year after trying and failing to import Messi, it took a long hard look at bringing in Ronaldo. The club had splashed out $140 million earlier that summer on a midfielder named Jack Grealish, but Guardiola remained anxious to add more firepower to his side. Whatever else you could say about late-career Ronaldo, he would certainly deliver that.

The sticking point was the transfer fee. City was willing to cover Ronaldo's hefty wages, but insisted on taking him from Juventus for nothing. The Italian club wouldn't settle for anything less than €30 million, because that's how much it still owed Real Madrid for signing him three years earlier. Days before the transfer window closed, talks between the two clubs reached an impasse.

That was Mendes's cue to ring one of his favorite customers in the game, the club he had plied with all kinds of players for years, from the brilliant to the distinctly mediocre: Manchester United. *You know*, he told them, *Cris is talking to Manchester City.* This was not Mendes's most subtle gambit, but he knew exactly how to push buttons on the red side of Manchester. At Old Trafford, the prospect of Ronaldo scoring goals in a blue shirt for the club down the road became an immediate source of consternation. Within hours, the wheels were set in motion.

Ronaldo himself was unsure about a return to United. The club hadn't won the league since 2013, nor had it won a Champions League final since Cristiano left in 2009. It took the intervention of a few old friends. Portugal teammate Bruno Fernandes pitched him on the strength of the current squad, while his former United colleague and next-door neighbor Rio Ferdinand stayed on the phone until 3:00 a.m. reminding him that any stint at Man City would be a stain on his career. He couldn't turn his back on the club that had made him who he was and take the money from its crosstown rival.

"Do you really want that to be your legacy?" Ferdinand asked him.

By early the next morning, United was negotiating a fee with Juventus. The move, hatched entirely in the space of 24 hours, was presented as an emotional homecoming, and fans ate it up. United's message on Instagram announcing Ronaldo's return garnered 13 million likes right away, making it the most-liked post by any sports team in the platform's history. Four days later, Ronaldo made his second debut for United, 18 years after the first, in a home game against Newcastle. He scored twice.

Unlike Messi at PSG, there was nothing jarring about this move for Ronaldo. Messi *was* FC Barcelona, a human emblem of a 123-year-old institution, a mascot in blaugrana stripes. Seeing him anywhere else looked deeply weird. But Ronaldo was always different. He was a one-man Galácticos project who had always wanted to play for the biggest clubs in the biggest leagues. He was so important that Manchester United wanted him twice.

What was unsettling were the weeks and months that followed, when it became clear that Ronaldo had signed up to spend the downswing of his career toiling away for a floundering and oddly joyless version of the world's most popular club. More confusing was how adding an all-time great, a global megastar, and a club icon to a squad that had finished second in the Premier League had somehow made United worse. Ronaldo was suddenly criticized all the time for everything from his body language to his defensive output—as though his contribution should be measured by defensive pressures per 90 minutes and not for the goals and assists that comfortably made him United's top performer. He was pilloried for disrupting United's tactical system and not running around as much as his younger teammates. It all felt faintly disrespectful.

No one piled on Roger Federer when he meekly slumped out of Grand Slam tournaments in the first week at age 39. No one killed Tiger Woods for missing the cut at majors after his first comeback. But that's the fundamental difference between individual sports and the crucible of European soccer. If Federer loses, that concerns only Federer, not 10 other players around him. A tennis player's feel-good farewell tour doesn't cost anyone else points, trophies, or money. Ronaldo, for the first time in his life, was being treated like a liability.

In his old age, Cristiano had grown highly attuned to these signs of disrespect. After 20 years spent burnishing his legacy, he wasn't about to let a couple of subpar seasons at the tail end of his career detract from it. His rivalry with Messi was over, but Ronaldo wasn't done feuding, particularly on social media, where any perceived slight was met with a two-footed lunge.

Two social media editors at a German soccer news website named Transfermarkt learned that the hard way in March 2020—before Ronaldo's move to United but after the drumbeat of criticism had begun. Transfermarkt had published an innocuous-looking Instagram post ranking Jorge Mendes's clients by their transfer values. Cristiano saw this, didn't like the site's assessment, and reached out directly. Why, Ronaldo wanted to know, had they assigned him a nominal fee of only €75 million? The Transfermarkt editors replied that the fee reflected the fact that he was now 35 years old, though he remained by far the most valuable player in the world in his age group. Ronaldo didn't think much of their answer. "He sent some smileys," one of the editors said, "and then he blocked us."

Then there was the time Cristiano replied to a social media screed from an Instagram fan account arguing that the Portuguese was more deserving of the 2021 Ballon d'Or than Messi, who had just picked up the award, in a sequined tuxedo in Paris, for a record seventh time. "For Ronaldo to win this award he has to be 300% unquestionable. It's no use scoring the most beautiful goal of the year, being champion of everything for a club, top scorer of everything and scoring a hat-trick in the World Cup," @cr7.o_lendario wrote to its half-million followers. "With Messi, it's the opposite. He can have a low season, way down, they'll always find a way to favor him and give him the award. Steal. Dirt. Shame. It's just unfortunate."

Ronaldo admired the reasoning. "*Factos*," he wrote.

"The biggest ambition of my career is to leave my name written in golden letters in the history of world football," Ronaldo explained later.

But the *facto* of the matter was that in 2021 Messi had authored one of the greatest achievements of his career. It didn't happen in his forgettable last season at Barça, nor during his quiet start in France. This was finally the moment of glory he'd been waiting for in an Argentina shirt. That summer, Messi had won the Copa America.

After more than a decade of heartbreak in sky-blue and white, everything had come together for him during a Copa held in empty stadiums around Brazil. Messi scored a tournament-high four goals and was at the center of every good thing Argentina did for that one dreamy month. And when his side knocked off Brazil in the final, inside the same stadium where he had lost the 2014 World Cup, Messi's teammates dedicated the trophy to him. When the prize was officially his, he sank to his knees and soaked in the relief. The victory was as much personal exorcism as sporting triumph, before the strangeness of moving to Paris. "I needed to remove the thorn of being able to achieve something with the national team," he said.

On the scoreboard for major national team trophies, it was now Ronaldo 1, Messi 1. (Portugal's triumph in the 2019 UEFA Nations League doesn't quite rise to the same level, despite what the CR7 Museu will tell you.) Ronaldo's prospects of adding something quite as significant to his résumé at this stage looked far dimmer.

Less than a full season into his return, Manchester United was already out of the title race, the dressing room mood was mutinous, and Ronaldo felt deeply unhappy. The whole experience hit rock bottom when the club's interim manager, a cranky German named Ralf Rangnick, informed Ronaldo that he'd be leaving him out of United's marquee clash with Manchester City in March. Uninterested in sitting on the bench, Cristiano decamped to Portugal instead without the club's permission. Man United called it an injury. A seething Ronaldo kept quiet. For a moment, it was unclear whether he was ever coming back.

The timing of Ronaldo's huff looked even worse considering it came days before Messi was due to take center stage in the Champions League. PSG had stamped its authority on Real Madrid at home and was now heading to Spain to finish the job and book its spot in the quarterfinals. Even without a Barcelona shirt on his back, Messi was returning to the Bernabéu to torment Real once again. The final days of the Messi versus Ronaldo rivalry suddenly felt like they might be quite one-sided.

That is, until Real Madrid rescued its old teammate. In yet another Champions League humiliation for Messi (and for Paris Saint-Germain), the French champions coughed up a 2–0 lead on aggregate to lose 3–2. The most surprising part wasn't that PSG could choke so badly in Europe—they'd already made a habit of it—but that the player the club signed to cure its stage fright seemed powerless to make a difference. Worse than that, Messi was anonymous. The biggest match of his short time in Paris had passed him by entirely. The first returns on PSG's Messi experiment pointed to a very expensive failure.

Whether Ronaldo was inspired by his old rival's misfortune or the presence of seven-time Super Bowl winner Tom Brady in the crowd at Old Trafford—"Another GOAT," as Cristiano called him—something seemed to click again for him that weekend. Ronaldo returned from Portugal tanned, rested, and angry. He channeled all of his frustration into personally dismantling Tottenham Hotspur with a hat trick of goals that captured all three eras of his career. The strike from 25 yards was classic United Ronaldo. The tap-in was the pure finisher Cristiano from Real Madrid. And the header, for which he seemed to float in the air above the Tottenham penalty area, was straight out of his target-man phase at Juventus. Together, they added up to the 59th hat trick of his career and pushed him over the mark to become the top goalscorer of all time, according to FIFA—one more achievement for the list. The pendulum had swung again, this time back to CR7.

That seemed to happen a lot now. In their shared final chapter, anything Messi or Ronaldo did took on outsize significance. Their era was clearly coming to an end, and the only discussion that mattered was legacy. That's why, in the space of a few days, the Debate could tilt so violently one way or the other. Every high or low became magnified, a weekly referendum.

Back in their primes, when Messi and Ronaldo spent their time rewriting the history books, the rivalry shifted like tectonic plates. The weight of everything they'd achieved meant that the movement was almost imperceptible in real time, except for the odd earthquake—a Champions League trophy here, a Copa America there.

But by this stage of their careers, even individual games could cause an aftershock. Just days after Ronaldo's masterpiece at Old Trafford, he was back in Spain experiencing the same fate as Messi: making a limp exit from the Champions League against a Madrid-based club in the round of 16. For the second year in a row, neither one of them would be in the quarterfinals of the tournament they used to own.

Fans weren't shy about reminding them of their mortality. When Messi returned to the Parc des Princes after PSG's Spanish exit, he was booed every time he touched the ball. Even after his team scored, Messi hardly celebrated. *L'Equipe*, which had plastered French soccer's most spectacular signing across its front page for weeks over the summer, now asked the previously unthinkable question: "Was PSG Right to Sign Messi?" Privately, Messi began to suspect the answer was no. Not long after, the rumors about a return to Barcelona kicked off.

By then, Ronaldo had long since realized that going back to Manchester had been a mistake. In his 12 years away, United had barely evolved as a club, something he wasn't shy about telling anyone in football who would listen. Ronaldo had set the standard for conditioning and recovery, leaning on every innovation and every new development in the field of sports science to keep himself in peak physical shape. Looking around at United, why wasn't anyone else as committed as he was? Nothing had changed since he left. By that summer, Mendes was again shopping him around to any Champions League club that might listen.

Ronaldo was so disgusted with the situation at Old Trafford—and the temerity of those who dared to blame it on him—that he summed it up bluntly to one senior executive during a FIFA event.

"This," he said, "is a disaster."

So WHAT WERE Messi and Ronaldo still doing there?

They were out of their natural habitats. They'd made more money than any two footballers in the history of the game. And most of the time they were chasing numbers that were no longer within their reach. Their era was clearly ending. Yet one thing kept them around above all else—more than setting records, cashing checks, or winning another Champions League. They felt there was still unfinished business on the international stage. Messi and Ronaldo stuck around for one more unlikely shot at the major trophy they were both missing: the World Cup.

The irony is that as much as anyone, they were responsible for knocking the World Cup off the pinnacle of soccer. During their epoch of dominance, it became impossible to deny that the standard of the club game far outstripped the level of international football. The highest quality came from the superteams of Europe, which brought together more talent in more sophisticated tactical schemes. The measure of all-time greatness for a player wasn't determined by what he did over a five-week stretch every four years. The true markers were how many times he won the Champions League or the Ballon d'Or. And yet something about the World Cup was unshakable. Messi and Ronaldo both knew that lifting that trophy still conferred a piece of sports immortality, the same way it had deified Pelé and Maradona. More importantly, winning it might settle the rivalry once and for all.

Because whatever they might have you believe, the rivalry was in their heads. It had lived there for 15 years, though modern athletes are too smart, too media-savvy to openly acknowledge grudges anymore. So for most of their careers Messi and Ronaldo either talked around the issue or skirted it entirely. But in their twilight, free from the recurring psychodrama of Barcelona versus Real Madrid, they could at last acknowledge that it spurred them on—even if all these years later the two men had never sat down for a meal together.

"It was curious, because we shared the stage 15 years, me and him," Ronaldo said next to Messi at a 2019 UEFA awards show in Monaco. "I don't know if it's ever happened in football, the same two guys, on the same stage, all the time. It's not easy, as you know. And of course we have a good relationship. We've not had a dinner together yet, but I hope in the future."

A YouTube clip of that fleeting moment of humanity between two godheads of global soccer has been watched more than 50 million times.

"It was a duel that will last forever because it went on for many years, and it isn't easy to keep at your highest level for so long," Messi said. "Especially at those two clubs we were at, which were so demanding, in Madrid and Barça, the best in the world."

The truth was that beyond the cartoonish differences between them, Messi and Ronaldo had more in common as players and as people than anyone was willing to recognize. Fans were suckers for the narrative that characterized them as polar opposites: Messi the humble hero, the ultimate team player, the guy who shunned celebrity and wanted to be remembered as a decent guy instead of a soccer great; Ronaldo the preening superman, an advertising billboard in aviator shades, the guy who always seemed mildly annoyed by the presence of his teammates.

But there is no such thing as a low-maintenance genius. When Ronaldo returned to Manchester United and demanded his old shirt number back, the Premier League bent its own rules to give him the number 7 jersey even though it was already the property of Edinson Cavani and supposedly set in stone for the season. It was another example of Ronaldo as prima donna, particularly given that Messi had allowed Neymar to keep the number 10 in Paris. Except Messi could be impossible too. His insistence on wearing number 30 also required a change of rules. In France, 30 was supposed to be reserved for goalkeepers.

Contrary to public perception, Messi and Ronaldo are not antitheses, they're two expressions of the same merciless drive, a physical and psychological need for perfection. It's their similarities, not their differences, that make it so difficult to weigh up one without the other.

"In the grand scheme of history, you almost have to consider them as one player," says Pascal Ferré, who oversees the Ballon d'Or. "They dominated at the same time, with crazy stats and albeit different styles. . . . But when you've got one scoring on a Saturday and the other scoring twice on a Sunday, it can't be a coincidence."

Having been so intimately acquainted with genius on a weekly basis for more than a decade, soccer fans and executives took it almost for granted. No one had seen Pelé or Maradona play this much. And they convinced themselves that this would be the game all the time now, driven by a blockbuster rivalry between legends. Clubs were inured to it, to the point that they believed they could reproduce it if they just looked hard enough and spent enough money. And if you happened to find a Messi or a Ronaldo, you could sit back and watch the trophies pile up for a decade. Decisions were deliberately made all over Europe on this very premise. PSG blew half a billion dollars on Neymar and Mbappé; Manchester United shelled out $140 million to sign Paul Pogba in 2016; and Atlético Madrid spent $142 million on a 19-year-old Portuguese wunderkind named João Félix in 2019. It had become easy to forget that a gap yawned between being very, very good and being magical. Messi and Ronaldo were unicorns.

That didn't stop the soccer world from seeing them everywhere. A hot young prospect could be "The African Messi" or "The American Ronaldo." Pep Guardiola once called his favorite knee specialist "The Messi of Medicine." Indian sports fans routinely ask whether Virat Kohli is "the Cristiano Ronaldo of cricket." Their duopoly even shaped the way people viewed the future of the sport. Soccer looked for its next geniuses two at a time.

It was no longer enough to have one era-defining player—whoever it was needed a foil as well. If Messi versus Ronaldo defined the 2010s, fans prepared for Kylian Mbappé versus Erling Haaland to shape the 2020s, even though the decade opened with Messi winning his seventh Ballon d'Or. The dinosaurs weren't extinct just yet.

The clubs they left behind, though, were much closer to being fossilized.

In the post-Messi-Ronaldo wreckage, Real Madrid and Barcelona found themselves scrambling for money, clinging to the remains of the Super League, and wondering what the two legacies did for them beyond a roomful of trophies and the longest highlight reels in the world. Barcelona was carrying an unsustainable level of debt. Attendances dipped so dramatically that for some matches Camp Nou was now half-empty. And the club grew so desperate in recent years that it launched a television studio to produce children's programming about kids at La Masia. The last time things were this grim, in 2003, Barça had turned to homegrown boys from the academy to strengthen the first team. In 2022, it was making cartoons about them.

As for Real, there was only one Galácticos signing to replace Cristiano—the Belgian playmaker Eden Hazard. He joined for €100 million and injured himself right away. Over his first two seasons, Hazard played fewer than half of Real's league matches and let his fitness deteriorate, even when he was healthy. Ronaldo's were big shoes to fill—since his departure, every major acquisition at the club has been criticized for not working hard enough.

It wasn't hard to see that the Messi-Ronaldo era in Spain had come at a crippling cost: Real and Barça were returning to the fallow eras that came before the pair of shooting stars. Only this time the two behemoth clubs were even more fragile. Their bank accounts were now dwarfed by those under the control of petro-state sovereign wealth funds and global oligarchs. By playing an old-school game under old-school rules, Real and Barça could no longer win the arms race.

Luckily for them, there was a glimmer of hope in the transfer market. One rational thought seemed to spread through Europe right as Messi was leaving Spain: the price of transfers had climbed so high that no one could afford to pay both the fee and a massive salary. Something had to give, and the bubble at the very top of the market finally seemed to be bursting. The consequence, as Arsène Wenger put it, is that "you will see the best players move around for free."

That freedom of movement should not, however, be mistaken for player power. Messi and Ronaldo ushered in a new level of celebrity in soccer and changed the economics of the sport, but even when they looked like the engines of the show, it turned out they still lacked agency. Total player power in the Messi-Ronaldo era remained an illusion. And when push came to shove, Messi was forced to leave Barça against his will. Ronaldo, no longer a net asset, was left searching for any landing spot that would have him.

Which is how they wound up spending the closing chapters of their careers in the last places anyone expected them. Manchester, to Ronaldo, was the beginning of the story, not the end. And Paris, to Messi, was EuroDisney, a shopping trip—the place that his buddy Neymar had spent years trying to escape.

Here they were, cashing their paychecks and waiting patiently for the World Cup, creating commotions wherever they went and only ever doing impressions of their former selves on the pitch. People flocked to watch them because of who they were—who they had been—and what they represented. You went to see them live because of what they'd done before, not for what they had left to offer in the twilight of the gods. Though they were still sometimes able to produce individual magic that others could barely imagine, these moments were the exceptions rather than the rule. They were flashbacks.

The conversation around them now more often highlights their ineffectiveness by their own bewildering standards. The days of 60 goals a season are gone. The days of blowing past defenders, leaving them on the ground, and circling back to humiliate them all over again are now physical impossibilities.

The overriding sentiment that comes with watching Messi and Ronaldo today is one of pilgrimage, a chance to bask in their shining presence—and maybe capture it in an iPhone video—before it's too late.

EPILOGUE

Winter in the Desert

O N A WARM winter night, a decade in the making, they stepped onto the pitch to the crackle of fireworks for the matchup the soccer world had been waiting for. Here they were, together again, one last time. Lionel Messi and Cristiano Ronaldo, head-to-head, in the Gulf.

For 10 years, the simple idea of it had been mere fantasy. Now, in a way that no one could have predicted, it was actually happening. Or rather, something close to it was.

This showdown in the Gulf wasn't the World Cup final, and it wasn't in Qatar. Instead, this was the most bizarre, absurd, and unnecessary exhibition match either Messi or Ronaldo had ever been a part of. After all those duels in the cathedrals of European soccer—Old Trafford, Camp Nou, and the Bernabéu—the two most precious commodities in the modern game had landed where so many other priceless collectibles ended up in 2023: Saudi Arabia.

The venue was an aging pile on the edge of Riyadh known as King Fahd Stadium. And no one was quite sure what they were doing there. Messi's Paris Saint-Germain had only turned up in the middle of its regular season because its original friendly in the Kingdom was delayed for a year by a Covid outbreak. PSG's coach made no secret of his displeasure—the squad remained in the country for less than 24 hours.

Ronaldo's team, meanwhile, didn't even exist. For tonight, he represented a one-off combo of Al Nassr, the Saudi club he had just signed for, and Al Hilal, the team he'd just learned was now his hated rival. The whole situation felt as if the Yankees and Red Sox had teamed up for a one-time showdown against Mars.

Yet with barely a week's notice, the match had come together, driven in large part by Messi's old friend (and Ronaldo's new friend) the MBS political enforcer and Saudi minister Turki al-Sheikh. He watched the entire spectacle while sipping tea in a plush chair on the stadium's VVIP terrace.

Once the strange affair kicked off, PSG strolled about the field. Messi scored in the first three minutes. Ronaldo took it far too seriously. He scored twice. The two men each played for an hour, fulfilling the precise terms of their contracts, and were substituted within a minute of each other to the raucous applause of around 60,000 fans. The Saudi all-star side, such as it was, eventually lost a wild game 5–4.

The night's only public interaction between the two men everyone had come to see amounted to a polite handshake and a little Spanish chitchat. Their 12 combined Ballon d'Or awards, won through sheer force of genius and will, had somehow brought them to this moment, but only as pawns of the larger forces that shape global soccer. Both men were happily on the Kingdom's petro-payroll—Ronaldo as the newest member of Al Nassr, and Messi as an ambassador for Visit Saudi, the country's campaign to drive tourism to the desert.

Neither player spoke publicly after the game. Messi needed to get out of there, out of the country, and back to Paris. Ronaldo dashed out too, though he wasn't traveling as far. He was stuck in the Kingdom now.

MESSI AND RONALDO couldn't have arrived in Riyadh in January of 2023 under more different circumstances.

Cristiano was there as the high-priced plaything of the regime after being fired by Manchester United in one of the ugliest, most public divorces in sports. Messi, meanwhile, was a world champion. For the first time in their careers, they were on the same pitch, but no longer belonged in the same debate. After a duel that lasted more than a decade, in which superiority ebbed and flowed season by season and sometimes by match, the matter had been settled in a matter of four weeks.

Back in December in Qatar, Messi had actually done it. At the age of

35, after more than a decade of angst in the blue-and-white jersey of Argentina, in what was likely his final appearance on the game's biggest stage, he had lifted the World Cup and resolved the debate forever.

As he hoisted the small golden trophy into the sky, draped in a ceremonial black robe placed on his shoulders by the Emir of Qatar, Messi joined a soccer pantheon of World Cup–winning GOATs that included only Pelé and Diego Maradona—and Messi had bolted the door behind him. Ronaldo's final moments at the Qatar World Cup had seen him traipse tearfully down the tunnel in Ultra-HD after coming off the bench in Portugal's defeat to Morocco. The question of who reigned supreme, Messi or Ronaldo, had consumed the world's most popular sport for so many years precisely because there was no clear answer.

Now, definitively, there was.

It demanded a series of stunning performances from Messi to make it happen, not to mention an astonishing save from Argentina goalkeeper Emiliano Martínez, a nerve-shredding penalty shootout, and the wildest final the World Cup has ever seen. But once it was all over, the final box had been checked. The trophy Messi had once given up on—the only major prize to have eluded him—was finally his.

His claim to immortality was assured before all that, of course. Messi and Ronaldo had done more than anyone to reshape the soccer landscape, recasting the Champions League as the pinnacle of the sport and its most prestigious prize. Even without a World Cup triumph, both of them had long since carved out their places in the ranks of all-time greatness. In a sport that ages athletes quicker than bananas, the fact that both of them had made it to Qatar was a minor miracle. Taking the field in a *fifth* World Cup had put Messi and Ronaldo in a club with only three members: two stalwarts from Mexico and the German diesel engine Lothar Matthäus.

What no one could have expected was that Messi was saving his greatest World Cup performance for his final shot at the trophy. Over the course of a month in the desert, Messi bent the tournament to his will. He scored in each of Argentina's knockout games, twice in the final, rolled home the opening penalty in the shootout, and was named player of the tournament. In retrospect, the whole narrative looked inevitable.

But it didn't start out like a coronation.

In fact, it started out like a blazing disaster. Entering the tournament on a 36-game unbeaten streak, Argentina lost its opening game against Saudi Arabia. At that stage, it looked as though Messi's last shot at World Cup glory would play out much like the previous four: high expectations, crushing disappointment, lots of obscene songs about Brazil.

Then, Argentina got angry. Lifted by a squad who accepted that it was all about their No. 10, Messi began to shape his legacy with a series of defiant performances. He carried his team into the knockout rounds, doing whatever it took to keep them alive. Nothing else mattered, not even preserving his nice-guy image. As Argentina progressed deeper into the tournament, Messi revealed himself to be the insidious trash-talker that a whole generation of Real Madrid players had always known.

He openly blanked Poland star Robert Lewandoski on the pitch, stomped on a Mexico jersey inside the locker room, and in a spectacularly ill-tempered quarterfinal against the Netherlands, taunted the Dutch bench by cupping his hands to his ears. His teammates—and the entire population of Argentina—ate up their new supervillain, Dark Messi.

The most shocking incident of all came after knocking out the Netherlands, when Messi took one look at Wout Weghorst, a giant Dutchman who was waiting patiently to exchange jerseys with a legend.

"*Que miras, bobo?*" Dark Messi barked at Weghorst. "What are you looking at, clown?"

The strange part was that the whole shift in persona actually made Messi more relatable. He was godlike with the ball at his feet, but kick the man too many times, and he got pissed off just like one of us. By the time Argentina reached the final, it seemed as if the whole world was willing him to go the distance. Or half the world, at any rate.

The other half had spent an uncomfortable month witnessing Ronaldo's career go into a sudden, violent, and self-inflicted tailspin.

The turbulence had been felt for months before the World Cup as Manchester United's manager Erik ten Hag made it clear that Ronaldo was no longer critical to his plans. From being one of the most valuable players ever, he'd been relegated to third-most useful guy off the United bench. Ronaldo took it exactly as you'd expect. At one point, when ten Hag called on him for a late cameo against Tottenham, Cristiano refused to enter the game. Ten Hag suspended him. Things only festered from there.

So, Ronaldo did what he always does. He took matters into his own hands and soon delivered one of the most devastating 90 minutes of his twilight years: a two-part, 1.5-hour long interview with the British TV pundit Piers Morgan in which he torched his relationship with the club that had made him a star.

"Don't tell me that the top players, the guys who want everything, the key players will play three minutes," Ronaldo told Morgan.

Ronaldo went on and on like this, speaking about respect and how no one was giving him any. He'd been betrayed, he said. The only human with 500 million Instagram followers had been treated like a nobody.

Inside Old Trafford, they'd seen enough. Within days, United issued a 67-word statement putting an end to the whole nasty business.

"Cristiano Ronaldo is to leave Manchester United by mutual agreement, with immediate effect," the club wrote. "The club thanks him for his immense contribution across two spells at Old Trafford, scoring 145 goals in 346 appearances, and wishes him and his family well for the future.

Cristiano was a free agent now, free to follow his ambition to a place that would truly value his talents, even as he approached his 38th birthday. This is what he wanted. Ronaldo had made it clear to Morgan.

"You want to keep playing at the highest level," Morgan had suggested. "You want to play Champions League football. You want to be breaking records. It comes back to my gut feeling: that if it was just about money, you'd be in Saudi Arabia earning a king's ransom. But that's not what motivates you. You want to keep at the top."

"Exactly," Ronaldo replied. "Because I still believe that I can score many, many goals and help the team."

The trouble was finding a team that actually wanted his help. Which is how, two months later, Ronaldo opted for Plan B: the king's ransom.

Worth some $210 million a year, his contract with Al Nassr instantly became the richest in sports history. He had trounced Messi's deal with Paris Saint-Germain and made LeBron James look like he was playing on a rookie salary. And yet, the distinction—another first/best/most— had also left Cristiano completely diminished.

"My work in Europe is done," Ronaldo said at his unveiling.

Just as jarring for Cristiano was the realization that his work with Jorge Mendes might be done, too. The longest association of his professional career had hit the rocks the previous summer when Ronaldo had tasked him with finding him a new, elite club. The one condition: it needed to be playing the Champions League.

Ronaldo's Champions League records are among his proudest professional achievements—and among the most extensively chronicled on the list of accolades he keeps close at hand. Cristiano was irked when he relinquished his title as Leading Scorer in the Champions League Group Stage (73 goals) to Messi the previous season. He wanted another season or two to burnish his stats in Europe's top competition.

But everywhere Mendes went, he was practically laughed out of the room. Napoli had a look and passed. Chelsea, under a new American owner, gave it only brief consideration, while Real said thanks but no thanks. Ronaldo felt that Mendes was clearly the person to blame in all this. So when it came to the Al Nassr deal, the job didn't fall to the most powerful agent in soccer. Instead, it fell to Ricardo Regufe, a former Nike PR man and a 20-year veteran of Cristiano, Inc.

Over the weeks that followed, as the dust settled on the madness of that month in Qatar and all its fallout, Messi and Ronaldo had to return to a semblance of reality.

Messi, back in his unhappy situation at PSG, looked checked out. Ronaldo, determined to live up to his Al Nassr price tag, looked oddly checked in. The only way he could justify the move to the Kingdom, after all, was if he started posting ridiculous numbers again, which turned out to be much easier against Saudi defenses than English ones.

But in the rest of Europe, where the top clubs were no longer whichever clubs happened to feature either Messi or Ronaldo, elite soccer was doing something that had been inconceivable just a few years earlier. The environment Messi and Ronaldo had turbocharged—full of star power, one-man heroics, and global branding exercises—was moving on without them. Even stranger was that in an era of unchecked capitalism in soccer's Wild West, the teams that had been lucky enough to enjoy Ronaldo or Messi in their primes had somehow failed to capitalize on them.

Two years on from his sudden departure from Italian soccer, it was clear that Ronaldo had merely rented his stardom to Juventus, leaving the club no better off than when he arrived. All of the new Juventus fans Ronaldo brought with him arrived just in time to watch the club hopelessly stagnate and run into trouble with the Italian tax authorities. Two years later, most of them had moved on to rooting for Manchester United. By 2023, they were getting acquainted with the yellow and blue of Al Nassr.

Real Madrid had at least enjoyed Cristiano's best years, but it didn't come out of its Ronaldo era in much better shape. The club that made the conscious decision to bid farewell to him in 2018 was still struggling with its transition to a post-Ronaldo future four years later. But a pair of holdovers from the Ronaldo era showed they had something left in the tank. An unlikely collection of young talent coalesced a rejuvenated Karim Benzema and Luka Modrić (combined age: 70 years old) to win the 2022 Champions League. Yet this vintage of Real Madrid, which relied on late-game heroics and baffling comebacks, remained a pale imitation of the dominant team that didn't lose a single Champions League knockout game for three straight years.

Still, that was more than Messi would manage over his two seasons in Paris. In the months that followed the match in Riyadh, it became clear that his stay at PSG was a complete bust. By the end of the 2022–23 season, Messi was booed at the Parc des Princes more often than he scored following yet another failure to win the Champions League. The most notable incident of his post-World Cup came when the club suspended him for missing a mandatory practice following a defeat. Messi had scampered back to the Kingdom, this time without the club's permission, to make an appearance for his paymasters at Visit Saudi.

From then on, it was clear that his days at PSG were numbered. The only question now was whether he would follow Ronaldo back to the Gulf.

The offer from Al-Hilal landed quickly. Hundreds of millions of dollars, tax-free, to putter around in soccer's most lavish desert retirement community, the Saudi Premier League. But in the background, Messi's camp was keeping an eye on a different part of the world known for its retirees: South Florida. Days after the French season wrapped up, Messi announced that, like Cristiano, he was leaving Europe.

The twist was that he was taking his talents to Inter Miami in Major League Soccer. MLS, where the highest paid player was earning around $14 million a season, was never going to compete with the richest on offer in the Kingdom—and Messi was never going to lower his salary demands.

While the league didn't quite move Heaven and Earth to secure his signature, it leaned on the next best thing: Apple and Adidas. Under the terms of Messi's unprecedented American deal, he would receive a percentage of every new subscription to Apple's streaming platform for MLS matches. (The company was in its first season of a $2.5 billion, 10-year deal to be the league's exclusive broadcaster in over 100 countries.) Adidas, too, was expected to chip in cash and a percentage of jersey sales.

In the space of six months, the Messi-Ronaldo era of European soccer had been consigned to history.

Though Barcelona had prayed that its favorite son might consider a return, even Messi couldn't see how the club could make it work. Two years after he left Catalonia in tears, Barça was still too much of a mess. The club still couldn't promise that it had the funds to add him to the roster.

The crackpot scheme that was the Super League had failed, so Barça had resorted to selling off anything it could, right down to the name of its home. Camp Nou, the house that Cruyff had built, had now been rechristened Spotify Camp Nou.

FC Barcelona in 2023 bears a striking resemblance to FC Barcelona in 2003: finances in tatters, stadium half-empty, and no closer to winning the Champions League. Club president Joan Laporta was signing the checks again, just as he had in the early 2000s, and promising that La Masia could churn out another team of geniuses, if only they gave it time. In other words, the club was hoping to replicate as much of the alchemy that led to Lionel Messi and Pep Guardiola and the rest as possible. But the truth was that they were out of ideas, running out of money, and increasingly desperate. The Super League fiasco was proof of it.

After Messi and Ronaldo, the clubs that made the greatest of all time were somehow back where they started before they'd ever met them— hoping, betting, and praying that lightning could strike again.

ACKNOWLEDGMENTS

The challenge of telling the story of two of the most famous people on the planet is that they are known to pretty much everyone, but also to no one.

So in tracking down the dozens and dozens of sources we interviewed in Cristiano Ronaldo and Lionel Messi's orbits, we relied heavily on the trust of many more people than we can name. In fact, many of them simply can't be named because they spoke to us on condition of anonymity since Ronaldo and Messi remain active, influential, and in a few cases, still in business with them.

That said, we would be remiss if we didn't thank the large, international cast of characters who guided us through this story in the middle of a global pandemic. In Portugal, we are grateful to three Carloses who worked with Ronaldo at different stages of his career: Bruno, Freitas, and Queiroz. We also gleaned insight and contacts from Pedro Pinto, Antonio Magalhães, and João Pinto, as well as a slew of Ronaldo's neighbors and acquaintances in Madeira. In Spain, we have to thank Ramon Calderon, Joan Laporta, Cesc Fàbregas, Víctor Vázquez, Victor Font, and Txiki Begiristain, among others—plus a special mention for La Liga's Joris Evers and president Javier Tebas, who offered us so much time to unpack this transformational era in Spanish soccer.

From across the rest of the football world, we are also grateful to Arsène Wenger, Carlo Ancelotti, Sepp Blatter, René Meulensteen, Peter Kenyon, David Gill, Garry Cook, Tim Howard, Wes McKennie, Phil

Thompson, Thierry Weil, Mike Forde, Robert Bonnier, David Piper, Pascal Ferré, Eric Eisner, Pere Guardiola, the team at Relevent, the executives and communications staffs of Real Madrid, Barcelona, Juventus, and Paris Saint-Germain, along with the current and former executives of Nike and Adidas who spoke to us anonymously.

There were, of course, many others in soccer who shared anecdotes, details, and documents with us on the condition that we kept their names out of it to preserve the secrecy that governs this crazy business. We are no less thankful that they believed in us.

At HarperCollins, we owe a huge debt of gratitude to the superbly thoughtful Matt Harper for his careful edits, his soccer chats, and the big-picture thinking that allowed us to unspool these two connected stories. And we would never have gotten the chance to tell them without our inimitable agent, Eric Lupfer, who saw the potential for this book, brought his signature clarity and sweep, and guided us through every step of the process—Jorge Mendes couldn't have done it better. Also at Fletcher & Co., Christy Fletcher and Melissa Chinchillo were invaluable in getting this book out to the world.

Pulling this off would have been impossible without the support of our bosses and colleagues at *The Wall Street Journal*, above all Global Sports Editor Bruce Orwall, Deputy Chief News Editor Jenn Hicks, Cynthia Lin, Mike Miller, and Matt Murray, who gave us the latitude and confidence to tackle this project. Our colleagues on *WSJ Sports* have had to cover for us more times than we can count, so we are deeply indebted to the people who carry that section every single day: Andrew Beaton, Jason Gay, Jim Chairusmi, Rachel Bachman, Laine Higgins, and Louise Radnofsky. The same is true for the digital platforms team, especially Brian Fitzgerald, Greg Rodewald, Roland Keane, Juju Kim, and Jim Jaworski.

Once the manuscript was finished—and often before—we ran it by the most trusted readers we know. Ben Cohen, a former *WSJ* sports writer, was there to reassure us that we hadn't entirely missed the point in analyzing two of the longest hot streaks the sports world has ever seen. Nick Kostov, of the *Journal*'s Paris bureau, was also always available to road-test an idea, often while actually on the road.

And of course, there were our home teams. They have always been our most devoted readers, cheerleaders, and fielders of late-night phone calls full of inane details that we had just learned. Joshua's parents and sister—Jeffrey, Aline, and Celine, who provided love, humor, and patience—now know more about the barrios of Rosario and Cristiano's workout routines than they ever bargained for.

Jon's parents, Lizzie and Ant, and his in-laws, Richard and Gloria Davies, gave support and encouragement. His brother, Dan, offered welcome feedback—and even more welcome distractions—during the writing process. That process depended on the generosity of two sets of friends—Henrik Tordrup and Ines Tordrup Bigaard, and Pravin and Anna Sathe—who offered up their homes as workspaces at a time when working anywhere was unusually tricky.

But the greatest thanks go to Jon's two children, Evie and Cooper, and to his wife, Katie, who once again proved herself to be the unquestioned GOAT.

Without all of that support, this book never would have seen the light of day. If we had our own *Museu*, you'd all be in it.

APPENDIX

MESSI VS. RONALDO: HEAD TO HEAD RESULTS
IN CLUB MATCHES (BOTH ON PITCH)

Date	Messi (M.)	Ronaldo (R.)	Venue	Score (M.–R.)
4/23/08	Barcelona	Manchester United	Camp Nou	0–0
4/29/08	Barcelona	Manchester United	Old Trafford	0–1
5/27/09	Barcelona	Manchester United	Olimpico	2–0
11/29/09	Barcelona	Real Madrid	Camp Nou	1–0
4/10/10	Barcelona	Real Madrid	Santiago Bernabéu	2–0
11/29/10	Barcelona	Real Madrid	Camp Nou	5–0
4/16/11	Barcelona	Real Madrid	Santiago Bernabéu	1–1
4/20/11	Barcelona	Real Madrid	Mestalla	0–1
4/27/11	Barcelona	Real Madrid	Santiago Bernabéu	2–0
5/3/11	Barcelona	Real Madrid	Camp Nou	1–1
8/14/11	Barcelona	Real Madrid	Santiago Bernabéu	2–2
8/17/11	Barcelona	Real Madrid	Camp Nou	3–2
12/10/11	Barcelona	Real Madrid	Santiago Bernabéu	3–1
1/18/12	Barcelona	Real Madrid	Santiago Bernabéu	2–1
1/25/12	Barcelona	Real Madrid	Camp Nou	2–2
4/21/12	Barcelona	Real Madrid	Camp Nou	1–2
8/23/12	Barcelona	Real Madrid	Camp Nou	3–2
8/29/12	Barcelona	Real Madrid	Santiago Bernabéu	1–2
10/7/12	Barcelona	Real Madrid	Camp Nou	2–2
1/30/13	Barcelona	Real Madrid	Santiago Bernabéu	1–1
2/26/13	Barcelona	Real Madrid	Camp Nou	1–3
3/2/13	Barcelona	Real Madrid	Santiago Bernabéu	1–2
10/26/13	Barcelona	Real Madrid	Camp Nou	2–1
3/23/14	Barcelona	Real Madrid	Santiago Bernabéu	4–3
10/25/14	Barcelona	Real Madrid	Santiago Bernabéu	1–3

M. Goals	M. Assists	R. Goals	R. Assists	Competition
0	0	0	0	Champions League
0	0	0	0	Champions League
1	0	0	0	Champions League
0	0	0	0	La Liga
1	0	0	0	La Liga
0	2	0	0	La Liga
1	0	1	0	La Liga
0	0	1	0	Copa del Rey
2	0	0	0	Champions League
0	0	0	0	Champions League
1	1	0	0	Supercopa
2	1	1	0	Supercopa
0	1	0	0	La Liga
0	1	1	0	Copa del Rey
0	1		0	Copa del Rey
0	0	1	0	La Liga
1	0	1	0	Supercopa
1	0	1	0	Supercopa
2	0	2	0	La Liga
0	1	0	0	Copa del Rey
0	0	2	0	Copa del Rey
1	0	0	0	La Liga
0	0	0	1	La Liga
3	1	1	0	La Liga
0	0	1	0	La Liga

APPENDIX

Date	Messi (M.)	Ronaldo (R.)	Venue	Score (M.-R.)
3/22/15	Barcelona	Real Madrid	Camp Nou	2–1
11/21/15	Barcelona	Real Madrid	Santiago Bernabéu	4–0
4/2/16	Barcelona	Real Madrid	Camp Nou	1–2
12/3/16	Barcelona	Real Madrid	Camp Nou	1–1
4/23/17	Barcelona	Real Madrid	Santiago Bernabéu	3–2
8/13/17	Barcelona	Real Madrid	Camp Nou	1–3
12/23/17	Barcelona	Real Madrid	Santiago Bernabéu	3–0
5/6/18	Barcelona	Real Madrid	Camp Nou	2–2
12/8/20	Barcelona	Juventus	Camp Nou	0–3

MESSI VS. RONALDO: GOALS AND TROPHIES (ALL
COMPETITIONS), SEASON BY SEASON

Season	M. Club	M. Goals	Appearances	M. Trophies
2002–03				
2003–04				
2004–05	Barcelona	1	9	La Liga
2005–06	Barcelona	8	25	La Liga, Champions League
2006–07	Barcelona	17	36	Supercopa de España
2007–08	Barcelona	16	40	
2008–09	Barcelona	38	51	La Liga, Copa del Rey, Champions League, UEFA Super Cup
2009–10	Barcelona	47	53	La Liga, FIFA Club World Cup, Supercopa de España
2010–11	Barcelona	53	55	La Liga, Champions League, Supercopa de España, UEFA Super Cup

M. Goals	M. Assists	R. Goals	R. Assists	Competition
0	1	1	0	La Liga
0	0	0	0	La Liga
0	0	1	0	La Liga
0	0	0	0	La Liga
2	0	0	0	La Liga
1	0	1	0	Supercopa
1	1	0	0	La Liga
1	0	1	0	La Liga
0	0	2	0	Champions League

R. Club	R. Goals	Appearances	R. Trophies
Sporting	5	31	Supertaça
Manchester United	6	40	FA Cup
Manchester United	9	50	
Manchester United	12	47	League Cup
Manchester United	23	53	Premier League
Manchester United	42	49	Premier League, Champions League, Community Shield
Manchester United	26	53	Premier League, League Cup, FIFA Club World Cup
Real Madrid	33	35	
Real Madrid	53	54	Copa del Rey

MESSI VS. RONALDO: GOALS AND TROPHIES (ALL
COMPETITIONS), SEASON BY SEASON (CONTINUED)

Season	M. Club	M. Goals	Appearances	M. Trophies
2011–12	Barcelona	73	60	Copa del Rey, Supercopa de España, FIFA Club World Cup
2012–13	Barcelona	60	50	La Liga
2013–14	Barcelona	41	46	Supercopa de España
2014–15	Barcelona	58	57	La Liga, Copa del Rey, Champions League, UEFA Super Cup
2015–16	Barcelona	41	49	La Liga, Copa del Rey, FIFA Club World Cup
2016–17	Barcelona	54	52	Copa del Rey, Supercopa de España
2017–18	Barcelona	45	54	La Liga, Copa del Rey
2018–19	Barcelona	51	50	La Liga, Supercopa de España
2019–20	Barcelona	31	44	
2020–21	Barcelona	38	47	Copa del Rey
2021–22	Paris Saint-Germain	11	34	Ligue 1

R. Club	R. Goals	Appearances	R. Trophies
Real Madrid	60	55	La Liga
Real Madrid	55	55	Supercopa de España
Real Madrid	51	47	Copa del Rey, Champions League, UEFA Super Cup
Real Madrid	61	54	FIFA Club World Cup
Real Madrid	51	48	Champions League
Real Madrid	42	46	La Liga, Champions League, FIFA Club World Cup
Real Madrid	44	44	Champions League, Supercopa de España, FIFA Club World Cup
Juventus	28	43	Serie A, Supercoppa Italiana
Juventus	37	46	Serie A
Juventus	36	44	Coppa Italia, Supercoppa Italiana
Manchester United	24	38	

SELECTED BIBLIOGRAPHY

Abellán, Jose A. *Asalto al Real Madrid: Diario de 838 días y noches al límite.* Madrid: Real del Catorce Editores, 2015.

Balague, Guillem. *Cristiano Ronaldo: The Biography.* London: Orion, 2015.

Ball, Phil. *White Storm: 100 Years of Real Madrid.* Edinburgh: Mainstream, 2002.

Buschmann, Rafael and Wulzinger, Michael. *Football Leaks.* London: Guardian Faber, 2018.

Carlin, John. *White Angels.* London: Bloomsbury, 2005.

Condo, Paolo. *The Duellists.* Liverpool: De Coubertin Books, 2017.

Cruyff, Johan. *My Turn: The Autobiography.* London: Macmillan, 2016.

Dudek, Jerzy. *A Big Pole in Our Goal.* Liverpool: Trinity Mirror Sport Media, 2016.

Ferguson, Alex. *Managing My Life: My Autobiography.* London: Hodder & Stoughton, 1999.

Hawkey, Ian. *Di Stéfano.* London: Ebury Press, 2016.

Iniesta, Andres. *The Artist.* London: Headline Publishing Group, 2016.

Juillard, Alexandre. *Insubmersible Messi.* Paris: Éditions Solar, 2016.

Juillard, Alexandre and Fest, Sebastián. *Le Mystère Messi.* Paris: Jean-Claude Gawsewitch Éditeur, 2012.

Keane, Roy and Doyle, Roddy. *The Second Half.* London: Orion, 2014.

Kuper, Simon. *The Barcelona Complex.* New York: Penguin Press, 2021.

Lowe, Sid. *Fear and Loathing in La Liga.* London: Yellow Jersey Press, 2013.

Mandis, Steven G. *The Real Madrid Way.* Dallas: Benbella Books, 2016.

Mendes, Jorge; Cuesta Rubio, Miguel; and Sanchez Mora, Jonathan. *La Clave Mendes.* Madrid: La Esfera de Los Libros, 2015.

Meulensteen, René. *René Meulensteen & Man Utd Methods of Success (2007-2013) Vol. 1.* London: SoccerTutor.com, 2020.

Nielsen, Per and Sorgenfri, Søren. *4: Per Nielsen—Brøndby for Evigt*. Copenhagen: People's Press, 2013.

Perarnau, Martí. *Pep Confidential*. London: Arena Sport, 2014.

Perarnau, Martí. *Senda de Campeones: De La Masia al Camp Nou*. Barcelona: Salsa Books, 2011.

Robinson, Joshua and Clegg, Jonathan. *The Club: How the English Premier League Became the Wildest, Richest, Most Disruptive Force in Sports*. New York: Houghton Mifflin Harcourt, 2018.

Smit, Barbara. *Sneaker Wars*. New York: HarperCollins, 2008.

Soriano, Ferran. *Goal: The Ball Doesn't Go in by Chance*. London: Palgrave Macmillan, 2012.

Strasser, J. B. and Becklund, Laurie. *Swoosh: The Unauthorized Story of Nike and the Men Who Played There*. New York: Harper Business, 1993.

Wilson, Jonathan. *Angels with Dirty Faces: The Football History of Argentina*. London: Orion, 2016.

Yergin, Daniel. *The Prize: The Epic Quest for Oil, Money and Power*. New York: Simon & Schuster, 1991.

INDEX

Kershaw, Les, 24–25, 80
Key Capital Partners, 248
Knight, Phil, 54
Koeman, Ronald, 39–40
Kroos, Toni, 219, 220

La Liga, 30, 62, 91, 121, 158, 162–65
La Masia, 32–45
    Generación 87, 40–45, 47–48
Laporta, Joan, 32, 62–63, 95, 97, 132,
    144–45, 163, 165–66, 251,
    256–60, 261–62, 286
Larsson, Henrik, 65
Law, Denis, 85
Lawrenson, Mark, 76
Lee, Spike, 262
Leiria, União de, 96
Levy, Daniel, 174
Lewandoski, Robert, 282
Liverpool F.C., 12, 112, 159, 160, 228,
    229, 231, 238, 246, 250, 254
Lowe, Sid, 139

McKennie, Wes, 236
Madeira, 13, 181–82
Madrid. *See* Atlético Madrid; Real
    Madrid
Major League Soccer (MLS), 54, 179
Makélélé, Claude, 122
Maldini, Paolo, 55
Manchester City FC, 211–14, 216,
    217–18, 220
    Messi and, 211–12, 213–14, 243
    Ronaldo and, 268–72
    Super League and, 253
Manchester United, 123–24, 145,
    146–47, 160, 212, 220–21
    2002–2003 season, 24–28, 29
    2003–2004 season, 9–11
    2005–2006 season, 72–74
    2006–2007 season, 77–80
    2007–2008 season, 81–87, 89–90
    2008–2009 season, 102–3

Manchester United, Ronaldo at, 4, 50,
    71–74, 77–87, 192, 234, 273–76
    2003 scouting and signing, 24–28, 29
    2021 signing, 269–70, 273–74
    2022 season and firing, 280, 282–83
Maradona, Diego, 69, 191, 195, 281
    at Barcelona, 113
    Messi and, 35–36, 59, 69, 88–89,
    148, 195, 196
    World Cup 1986, 41, 88, 195
Martínez, Emiliano, 281
Martinez, Ramon, 12
Martino, Gerardo, 173, 187
Mascherano, Javier, 25, 184
Matthäus, Lothar, 77, 281
Mayorga, Kathryn, 206–9
Mbappé, Kylian, 215, 218, 276–77
Mediapro, 162
Mee, Ben, 254
Mendes, Jorge, 1–2, 11–12, 77, 91, 92,
    93, 168, 185, 217, 219, 284
    background of, 48–51
    branding and endorsements of
    Ronaldo, 167, 168
    Juventus signing, 232–38
    legal troubles of Ronaldo, 203, 204,
    206, 210
    Manchester City and, 267–69, 270
    Manchester United signings, 26–28,
    269–70
Mendes, Nuno, 182
Menotti, César Luis, 216
Messi, Jorge, 36, 47–48, 165–66, 261–62
    branding and endorsements, 51,
    58–61, 65, 168
    contracts, 48, 62–63, 165–66, 185,
    186, 210, 230
    legal troubles of, 209–10
Messi, Lionel
    2006 World Cup, 69–72
    2007–2008 season, 87–97
    2008–2009 season, 99–101
    2010–2011 season, 163

Relevent Sports, 177–78, 249
Rexach, Charly, 36–37
Rijkaard, Frank, 4, 63–65, 95, 97, 100, 142–43
Riquelme, Juan Román, 68, 70
Roberto, Sergi, 238
Robson, Bobby, 96
Roca, Fernando, 161
Rodríguez, James, 221
Rodríguez, Maxi, 70
Ronaldinho
    at Barcelona, 3, 29–30, 32, 63, 87
    Nike endorsement, 58, 59
Ronaldo (Ronaldo Luís Nazário de Lima), 56–57, 156
Ronaldo, Cristiano
    2003–2004 season, 9–11
    2005–2006 season, 72–74
    2006–2007 season, 77–80
    2006 World Cup, 74–78
    2007–2008 season, 81–87, 89–94
    2008–2009 season, 97–103
    2010–2011 season, 163
    2016 European Championship, 197–200
    2017–2018 season, 219–20
    at Al Nassr FC, 279–80, 283–84, 285
    Ballon d'Or, 3–4, 89, 149, 155–56, 180, 181–82, 189–90, 235, 271, 280
    branding and endorsements, 57–58, 165–70, 179, 192, 206, 254–55
    early life and soccer career, 12–23
    empire in Madeira, 181–82
    FIFA World Player Gala (2007), 1–5
    Football Leaks, 203–9
    at Juventus, 12, 232–38, 257, 267–68, 269, 285
    at Madrid. See Real Madrid, Ronaldo at
    Manchester City and, 268–72
    at Manchester United. See Manchester United, Ronaldo at

Messi vs. See Messi–Ronaldo rivalry
    origin story of, 9–12
    rape allegation against, 206–9
Rooney, Wayne, 12, 73–79, 81, 84
Rosario, Argentina, 2, 35–36, 47, 182–83
Rosell, Sandro, 166, 174, 184
Ross, Stephen, 177–78
Royal Spanish Football Federation, 62, 164
Ruth, Babe, 141

Sabella, Alejandro, 183, 195–96
Sala-i-Martin, Xavier, 171
Salas, Marcelo, 12
Salgado, Míchel, 120
Sampaoli, Jorge, 196
Samui Video, 48–49
Sánchez, José Ángel, 124
Santo, Nuno Espírito, 49–50
Santos, Fernando, 9, 199–200
Santos FC, 171–72
Sanz, Lorenzo, 115–17, 120–21
Sarkozy, Nicolas, 262
Saudi Arabia, 80, 177, 204, 216–17, 279–80
Saudi Premier League, 279–80, 285–86
Saviola, Javier, 69
Scholar, Irving, 159
Scholes, Paul, 56, 86, 89
Schuster, Bernd, 91
Schwarzstein, Diego, 36
Scolari, Luiz Felipe, 72, 75–76
Shevchenko, Andriy, 195
Siemens, 126–27
Smit, Barbara, 52
Smith, Walter, 84–85
soccer boot, 51–61
social media, 167, 191–92, 208, 254–55, 270–71
sociedad anónima deportiva (SAD), 114
Soriano, Ferran, 31, 34, 97, 145, 162, 165, 166, 214

ABOUT THE AUTHORS

Joshua Robinson has been the European sports correspondent for the *Wall Street Journal* for over a decade. In addition to soccer, he has covered everything from the NFL and the Olympic Games to the Tour de France, and the World Chess Championship. Robinson's work has also appeared in the *New York Times*, the *Washington Post*, and *Sports Illustrated*. A native of the South of France, he was raised in London and is a graduate of Columbia University. He is based in Paris.

Jonathan Clegg is a senior editor for the *Wall Street Journal*. He joined the *Journal* in 2009 as the paper's first Europe-based sports reporter and has since written about every major sport, covering the Super Bowl, the College Football Playoff, the World Cup, and the Olympics. He is a graduate of the London School of Economics and lives with his wife and two children in Brooklyn.